History B

"François Davoine and Jean-Max Gau   ..re remind us, convincingly, that madness can only be genuinely understood when seen in its proper personal, social, and historical contexts. *History Beyond Trauma* is a genuine labor of love and stands in stark, and refreshing, contrast to the current dominance of a simplistic biogenetic ideology with its unhelpful overreliance on diagnoses and drugs. The authors are to be congratulated on a truly personal approach to a topic that has been depersonalized for far too long."
  —Dr. John Read
    Director of Clinical Psychology, University of Auckland, New Zealand;
    Editor, *Models of Madness* (Brunner-Routlege 2004)

"This is one of the most compelling examples of what can be gained by crossing boundaries. In a work that cannot be pigeonholed as clinical, anthropological, philosophical, or historical, the authors succeed in weaving together the results of their many years of clinical experience in different cultures with a profound rereading of philosophy, history, and psychoanalytic theory. Never lost from sight are the compelling individual stories of madness and war that serve as the touchstone for a rich series of meditations on the meaning of our links to each other and to our individual and social histories."
  —Lynn Hunt
    Eugen Weber Professor of Modern European History, UCLA

"In their wide-ranging and erudite study of the psychoanalytic treatment of the psychoses, a deep consciousness of shared humanity gives the authors the courage and imagination to cross the psychotic break to discover the human being on the other side. *History Beyond Trauma*

encourages us to be equally brave and creative in facing the human condition we call madness—in others, in society, in ourselves."
—Thomas A. Kohut
Sue and Edgar Wachenheim III Professor of History and
Dean of the Faculty, Williams College

"Written in a nonlinear style that tracks transferential movements, *History Beyond Trauma* assembles insights derived from both clinical practice and teaching at the prestigious Ecole des Hautes Etudes en Sciences Sociales. The authors not only explore the intricacies of transferential relations with respect to those diagnosed as psychotic or 'mad,' but also boldly bring psychoanalysis and history into thought-provoking dialogue and elucidate how the analysis of trauma necessarily comes up against 'pieces of the Real' embedded in historical experiences (notably the atrocities of war and genocide). In exploring the role of trauma and its haunting symptoms, the authors themselves respond to the call of the book's Wittgensteinian subtitle and indicate how what cannot be spoken can be shown in symptoms and to some viable extent possibly worked through."
—Dominick LaCapra
Bryce and Edith M. Bowmar Professor of Humanistic Studies and
Director, School of Criticism and Theory, Cornell University

"Davoine and Gaudillière give us the benefit of three decades of working as clinical analysts and researchers with survivors of trauma. Their wide-ranging book speaks miles about how society views the madness of war and other horrors. *History Beyond Trauma* offers a masterfully original perspective on those who are mad, and also on those who seek to help them."
—Elizabeth Loftus, Ph.D.
Distinguished Professor, University of California-Irvine;
Past President, American Psychological Society

"History Beyond Trauma is compelling. The authors are insightful— and compassionate—readers of the human condition."
—Dr. Gregory Nagy

Whereof one cannot speak . . .

History Beyond Trauma

. . . thereof one cannot stay silent.

Françoise Davoine
and
Jean-Max Gaudillière

Translated by Susan Fairfield

OTHER
Other Press
New York

Copyright © 2004 Françoise Davoine and Jean-Max Gaudillière

Production Editor: Robert D. Hack

This book was set in 11 pt. Apollo by Alpha Graphics of Pittsfield, NH.

10 9 8 7 6 5 4 3 2 1

Library of Congress Cataloging-in-Publication Data

Davoine, Françoise.
  History beyond trauma / by Françoise Davoine & Jean-Max Gaudillière ; translated by Susan Fairfield.
      p. cm.
Includes bibliographical references and index.
  ISBN 1-59051-111-5
1. Post-traumatic stress disorder.   2. Psychic trauma.   3. Psychoanalysis.
4. War–Psychological aspects.   5. Mental illness–Social aspects.
6. Intergenerational relations.   I. Gaudillière, Jean-Max.   II. Title.
  RC552.P67 .D386 2004
    616.85'21–dc22

                                        2003022677

Contents

Foreword

In 1979 Françoise Davoine and Jean-Max Gaudillière visited the Austen Riggs Center in Stockbridge, Massachusetts, for the first time. Riggs is a small, unusual psychiatric hospital in that it treats severely disturbed patients with intensive psychoanalytic psychotherapy in a completely open therapeutic community. Its treatment program was established in the late 1940s by Robert Knight, David Rapaport, and a number of other brilliant young psychoanalysts from the Menninger Clinic. Joined soon thereafter by Erik Erikson, this group made major contributions to the theory and clinical practice of psychoanalytic ego psychology.

When Otto Will became Riggs's medical director in the late 1960s, he guided the hospital toward treating the more obviously psychotic patient. Having had years of experience at Chestnut Lodge, Dr. Will was a charismatic clinical genius whose work with schizophrenic patients included a rugged fearlessness, a Sullivanian conviction about the ordinary humanity of all people, and the strong impression that he knew his patients' suffering at first-hand. But an ongoing tension— sometimes creative and sometimes problematic—developed at Riggs between the ego-psychology emphasis on the patients' adaptation to their community (including the hospital community, which was the context for treatment) and the interpersonalist emphasis on meeting the patient in his or her regression.

Into this unsettled mix of treatment perspectives came Drs. Davoine and Gaudillière. They presented a clinical case, a story of work with a psychotic patient, and it somehow spoke across the language barrier to all segments of the Riggs therapy staff. It left no doubt that they did indeed meet their patients, but it also suggested that the patient's psychosis was not simply an attack on the social order, but, at a deeper level, a frantic effort to bring a foreclosed social connection into existence.

Since that time, Drs. Davoine and Gaudillière have presented at Riggs on a number of occasions and have offered many individual consultations to staff. As is true in the various parts of the world where they teach, the therapists who consult them find the experience illuminating, relieving, and, to some degree, magical. They feel not only that they understand their patients better and differently, but that they understand themselves with their patients in a new way. They also find themselves freed from whatever doctrinaire positions they may have accepted in their training. Most of all, they feel grateful to discover that both they and their patients are situated in a larger dimension of history, that history pervades the individual lives of each, and that recognizing this endows the patients' symptoms, and their use of the analyst, with hitherto unformed meaning.

Some Riggs staff members have also had the opportunity to present at the seminar Drs. Davoine and Gaudillière have led for many years at the Ecole des Hautes Etudes en Sciences Sociales in Paris. Their general topic is always the same: madness and the social link. Specific topics change from year to year (Harry Stack Sullivan, Wittgenstein, Bion, the crazy mother of medieval drama, Don Quixote), but, within each, they investigate what deep madness is trying to accomplish, what social meaning it is trying to bring (or bring back) into existence. Through them, their patients are active members of the seminar, and what they have to say, as well as how Drs. Davoine and Gaudillière join them, is the subject of this book.

History Beyond Trauma is not a book about the individual's developmental and psychodynamic history prior to trauma and breakdown. It is about the history of families on the other side of—lying beyond—the societal trauma that has devastated them and about the forces within their social structure invested in cutting that history out of the sanctioned social narrative. It is about the actual social history, crucial to the patient's emergence from madness, to be discovered, perhaps to be formed for the first time as something one can truly think, from the encounter with the remnants of trauma carried forward by the patient.

In 2001 Drs. Davoine and Gaudillière organized a conference that they called Casus Belli. The twenty or so invited participants from throughout Europe and the Americas were each asked to present a clinical case, relating somehow to larger societal trauma and involving a turning point in the treatment. Most important, we were to introduce ourselves not with our official, professional designations, but with something more personal about ourselves, especially as that might relate to the patient we had chosen to present. The stories unfolded with an unconscious logic, each illuminating one of the points to be found in this book and each case building on the preceding one.

To my surprise, in those rare instances when the presenters did not introduce themselves personally, they did so unconsciously through their patients. This phenomenon turns out to be central to what Drs. Davoine and Gaudillière are trying to teach us: stories of deep connection and pain must be told. If, for some reason, they cannot be spoken, they are told through an other. If they are unthinkable, their traces or debris are carried generationally and lived as madness by someone charged—in the double sense of an energy and a duty—to represent what Freud called the family's archaic heritage. And, in the transference with psychotic patients, it is analysts' responsiveness within their own archaic heritages that creates a field in which analysts may be charged by patients to represent something for them.

Drs. Davoine and Gaudillière have given us a book that is personal, demanding, and original. It is personal insofar as it is the record of their experience with mentors, colleagues throughout the world, and, most of all, their patients, each of whom has called into existence foreclosed aspects of his or her life and family history at crucial moments of the treatment. The authors' requirement that we as therapists become personal with our patients (within an analytic framework) is one reason that what they have to say to us might feel demanding. It is indeed a demand, one they would say our patients make upon us, to be there, person to person, at those moments when the patient is calling upon, and needs to use, something in us and in our own histories. One of the mentors cited in this book, Martin Cooperman, once commented that in psychotherapy the patient comes with his symptoms and the therapist comes with his technique, and if things go well, they both come out from hiding.

Drs. Davoine and Gaudillière would certainly agree with that, and, like Dr. Cooperman, they would not mean abandoning the treatment task in a glorification of the putative curative power of the dyadic relationship. Rather, they would mean that madness has to do with the radical dislocation of human beings from their social context by way of generational trauma and the patient's driven and nearly incomprehensible effort to link to that social context through the medium of the analyst, whose own connection to or dislocation from the social field is used by the patient in this process. Psychoanalysis is not a method of treatment applied by one person to another; it is a process engaged in by two people on behalf of one of them—and on behalf of all those family members and ancestors represented by that person.

This book is also demanding, especially to the American reader, because English is not the authors' first language, and their style of communicating is "French," by which I mean it is elegant, associative, and a bit elliptical. It bathes the reader in experience and culture rather than making its points in a more linear and deductive fashion, and it also includes easy and erudite references to Western history. Educated Europeans know and live in history much more fully than we Americans do. Their sense of time and of the flow and intersection of great and small events is broader and deeper than ours. The major wars of the twentieth century were fought on their soil, and so they know more immediately the relationship between social catastrophe and the breakdown of families and individuals.

But Drs. Davoine and Gaudillière have written this book for Americans. They are publishing it first in America, and in English, as a way of returning something for the learning that has come from the sharing of clinical stories over the years with American colleagues. (In some ways, their book is a work of gratitude to mentors like Otto Will, Ess White, and Martin Cooperman, and a delightful aspect of this book is the people the reader meets in its pages.) Lacanian writing has been accused of obscurantism, but Drs. Davoine and Gaudillière want their work to be understood and used. I urge readers in the "New World," often so unknowing about history and, until recently, so inclined to feel invulnerable to social catastrophe, to open themselves to this European sensibility and knowledge. Drs. Davoine and Gaudillière are listening to History. Its characters, like those in Greek drama, are trying to represent something as part of the healing of the human community. These historical characters are mentors too, and though some may come from different fields of specialization, they are speaking to a critical aspect of the human condition regardless of the era or angle from which they are approaching it.

Finally, this is an original work. It is fresh, daring, and authentic. Its clinical experience rings true. I know of nothing else like it in the analytic literature, though, like most good analytic writing, it consists, first of all, of believable stories about patients and treatments. It is a journal of its authors' learning: by way of their travels, their chance encounters with colleagues similarly involved with the meaning of madness, and, of course, their figurative travels and analytic encounters with patients in their consulting rooms. Drs. Davoine and Gaudillière are, as they say, co-researchers with their psychotic patients, "seconds" in the combat with which their patients are engaged as they try—madly, but, as we follow the clinical data, with deep sense—to restore the links to a foreclosed but essential social context.

M. Gerard Fromm, Ph.D.
Director, Erikson Institute
Austen Riggs Center
Stockbridge, Massachusetts
August 2003

Preface

The first draft of this book was completed in mid-August 2001. We had begun it in September 2000, and we brought it to the publisher in New York at the end of August 2001.

It was a very beautiful day. To show the horizon to some young people who were with us, we went up to the top of the World Trade Center. One week later, when we were back in Paris, we heard the news in the middle of the afternoon. Impossible to believe it; it wasn't true. All those people dead, all those missing. Suddenly we realized that we were at war. War was right there. The collapse of the towers and lives made time stand still.

Several months later, life resumed its course. The war had apparently taken place far away from us. Others, in Afghanistan, in the Middle East, were undergoing those collapses of time. As they had so recently done in Rwanda and Yugoslavia. . . . For a moment we thought we were living through World War II again, or even World War I. As in the last century, totalitarian slogans were chanted to a familiar tune, sounding hackneyed.

Within a few months' time, we had experienced concretely what we are talking about in this book:

Denial: what happened didn't happen.
Survivor guilt: "Why them and not us?"
Identification with the aggressor: "We had it coming."
Perversion of judgment: the victims were guilty and vice versa.
The fascination with criminals and mass destruction noted by Hannah
    Arendt in *The Origins of Totalitarianism*.[1]

---

1. Arendt 1951, pp. 326–340 (Chapter 10, "The Temporary Alliance between the Mob and the Elite").

The revival of the catastrophes: the old people were sounding the alarm to us; we're in 1938: Munich; we're in 1939: the Blitzkrieg; we're in 1941: Pearl Harbor, and the United States is entering the war. Nothing will ever be the same anymore.

And, finally, trivialization: the sophistication of the commentaries going hand in hand with the anesthetizing of feelings.

In all this we recognized the scansions of our work as psychoanalysts: in the psychiatric hospital, in the clinic, and in our offices, with patients whose madness, transient or ongoing, keeps on exploring these traumatic breaks in the social link and the political results of such traumas. When psychoanalysis grapples with madness, it is essential that analyst and patient pass through these moments and not just denounce them.

LACAN, WAR, MADNESS

Jacques Lacan, whose seminars we attended during our years of training, went to England as early as 1945 to see Wilfred Bion. In his 1947 paper on British psychiatry, he gave an account of the field of research opened by the war.[2] In passing, he cited the pioneering work, in the

---

2. When I was in London in September 1945, the fireworks had just recently been falling on the city on V-Day, when it celebrated its victory. The war had left me with a keen feeling of the kind of unreality under which the French as a collective had lived through it from beginning to end. I am not referring to those carnival ideologies that had counterbalanced phantasmagoria about our greatness. . . . What I mean instead is everyone's systematic misunderstanding of the world, those imaginary refuges in which, as a psychoanalyst, I could only point out on behalf of the group, at that time in the throes of a truly panicky dissolution of its moral status, the same defensive modalities used by the individual in neurosis against his anxiety, and with a not less ambiguous success, as paradoxically effective, and similarly, alas!, confirming a fate that is handed down through generations. [p. 101]

In the early 1970s, a copy of this paper, originally published in the journal *L'évolution psychiatrique* and not reprinted since then, was given to us by the psychiatrist and psychoanalyst Edmond Sanquer, medical director in various public psychiatric hospitals where we would be working as analysts for over twenty-five years. [Translator's note: Wherever works are cited in languages other than English in the Reference List, the translations are mine.]

preceding war, of Thomas W. Salmon, already pointing ahead to the importance that the social link would assume in his theory. This topic was chiefly developed in the seminars following the events of 1968, especially in *L'envers de la psychanalyse* (1969–1970). This was exactly the time when we began attending Lacan's seminar.

Throughout his work, Lacan sets forth concepts for the psychoanalytic exploration of the field of madness. But in his seminar on the psychoses and the paper in *Écrits* that summarizes it (1955–1956), he deliberately stops short of the issue of handling the transference in psychosis.[3] Psychiatry in France after World War II was oriented toward reforms that were primarily institutional. The institution of imprisonment in all its forms, along with its historical critique, had also been the axis chosen by the philosopher Michel Foucault (1961).

This was just the right moment for the translation of the collected papers of Harold Searles (1965), describing his clinical work with madness, published in French under the title of one of his papers, "The Effort to Drive the Other Person Crazy." We immediately recognized in this book one of the transferential modalities we had encountered in practice.

MADNESS WITHOUT BORDERS

Reading Searles committed us to crossing the ocean separating the two traditions, Anglo-Saxon and French. In 1979, we were invited by Jim Gorney (cf. 1994, 2000), John Muller, and William Richardson (Muller and Richardson 1982, 1988) to present our clinical work in the light of Lacanian concepts at the Austen Riggs Center, in Stockbridge, Massachusetts, which is dedicated to the analytic psychotherapy of the psychoses. This initial contact with clinicians coming from diverse theoretical horizons (Kleinian, Winnicottian, Anna Freudian, etc.) was as beneficial as could be for us. After our talk, some elements of which are to be found in the present book, Dr. Ess White, director of admissions, asked us simply, "This is all well and good, but now tell us how you do it."

---

3. As we go along, we shall be presenting the aspects of Lacan's teaching that have been of use to us. For a fuller understanding of his work, see Dor 1985 and 1994.

In our pidgin English, without thinking, we found ourselves telling stories of sessions in front of predecessors for whom we did not know the respective theoretical references. The work of Sullivan and Frieda Fromm-Reichmann was for the most part unknown to us at the time, among other reasons because there were no translations. We were amazed to find how pleasurable this impromptu exchange was. For what the Austen Riggs clinicians did was to offer their own clinical vignettes, their chief aim being to describe the impasses in which patients drive their analysts into a corner—patients who came to see us, as they came to Riggs, drained, out of breath, after exhausting the theories and ideologies of their former therapists.

We rediscovered this form of clinical exchange several months later, with Sioux medicine men in South Dakota to whom we had been introduced by Gerald Mohatt (Mohatt and Eagle Elk 2000). Mohatt, who was also invited to give a paper at Austen Riggs the following summer, had found our Lacan to be a close kin of the Plains Indians. The puns and the theory of lack and loss as the basis of desire reminded him of "give-away" rituals. And in fact this notion was anchored, for Lacan, in Marcel Mauss's *The Gift* (1924), which was itself influenced by the Amerindians. So we were moving on to one of the sources of Lacanian theory. Thus, for several consecutive summers, on the Rosebud Reservation, then on Manitoulin Island in Ontario (Mohatt and Eagle Elk 2000, Muller 1995), we exchanged clinical stories with medicine men and analysts.

In the ceremonial context, a person is received not just as an individual but in the name of all those to whom he is connected. This bond is conveyed through the word and through pledging one's word. We were surprised, therefore, to find direct experience of a theory of speech and language that was familiar to us (Lacan 1953), right down to the comic use of jokes and double entendres during the meal following the ceremony. In the past, in medieval Europe, laughter had been part of the rite. Had we, then, come all this way to find the near and distant trace of language games that had been in use in our own part of the world? In any case, this is how Stanley Red Bird (1984), one of the leaders of the Rosebud Reservation, put it during one of these meetings: "You're finding here what you also have at home."

But in France, at this time, the art of telling clinical stories was hardly in favor. As a rule, in the human sciences, seriousness of conceptualization relegated such stories to the rank of anecdotes. In retrospect, the pleasure of such an exchange—at Austen Riggs in Massachusetts, at the Sinte Gleska University on the Rosebud Reservation in South Dakota, on Manitoulin Island in Lake Huron, at the University of Alaska in Fairbanks—had to do with one detail that, though often forgotten, is fundamental: the therapists admitted that they did not always play the right role or offer the right interpretation but were working on the basis of their own flaws. This work was part of the path they had to walk in the transference to a chosen other, analyst or medicine man. Such a skill had not been gained once and for all in moving up through the stages of official training. Jacques Lacan had already been ironic about the "Lacan label" marking the boundaries of all the conformities and registered trademarks and, obviously, providing no definitive passport for clinical experience.

HISTORY'S STORIES

The stories we were beginning to tell then, with complete freedom, seemed from the outset to be the stories of history,[4] the history to which we never stopped bringing these patients back. Thirty years later, the title of the present book still emphasizes this point. As Lynn Hunt, a historian of the French revolution (1992), has recently noted in juxtaposing history and psychoanalysis (2002), the two disciplines were made to encounter one another. But the meeting has been a difficult one. According to Hunt, the trouble stems from the incommensurability between the historical approach, based on the analysis of social forces, and the clinical approach that is so quickly reduced to the individual scale. Between the "tyranny of the social and that of the individual," the outcome, as always, cannot be found in dichotomy.

Where it occurs is in the gap opened up by those patients who rightly lament that they have no self, no "me," no individuality. They teach us that this absence of boundaries is the source of their ability to bear witness to the stories that have been erased from history, the history of breakdowns in the social order, whose disaster they reveal at

---

4. Translator's note: In French, the same word, *histoire*, means both "story" and "history."

the price of their own identity. They enable us to see in the "decided simplification of the ordinary life situation [met with in schizophrenics] manifestations of the subject matter of each of the social sciences" (Sullivan 1974, p. 223), as well as concrete examples of the encounter described by Hunt (2002). Indeed, in the very place where the analyst and the historian find it hard to connect with one another, analytic experience returns to another of its roots, one that is even more deeply buried: the epic function that confronts what has never before been said. In so doing, it once again discovers the rhythms and landmarks of the oral traditions, beginning with the *Iliad*, discussed by the Hellenist Gregory Nagy (1979).

Epics always relate stories of war and battles. In our experience as psychoanalysts, war and madness have an odd relation to one another. Like Socrates at the beginning of Plato's *Gorgias*, analysts usually arrive after the fighting is over.[5] And yet we always go back there. Is this just our "hobby horse," making us the heirs of Don Quixote or of the Uncle Toby of Sterne's *Tristram Shandy* in order to make contact with difficult patients?

IN EXTREME CONDITIONS, A SOCIAL BOND OUTSIDE THE NORM

At any rate, it is hard to pinpoint such patients without discrediting them; euphemisms like that adjective "difficult" are hardly more illuminating. And so we shall speak of madness. Starting right now, we have to make it clear that we never use this word to describe the structure of an individual but instead to characterize a form of social link in an extreme situation. Wars on whatever scale—worldwide, civil or ethnic wars, wars of decolonization—are such extreme circumstances, in which the breakdown of all reference points gives rise to links outside the norm. People said to be crazy, in the ordinary sense of the term, show us what it was necessary to do in order to survive.

---

5. CALLICLES: This is how they say you should take part in warfare and battle, Socrates.

SOCRATES: What, have we arrived at the latter end of a feast, as the saying goes? [447a, p. 230]

Thus, in our experience, the successive shocks that constitute the rhythm of an analysis of madness always lead us back to the same region, the field of historical and social traumas. In the symptoms of patients who never directly experienced battlefield traumas there persists the evidence of such collapses of time and of guarantees of speech, to their own generation, in "the long week-end" between two wars (Bion 1982).

But no sooner have these areas been perceived and recognized than they are actualized here and now, in the work of the transference. It's war in the analysis, without metaphor. Analytic experience shows that long-ago wars form a precipitate in the sessions on the basis of resonances with the analyst's historical bearings or lineage. Such bizarre, uncanny interferences add dimension to these erased catastrophic areas and bring them back into awareness. Their historicization results in unarguable improvements on the individual level, spreading out into the social fabric by means of different language games that are equivalent to "forms of life" (Wittgenstein 1945–1949, §23).

A MEMORY THAT DOES NOT FORGET

What about people living today in countries or on continents that were not territorially affected by world wars? And what about their therapists, who are also too young to have been touched by these historic earthquakes? When someone like this from overseas asks us such questions, we simply reply, "How about your grandparents and your ancestors three or four generations back?" The same comments, the same questions, hold true for analysts' forebears.

To mention only the United States, which is entirely oriented toward the future to be constructed, these resistant symptoms keep on asking, "Your families that immigrated: where did they come from, when did they leave their country of origin, under what catastrophic circumstances? And what about the frontier, and the Indian Wars, the Hispanic Wars, the Civil War? And the African, American, Canadian, Australian, English, and other national cemeteries on French soil? And the wars in Asia and Africa, and social, economic, and natural disasters, on whatever scale?" It would take too much time to list all the countries from which refugees have fled in order to start a new life and forget.

Despite the understandable determination to forget the past, all we had to do was mention this connection between psychoanalysis and the madness of wars for the audiences at the seminars in which we set forth this experience to be reminded, hesitantly but so easily, of the ruined worlds from which their patients' ancestors had escaped. And the analysts' forebears as well: "My father was wounded in Italy and my grandfather was a prisoner for five years; when they came back they were never the same again," we were told at a lecture in Vermont.

At the invitation of the Appalachian Psychoanalytic Society[6] we gave a talk in Knoxville, Tennessee, on *Absalom, Absalom* (Faulkner 1936), which was in the forefront of our seminar. That evening, one of the participants continued, over drinks, reconstituting for us in detail the battle of the War of Secession in which two of his ancestors had taken part on each side of the frontline: here was the escarpment, the steep slope (fascinated, we watched the great-nephew's hands), over there was a safe zone, but here one was sure to be killed. As though it were yesterday, and more intensely than in the movies, this analyst seemed to us to be stepping right out of the smoke and dust of battle with mustache, tunic, large hat, or peaked cap. Patients, too, speak in a temporality outside of time.

During these conferences it happened that Americans, in turn, reminded us of a memory that does not forget. In a powwow on Manitoulin Island, in Canada, at a dance around the feather that falls for each warrior killed in combat, someone mentioned those who lie dead in France under wooden crosses. In Alaska, a former World War II pilot took us to task, mentioning his buddy killed in the sky over France.

In 1995, when, invited by The Washington School of Psychiatry, we began working on the relationship between war and the psycho-analysis of the psychoses, Nancy Balakar, M.D. (Commander, U.S. Navy, ret.), spoke to us at the end of our seminar about "forward psychia-try" and "the Salmon principles," about which we hadn't the slightest idea. We had seen the name Salmon twenty years earlier in Lacan's

---

6. William MacGillivray, at that time president of the Appalachian Association, gave us the opportunity to get to know Pat Barker's *Trilogy* (1992, 1994, 1995).

(1947) paper without realizing how important it was. Balakar sent us articles that we shall be citing in the course of this book.[7]

During a stay in Paris, Skip Meade, the descendant of an African-American fighter in World War II, offered our seminar excerpts from the writings of W. E. B. Dubois (Dubois 1921) on the role of black U.S. soldiers during the First World War. He told us about how the Red Hand Division distinguished itself heroically under French command.[8] Had we too, then, forgotten, withdrawing into some sort of unawareness?

TRAUMAS WITHOUT A LESION

It is precisely with the critical question of unawareness that we begin this book. In the first part, we discuss the arguments of the neurologist Antonio Damasio (1995, 1999). But, as it happens, the relationship between insanity and neurology has a history that once again takes us back to the war of 1914. The English historian Ben Shephard (2000) gives a detailed account of this in *A War of Nerves: Soldiers and Psychiatrists in the Twentieth Century*. To some extent, the psychoanalysis of the psychoses got its start on this front, exposing psychiatrists from the outset to the confusion between madness, psychic trauma, and cerebral lesions.

How, then, does the question present itself? Patients who are clearly afflicted with a cerebral lesion retain an intact intelligence. But, disconnected from their affects, that intelligence leads them to make incoherent and disastrous decisions. Yet a very specific transference joining the researcher to his patient, and attested by the neurologist himself, opens up a fertile area of contact between neurology and psychoanalysis. This prompts us, personally, to think about symptoms that

---

7. We presented them in 1996–1997 in our seminar entitled "The Madness of War," at the Ecole des Hautes Etudes en Sciences Sociales in Paris.

8. Dubois cites the letter of December 15, 1918 from the French general Goybet, who led the Red Hand division for eight months, when he transferred it to American command. He praises the men for their performance in the battle of Champagne in September of that year: "The Red Hand Division has, during nine hard days of battle, been ahead in the victorious advance of the Fourth French Army . . . and led us to victory. Soaked in the blood of the brave, those bonds will be indestructible" (p. 66).

are similar but that are not related to any lesion. Damasio (1995) goes as far as to extrapolate this paradox to a "sick culture" (p. 178) and wonders about the brilliant and affectless intelligences that may constitute its breeding ground. For totalitarian systems and "scientifically programmed" mass exterminations are still in the news today.

TEMPORAL PARADOXES OF THE TRANSFERENCE WITH MADNESS

For us, three factors have constantly brought us back to these war zones:

1. Our patients' crises open an investigation of the sociopolitical fault lines in which the self has exploded.
2. These crises resonate with our own situation during World War II. Both of us were born during this troubled period, and it is activated for us by the analogous area in the space-time of our patients, even if they are bringing us experiences from the other end of the planet with decades of intervening years.
3. The analysts who oriented our research and our clinical work were directly involved in these wars. We shall be describing this dialogue that has gone on for over twenty-five years, either face to face or through their books and papers.

In this way the principles of war psychiatry gradually came to seem to us like a framework and a method that were familiar to us in practice even before we discovered their formalization by Thomas Salmon. Salmon had presented them on the basis of his reconnaissance mission in France in 1917. They underlie the presentation of our clinical and theoretical work in the second part of this book.

Still, we are not claiming to provide an extensive treatment of the field of trauma, war, or madness, already covered by an abundant literature,[9] nor to add to a semiology that is, to say the least, problematical when it comes to psychoanalysis. An objective presentation would

---

9. See, for example, on traumatic dreams Barrett 1996 and, recently, Belau and Ramadanovic 2002.

classify mass or individual trauma on a quantitative basis. In a cultural relativism, it would differentiate what is normal here and what seems intolerable over there. It would make a chronological distinction between wars in past times and wars today.

We have made the opposite choice. We cannot, of course, support the fraudulent notion of an ahistorical and universal psychic reality. The constant changes of scale and the temporal paradoxes we encounter in the examples we give imply precisely that they are located with the greatest exactitude in history, space, and time. But we have emphasized the critical moments of the transference where the exactitude of these references gets blurred and becomes irrelevant. The crises of the planet are the objects of rigorous studies in each discipline charged with analyzing them. But these analyses change their frames of reference abruptly as soon as the event touches you personally.

At these times when he is somehow *touché*, as they say in fencing, the analyst is caught up in the catastrophic area of the investigation. Subject and object are confused: here and there, inside and outside. The past is present, the dead return. It is a child's voice that is speaking, in a session, through the mouth of the adult he has become, in the name of an entire society threatened with disappearance. Killings on the far-off African shores take up residence in a massacre that occurred in the mountains where the analyst was born, at the same time or years earlier.

Our work brings into existence zones of nonexistence wiped out by a powerful blow that actually took place. But whatever the measures chosen for erasing facts and people from memory, the erasures, even when perfectly programmed, only set in motion a memory that does not forget and that is seeking to be inscribed. In Greek, non-forgetting is, literally, *a-letheia*: this is the very name of truth, at stake in this specific memory as in the scientific approach. Hence we do not have to choose between the minute detail and the global fact. Sometimes a fit of madness tells us more than all the news dispatches about the leftover facts that have no right to existence.

SHORT STORIES FOR A MICROHISTORY

Our accounts of the ways in which these remnants make themselves felt will be intentionally short. In their straightforwardness, they correspond to the critical, heuristic moments of analysis, and to the moments of impasse as well, when the available ways of knowing are no longer effective. These pivotal episodes involve a small number of sessions. We wanted to capture them in their conciseness. In these accounts of when the analytic process founders, the findings and the interpretation always have to do with a piece of the story that escaped history. Actualized in the transference, it sometimes allows time to start moving forward again. These examples are not so much illustrations of a theoretical schema as they are instants of on-the-spot discovery, and so they do not call for an exhaustive case presentation. Nor can they be assimilated through a statistical treatment or measured against standard scales, forcing them into a pseudo-scientificity.

It is true that, today, psychoanalysis looks antiquated. Its vignettes seem outdated when everything comes down to averages. An almost picturesque vestige, it has left the Broadway footlights of conferences on mental health. Hence the idea of this book: off-Broadway, where psychoanalysis can be found in the company of Quixote-like ex-servicemen, a bit ridiculous, not very brilliant. But, in the case of madness, when the time is out of joint, hasn't offstage always been where rather foolish old warriors who keep on saying the same thing meet up with those—little children or therapists—who can't help listening to them and, in different ways according to the time and place, keep trying to make a story out of what has not been received by any form of speech?

One of the important tasks we have set ourselves in this book is describing how the coming into being of the subject of speech, in circumstances created for its destruction, is a matter of life or death. The destruction—this is no metaphor—of the guarantees of speech, and the deconstruction of all reference points, leave the subject who is confronted with them in a state of total estrangement, of absolute aloneness with regard to all the ties that, up to that point, were familiar (Shapiro and Carr 1991). This alienation from the world is transmitted to whichever of the person's descendants try, in some outburst of madness, to communicate and demonstrate the deafening screams that were left in a state of suspension, until they find someone to whom it has been given to accompany them to those places that no one wants to look at or hear about anymore, so that they can begin a transmission. In this way, a child's gaze can transmit the reflection of a people's disappearance or the vanishing of a social bond on whatever scale. Must we really try to subdue this hypersensitivity? And, most important, how is it to be described?

BACK TO GROUND ZERO WITH DESCARTES AND WITTGENSTEIN

We would have liked to proceed in a linear exposition, going from premises to conclusions, unfolding arguments in fine logical order. But the only way we could approach this subject was through the progressive impressions left on us by the strange worlds into which we were led, often against our will.

Recently or long ago, our American readers, too, came from one of these "elsewheres." They or their families left the "back there" of disaster zones. They survived, they made it through, they left their loved ones there. When we returned to New York at the end of October 2001, we stood in remembrance near Ground Zero. It happened to be Halloween. After September 11, everyone was expecting craziness and universal breakdown. But, amid the horror and the traumas, there appeared a resistance to the disasters and the terror that everyone must, after all, get from somewhere, and why not from one of those "elsewheres"?

To conclude this preface, we want to let two veterans speak, philosophers who will reappear in the course of this book: Ludwig Wittgenstein in connection with the two world wars and René Descartes with the Thirty Years War.

In his preface to the *Philosophical Investigations* (1945–1949) Wittgenstein excuses his inability to keep from "jumping from one topic to another," comparing his book to a journey "over a wide field of thought, criss-cross in every direction." This is exactly the movement of the transference, which can be described only across a discontinuity similar to Wittgenstein's "sketches and landscapes made in the course of these long and involved journeyings." He adds: "It is not impossible that it should fall to the lot of this world, in its poverty and in the darkness of this time, to bring light into one brain or another, but, of course, it is not likely" (p. 33).

Without being so pessimistic as this, we shall simply join Descartes (1637) in offering our readers an account that stems less from what we know than from what we don't know:

> I would very much like everyone to know that what little I have learned up until now is almost nothing in comparison with that of which I am ignorant and which I am not despairing of being able to learn. For it is almost the same with those who little by little discover the truth in the sciences [as it is for those] who need more leadership to maintain themselves after the loss of a battle than they do to take cities or provinces after having won one. For to try to vanquish all the difficulties and the errors that prevent us from arriving at the knowledge of the truth is truly to engage in battles, and to accept some false opinion concerning a matter even a little general and important is to lose one of them. [pp. 91–92]

What we shall be doing, then, is chronicling the battles to which our patients incited us. These critical moments are also moments of theoretical encounters that lead us, each time, to understand that the connection between madness and trauma is not a causal one. For there can be no transition from the past to the present when the impact of disaster has immobilized time. Thus the stories we shall tell are those of descendants whose task it was to transmit, from generation to generation, pieces of frozen time. The problem is to recognize that these moments excised from history are actualized in the present of the analytic work. As Descartes says, it would be "to accept some false opinion" if we were not to do battle with[10] these patients who literally fight with their backs to the wall in order to bring forth rejected truths.

---

10. "With" in both senses: "alongside" and "against."

I

LESSONS OF MADNESS

I

From the Collapse of a World to the Search for Insanity

I.I. FOLLY SPEAKS[1]

I.I.I Auguste: In the Beginning Was Shame

"I'm a dissident of the Western world. My madness appeared at the intersection of the history of the last war and the story of my family. I'm carrying a *samizdat*,[2] a secret message that I myself don't know about. My mission is to see that it arrives at its destination, at the risk of my life. I threw all my clothes into the water from a bridge over the

---

1. The Latin title, *Encomium Moriae*, of Erasmus's (1508) *Praise of Folly* puns on the name of Thomas More, to whom it is dedicated. Composed on horseback, while Erasmus, returning from a visit to the Italian humanists, was crossing the Alps, this work was a success throughout Europe during the time of the wars of religion. The allegorical figure of Folly (sometimes translated here as Madness) plays on words, and, in its time, the verbal virtuosity of the book went far beyond Lacan's passion for punning on signifiers. Lacan (1974) placed his own work in this tradition: "Be more relaxed, more natural when someone comes to you to ask for analysis. Don't feel that you have to be pushy. You're even justified to be clownish. All you have to do is look at my "Télévision." *I'm a clown. Model yourself on that, and don't imitate me"* (p. 547, emphasis added). With all due respect to sensitive ears, when it comes to choosing between avoiding pejorative diagnoses and using euphemisms that fool no one, we have no hesitation in calling madness by its name; as they say in English, we shall call a cat a cat.

2. The word *samizdat*, borrowed from the Russian, literally means "self-publication," on the model of *gosizdat*, "state publication." Censorship was so extensive that the word did not occur in official Russian dictionaries, although it had been used quite normally before the period of liberalization. *Samizdat* refers to the clandestine dissemination of works forbidden by the censors in the Soviet Union, and, metonymically, a work thus disseminated.

Seine, along with all my papers, so that no one would recognize my identity."

This theory of madness, uttered during one of the initial interviews with the analyst,[3] seemed to belong to a case of madness. Moreover, in the way he carried himself, his retiring gaze, and his toneless voice, the man sitting opposite her did all he could to make himself forgotten, like a child at the edge of a family photo. We shall call him Auguste, like the Roman emperor and like the clumsy clown, partner of the white clown in French circuses.

His insanity had, in fact, broken out on the hills of Rome. Sent back to France in order to be committed to a mental institution, he asked to be hospitalized in an avant-garde clinic, where he hoped that the validity of his *samizdat* would be acknowledged. Electroshocks wrapped in fine words took the place of the interlocutor he trusted he would find there. After several months, he left against medical advice, remained catatonic at home, and finally rang the analyst's doorbell.

It took time for the *samizdat*, which showed the history of his lineage, to be woven between Auguste and the analyst. His family, which had done business with Germany for a long time, had been caught up in the settling of scores during the purge after the war.[4] Afterward, his parents began a new life. His birth helped them to forget the past. The pampered child was to know nothing, while his mother, in silence, was slowly dying of cancer. He cherished a very tender memory, without drama, of this fatal illness. Then life resumed its course, as if nothing had happened. Now this "nothing" was brought to the analyst in condensed form, as though frozen in that strange-sounding Russian word. In this way, Auguste opened for the analyst the pathways and voices of the war, where history intersects everyone's story, resonating equally with the analyst's. Little by little, the impasses of his life gave way to creative outcomes.

---

3. Throughout this book, "the analyst" refers to either Françoise Davoine or Jean-Max Gaudillière. In the case histories, the use of feminine or masculine pronouns will identify which one is meant.

4. During the French Revolution, the word *purge* was used to refer to the elimination of undesirable elements in a party or society. It was revived in connection with the measures taken in France after the liberation, with regard to persons accused of having collaborated with the German occupiers.

It was difficult simply to say that the war had made him crazy; Auguste had not lived through that period, and he was the only one among his siblings to present these striking problems. Objective causality comes up against serious limits here. On the other hand, his family's tragedy can be reconstructed on the basis of the shame and silence surrounding the time of purge and collaboration. In any event, Auguste rejected these constructions as irrelevant. He had the art of making the analyst fall on her face. The failure of these attempts at interpretation gradually came to turn the analytic work into a disaster area in which he was no longer the only one to wander. The analyst often felt herself to be inadequate and foolish. At least this unpleasant feeling was the preliminary stage of a relationship. It was better than "nothing."

The only proposition that holds good in this case can be summed up in the words of the master clown, Glock[5]: "Want to play with meee?" Each session was a battle against non-sense; each session was the last session.

One day, shame appeared on the scene. As usual, Auguste was talking about ending his analysis, but this time for good. Urged by the analyst to explain, he finally said, not without reluctance, "I think you're namby-pamby." The onomatopoeia condemns the absence of energy along with a whiny, self-satisfied attitude. Touched to the quick, the analyst replied, "And what does that remind you of?"

This analytic reflex enabled her to gain time, first of all in order to justify herself internally. Wasn't it *his* apathy that was blocking the sessions? But an association, a painful one, was hovering about, one that she found it hard to catch on the wing. That day she was awaiting the results of a laparoscopy that would inform her whether or not she had cancer. After a period of reflection, she finally told him about this suspense, realizing only then the extent of her own despondency: "I'm waiting for the results of medical tests; no doubt you've noticed my apprehension."

As if this confession on the part of the analyst were something he took for granted, he began to recount, for the first time, the shame he

---

5. Adrien Wettach (1880–1959), known as Glock, was the most famous of the Augustes. According to tradition, the name Auguste was coined, in 1898, from the German expression *dummer Augustus*, meaning "idiot."

felt when his mother came to take him home from school, prematurely aged by her illness, alongside the mothers of his pals. Then gradually, as the sessions went on, the unbearable shame represented by his mother was joined by The Shame that, after the liberation, marked those who, directly or indirectly, had had moments of weakness with the enemy. Afterward time dulled these strong impressions; everyone came to terms with the past and rewrote history in his or her own way.

Auguste had made it necessary for the historical truth of shame first to be embodied, then to be spoken, and finally to be inscribed. He was somehow able to go back to the topic of his dissertation in philosophy, which had been interrupted for many years, because of the topic of the insanity of truth and the truth of insanity.

In this way, little by little, patients like Auguste pointed us in the direction of war and led us to find the traces of a particular branch of psychiatry, one that appeared in connection with the major conflicts of the last century. Paradoxically, this was the crucible in which a psychoanalysis of the psychoses was developed. At the end of each conflict, these principles fall into disuse and must be reinvented to confront the psychic losses of the next conflict.

On the basis of these investigations, clinical and historical at the same time, what we are setting out to do here is formulate the conditions of possibility for an analytic approach to the symptoms that reveal the rupture of transmission along the fault lines of the social link. In this perspective, the handling of the transference is very different from its classical use in psychoanalysis. Here, it is aimed at inscribing the pieces of dissociated—not repressed—history, at the crossroads of the most particular and the most general (Davoine 1990, 1992).

1.1.2. The Twofold Tradition of Folly: Speaking of, Speaking to

Other scientific rationalities approach symptoms like these in terms of neuronal lesions or genetic transmission. They thereby construct an object of observation by defining their field on the basis of objectivation. Indeed, ever since antiquity madness has been received in a twofold tradition, one aspect having to do with the interior of the skull, the functioning and breakdowns of the cerebral machinery, and the other with the dimension of speech and the language games that madness brings forth. Recent advances in biology in no way disconfirm the rationality of the transferential approach.

But madness undermines the most rationally based certainties. It puts boundaries in question, for example those separating the physical sciences and the humanities (Schrödinger 1954).[6] Challenging psychoanalysis, it, too, is given to reification. Its first movement, as is shown by Auguste on his bridge, is to efface all the criteria of the subject, even those of identity. Thus, as soon as we arrived in the first hospital where we were beginning to work, one of the chronic patients said to us, "The little mice, you know? I'm your guinea pig. I'm giving my soul to science. Do whatever you want with me."

He knew perfectly well that we were not psychiatrists, neurologists, or experimental pharmacologists. What he was actually doing is summoning us to respond to him. From what place? From the place where there is no other who is responding. In speaking to a wall, to the TV, or to the universe, madness challenges its interlocutor to find the place of otherness to which it can speak.

Scientific investigation of the nervous system and the interior of the skull nowadays makes use of the latest refinements in brain scanning and biochemistry. But, in psychiatry, investigation is debased into a mechanistic theory, heir to the medieval science of humors. And, as in

---

6. Schrödinger (1954) explains his reasons for returning to ancient thought as follows:

> There was need to explain (though I was myself not so thoroughly convinced of it) that in passing the time with narratives about ancient Greek thinkers and with comments on their views, I was not just following a recently acquired hobby of mine; that it did not mean, from a professional point of view, a waste of time, which ought to be relegated to the hours of leisure. . . . Far from following an odd impulse of my own, I had been swept along unwittingly, as happens so often, by a trend of thought rooted somehow in the intellectual situation of our time. [p. 4]

He continues: "One regrets to see mankind strive towards the same goal along two different and winding paths, with blinkers and separating walls, and with little attempt to join our forces. . . . This is regrettable, I say, and would be a sad spectacle anyhow. . . . However, the loss might perhaps be endured if it were actually two separate crowds who follow two paths. But it is not so" (p. 12).

the Middle Ages, psychiatry dispenses shock treatments and amnesiac drugs. At that time, as is the case today, there were a variety of discourses concerning madness—juridical, theological, and especially medical—that argued over it without managing to contain it (Fritz 1992).[7] At the same time, the words, actions, and behaviors of people said to be "out of their minds" were the focus of an intense curiosity, no doubt livelier than is the case today (Dufournet 1974).

This state of being "out of one's mind," coming from the borderlands of discourse, did, to be sure, concern the human, but it was understood that it could be captured or tamed only through fictions, oral or written. The madman, the fool, the jester, ancestors of the clown Auguste, descendants of the ancient know-how of the oral tradition, used carnivalesque and unseemly gestures to show what cannot be said. They were the heirs of the indigenous spirits, of the pagan festivals and trances in which they could bring the ancient deities to life (Nagy 1996)[8] with the suspicious blessing of the Church.

They were the *histriones*[9] who relate unofficial history by means of gesticulations and who, by virtue of being "out of their minds," deconstruct constituted discourses. With no permanent dwelling place, they were thus like the wild men of legend, finding refuge, in their wanderings, in the forests and mountains at the edges of our world, and above all finding refuge in literature, written and oral, which was a favored place for them.

---

7. Fritz describes the discourse of the madman as one of restless wandering, of being "everywhere and nowhere, at the crossroads of speech" (p. 11). The madman was a major subject in medieval literature, for example in the anonymous *Amadas and Ydoine* from the thirteenth century, *The Tale of Tristan's Madness* from the end of the twelfth, and Adam de la Halle's *Jeu de la Feuillée* (1276). Medieval medicine is restricted to a strictly somatic viewpoint. Contrary to the stereotypes conveyed, according to Fritz, by most historians of psychiatry, this "humoral" medicine, the legacy of the Roman physician Galen, was in no way a practice of exorcists or theologians.

8. "When the rhapsode says . . . : 'Tell me, Muses!' this 'I' is not a representation of Homer; it is Homer. My argument is that the rhapsode is re-enacting Homer by performing Homer, that he is Homer so long as the mimesis stays in effect, so long as the performance lasts. In the words of T. S. Eliot ("The Dry Selvages"), 'You are the music while the music lasts'" (Nagy 1996, p. 61).

9. Schmitt (1990) emphasizes that Isidore of Seville cites a possible etymological connection between *histriones* (actors) and *historiones* (historians).

In such a desert, the wasteland that T. S. Eliot (1922) described right after the war, there is an opportunity for the wild men and women of today to be first welcomed, as in ancient times, by the knock on the head, nowadays provided by ever more modern and miraculous mechanics.[10] Nevertheless, they may also happen to find someone to talk to.

It may be useful to recall at this point that at the end of the long Middle Ages a large part of Europe had been decimated by the plague and by the Hundred Years War. From the fourteenth to the sixteenth century in France, one of the systems, social and literary, that formalized the different phases madness required in order to deliver its message of the end of the world was the "Fools' Theater," the Follies (Aubailly 1984).

Around the central character, Mother Fool or Mother Crazy, who started by uttering a loud cry, the madmen, her subjects, came bursting onto the small fairground stage. Having shed all identity as citizens, they answered only to a number: Fool Number One, Fool Number Two, and so on. They gesticulated and pirouetted in disorderly fashion, with their fools' baubles, their green and yellow costumes, and their horned hats that were supposed to make them invulnerable. Necessary precautions, since what they were doing was judging the crimes and abuses of the times: the fools dragged along the tyrants of the day (kings, popes, generals, notables), dressed in the pompous garments of their office, and proclaimed out loud what "Everyman"—the indeterminate *quidam* representing us, incarnated onstage by this general term—was thinking quietly to himself.

---

10. As Sullivan (1974) observes,

The obverse of the devil-doctrine is the old doctrine of mind and body. The demented have lost their mind, if not by dispossession by an evil spirit, at least by some strange machination which is formulated in the likeness of other magic; this is a glaring instance of magical thinking, and the more enlightened do not tolerate it. No, indeed. They show the same superstition, however, in their anxiety to *eliminate* "mind." They are the laymen who relate Johnnie's psychosis to a bump on the head and the psychiatrists who write of psychology as a division of "brain physiology." This is materialistic twaddle, and the succeeding mechanistic explanations are energized by the same old magical idea of antithetic mind and body. [p. 142, emphasis in original]

Sometimes kings protected this theater so as to have a better idea of what was going on in the realm (Zumthor 1978). At other times, the jugglers, actors, authors, and producers of the follies were persecuted and even hanged, for this political theater was highly virulent. But the most remarkable thing about it was its verdict. This was always the same: when he least expected it, the Great Man, dragged before the tribunal, was assailed by throngs of fools, who undressed him. At the end of this strip-tease, conducted in the hellish rhythm of a real verbal delirium, with a great deal of extremely skillful word-play, he appeared before everyone's eyes, not entirely naked, but, under his purple and gold, clad in motley, yellow and green: the fool's costume.

This was the scenario of the Judgment Follies, the canonical form of these plays, simultaneously political and therapeutic. They seem to us to be very close, in their structure, to the stages of an analysis of madness and trauma, in which the mere reviving and denunciation of the abuses is of no use without the vehement undressing of the tyrant, embodied by the analyst when he least expects it (Davoine 1998).

During the entire show, one of the fools carried a mirror among the audience, so that Everyman could recognize himself and observe that the boundary between the actors and the spectators was not watertight. For, at certain times, Everyman can be this Mother Crazy, this jester, and—why not?—this tyrant.

"Folly speaks": with these words, Erasmus (1508, p. 30) begins the famous personification in *The Praise of Folly*, a linear descendent of the follies. Madness, Folly, is Mother Crazy, the *subject* of a critical discourse that reviews the psychopathology of everyday insanities. A best seller in Europe, and very soon published in the New World, it was bedside reading for the more literate of the conquistadors (Fuentes 1990). At the beginning of the book, Folly states: "It is Folly speaking, . . . and I know no one who knows me better than I do myself" (p. 33). At the end, she says, "If anything I have said seems sharp or gossipy, remember that it is Folly and a woman who has spoken" (p. 123).

Dame Folly, this Fury, forcefully expresses an unalloyed knowledge. Nowadays the analyst, who is trying to become the person to whom it is addressed, must recognize this knowledge, whereas other discourses—medical, juridical, and social—try in their respective ways to calm it or to silence it. The analyst's office becomes a restricted space, highly delimited, no larger than the stage of the follies, where, slowly and painfully, something of this knowledge comes to be shared.

But at first the analyst is reluctant and, like the others, secretly wishes things would keep quiet or calm down. At the same time, he is defied: "No one knows me better than I do myself" is to be heard as a *casus belli*. If the analyst, too, manages to know something about it, it is because he has been shaken up, dragged onstage against his will, pushed to reveal the role of folly, of madness, that he is playing in this process. Sometimes jester, sometimes even tyrant, he will then speak "to" madness instead of speaking "of" it. It is at this moment, brief as it is in the course of a treatment, that there truly occurs the analysis of a riddle that has taken so much time to let itself be approached and circumscribed.

To whom, then, is Erasmus's Folly speaking? The humanist, following a secular tradition of "follisophy," teaches us that it is we— "The People," who is also a character in the follies—who are being addressed.

1.1.3. When Folly Is Speaking to No One, to Whom Is It Speaking? A Social Link in the Making

In order to constitute an addressee for its discourse, madness demands a change in the interlocutor on whom it falls and whom it causes to fall with its symptoms.[11] It goes in search of an echo, in this improbable other, of what official history has marginalized or trivialized, evoking in the analyst details and anecdotes that have been unclaimed, even in his or her own analysis. Here again psychoanalysis is in touch with the oral tradition, which is not confined to the preliterate history of antiquity or to societies said to be "without history" before their encounter with writing. It is precisely in the space of this atemporality that madness juggles, gesticulates, and resists.

Without time, without place, a piece of history that had escaped History now arrives, at the intersection of the singular and the plural, in the form of "a social link in the making" (Revel 1996, cf. Revel 2001)—but only if the symptom finds someone to speak to. For, in seem-

---

11. From the Greek *sympipto*, "fall with."

ing to refer only to itself, it is simply showing that it is alone in trying to be understood. This is not to imply that there can be no one else. Wittgenstein (1914–1916) asks, "Can't I say something to nobody, neither to anybody else nor to myself? What is the criterion of saying it to myself?" (p. 45) and states, "When one says, 'I talk to myself,' one generally means just that one speaks and is the only person listening" (p. 15). It takes time to leave the objectivation of this position, all the time that is needed to pass from what falls on you, and makes you fall, to a case history, that is, to the account of an *agôn*, an action in which the analyst becomes the antagonist actor.

On the basis of thirty years of work in the clinical psychoanalysis of madness—in a psychiatric hospital, in a health center, and in private practice—what we want to do here is describe a kind of anthropological constant: every interruption in the transmission that links people to one another is, paradoxically, searching for the pathways of an inscription. Most often, this dynamic seems to come up against the irreparable. But madness is one of the social relations dedicated to this hard and exacting task, to contact with the impossible. It sets in motion a conjoint search in which the analyst takes the second place, thereby becoming part of the field to be analyzed.

Psychoanalysis is, as it were, one of the pathways that madness has found in this century in order to make itself understood by us. Through the slowness, regularity, and rigor of its setup, it enables the analyst to come into contact with, and to exist in, the patient's zones of non-existence.[12] This process is as old as human societies, passing first

---

12. As Benedetti (1980) puts it:

The more we pile up interpretations of genetic mechanisms and behavioral models, the more we add to the weight of the things the poor ego of the patient has to bear. And in this way we are promoting its dissolution. The old saying that psychoanalysis is counterindicated in the therapy of the psychoses remains completely valid here. On the other hand, the psychotherapy of psychosis is analytic only to the extent that *we are prepared to analyze ourselves continually in the encounter with the patient*. . . . At the outset, psychotherapy does not consist in analyzing the experiences that led to non-existence. It begins with the therapist's attempt to exist in the patient's non-existence, with the attempt to transform it into existence by means of a presence in it. [p. 25]

through language games[13] to weave a social bond that was impossible up to then and to make a "text,"[14] a memory, and thus a possible forgetting. For the madness that speaks to itself—or to everyone, that is, to no one—shows outside of temporality what no one wants to know anything about and what is not inscribed as past.

Thus we shall be telling stories as a certain number of particular cases,[15] which will enable us to reveal lapsed, eradicated social relations on whatever scale. These disappearances are sometimes all too evident, too known. Or, on the contrary, they remain unperceived, anecdotal, and erratic with regard to broad sociological, historical, or political currents. The particular case, here, is the sole level of relevance and, with all due respect to the law of large numbers, we do not have to be ashamed of that. "The world is everything which is the case."[16]

The signs, the symptomatic details emphasized by crises of madness, thus point to the disaster areas in which the social fabric creases (crises/creases) or tears. These are the contexts in which it is normal to be crazy—on condition that the analyst is located there and is asking himself what the social link consists of in such a case and how, in this case, with this patient, "there could be a social link instead of nothing" (Revel 2001). For the social link cannot be taken for granted. Each case of madness requires the analyst to respond to the leftovers, the residue of the generalistic discourses of the social sciences, including psychoanalysis.

---

13. "[T]he term of language game is meant to bring into prominence the fact that the speaking of language is part of an activity, or of a form of life, including the tone of voice and the look with which the words are uttered. . . . There are countless kinds" (Wittgenstein 1945–1949, § 19, 22, 23).

14. "The singer, rhapsode, *rhapsoidos*, [is] he who sews together (*rhapto*) the song (*aoidé*). . . . Song is visualized as a web, a fabric, a textile (Latin *textilis*, from *texo*, weave), or, to use only for the moment an English word which no longer retains its metaphorical heritage, even a text (Latin *textus*, again from *texo*)" (Nagy 1996, pp. 64–65).

15. Latin *casus*, from *cadere*, "fall." Again we cite Wittgenstein: "I want to say here that it can never be our job to reduce anything to anything, or to explain anything. . . . Instead of 'craving for generality,' I could also have said 'the contemptuous attitude toward the particular case'" (1933–1934, p. 18).

16. Wittgenstein 1918. This is the first sentence in the *Tractatus*; the last, "*Wovon man nicht sprechen kann, darüber muss man schweigen*" ("Whereof one cannot speak, thereof one must be silent" [p. 85]), inspired the subtitle of this book.

These little nothings jam the signifying machines, wreck the serious mood. Survivors of extreme situations bear witness to the fact that the line between the tragic and the comic is unpredictable. It takes nothing to pass from laughter to despair. The Marx brothers and all the masterpieces of comic film between the two world wars make us collapse with laughter by showing a world in a never-ending state of catastrophic collapse.

But, in the years between the wars, the invention of the social in catastrophic moments in which all trustworthiness goes under was also characterized by epistemological ruptures. Freud passes from the topographic to the structural theory, and Wittgenstein sets out on the course that will lead him from his first to his second philosophy. Between the burning of his books in 1933 to his death in 1939, Freud will wonder how a culture can be transmitted despite its eradication.[17]

During the same interval, the philosopher, struggling with major suicidal crises, passes from the conclusion of the *Tractatus* ("whereof one cannot speak, thereof one must be silent") to the elaboration of a philosophy that, for him, functions as a therapy.[18] Wittgenstein's three

---

17. Speaking of the composition of *Moses and Monotheism*, Freud (1939) says:

I found myself unable to wipe out the traces of the history of the work's origin, which was in any case unusual. Actually it has been written twice: for the first time a few years ago in Vienna . . . , where I did not think it would be possible to publish it. I determined to give it up, but it tormented me like an unlaid ghost, and I found a way out by making the two pieces (Moses an Egyptian, if Moses was an Egyptian) of it independent and publishing it in our periodical *Imago*. The remainder, which included what was open to objection and dangerous, the application of these findings to the genesis of monotheism and the view of religion in general, I held back as I thought forever. Then in March 1938 came the unexpected German invasion, which forced me to leave my home but also freed me from my anxiety lest my publication might conjure up a prohibition of psychoanalysis in a place where it was still tolerated. I had scarcely arrived in England before I found the temptation irresistible to make the knowledge I had held back accessible to the world, and I began to revise the third part (this actual Part II) of my study to fit it on the two parts that had already been published. [p. 129]

18. "There is not a philosophical method, though there are indeed methods, like different therapies" (Wittgenstein 1945–1949, § 133). Earlier, he had written:

brothers (he was the last born of eight siblings) committed suicide (McGuinness 1988, Monk 1990). Such sacrifices are always a threat in the investigations into which patients draw us. For we enter with them into a realm in which representation, guarantees, ideals, and legitimacies are reduced to nothingness.

Jacques Lacan was in the habit of calling this realm "the Real": that which knows neither name nor image and "always returns to the same place" outside of symbolization. The Real is "the impossible,"[19] that which "doesn't stop not being written."[20] It irrupts where the oppositions that structure our common reality—inside and outside, before and after—no longer function, where the guarantees of legitimacy that underlie the social link are flouted.

Thus, by definition, the irruption of the Real makes all otherness impossible, whether it be the other who is similar to me, my brother,[21]

Now, suppose that the tool with the name "N" is broken. Not knowing this, A gives B the sign "N." Has this sign meaning or not? What is B to do when he is given it? We have not settled anything about this. One might ask: what will he do? Well, perhaps he will stand at a loss, or shew A the pieces. Here one might say: "N" has become meaningless, and this expression would mean that the sign "N" no longer had a use in our language game (unless we gave it a new one). . . . *But we could also imagine a convention whereby B has to shake his head in reply if A gives him the sign belonging to a tool that is broken.* In this way, the command "N" might be said to be given a place in the language game, even when the tool no longer exists, and the sign "N" to have meaning even when the bearer ceases to exist. [§ 41, emphasis added]

19. "Here we once again find the terms that are the ones I defined as fixing the category of the Real, insofar as it is radically distinguished, in what I am articulating, from the Symbolic and the Imaginary—*the Real is the impossible.* Not as being simply the abutment against which we bump our foreheads but as the logical abutment of that which, from the Symbolic, is pronounced impossible" (Lacan 1969–1970, p. 143, emphasis added).

20. "What doesn't stop not being written is a modal category, and it's not the one you might have expected to be opposed to the necessary, which instead would have been the contingent. Imagine that the necessary is linked to the impossible, and that what doesn't stop not being written is its articulation" (Lacan 1972–1973, p. 59, translation modified).

21. This is Baudelaire's famous address to the reader: *"Hypocrite lecteur, mon semblable, mon frère"* (1861, p. 82).

with whom I identify and with whom I compete (in the register Lacan calls the Imaginary), or the Other invoked to guarantee alliance, promises, and good faith in the register of the Symbolic. Thus the register of the Real is defined by a repudiation, a foreclosure of symbolization: "what has not come to light in the Symbolic appears in the Real."[22]

This register also pertains to everything in nature that has not come to the light of symbolization (for example, into scientific formulation) but spreads with a blind and nameless force, encountering no limits. But this same register of the Real also denotes what appears among men when, possibly in the name of science, social links are destined to annihilation. When the guarantees of speech have been destroyed, how to construct an Other to whom to speak?

1.1.4. Adam, Holzminden: The Return of the Real

Several years ago a novel appeared whose author had gone to the other end of the world to write it after having stopped his analysis. The plot involved the tragic end of a character who had made his fortune from

---

22. In connection with Freud's concept of repudiation (*Verwerfung*), Lacan (1954) makes the following observation:

> *Verwerfung* has cut short every manifestation of the symbolic order, that, is, the *Bejahung* [affirmation] that Freud posits as the primary process in which attributive judgment takes root and that is nothing other than the primordial condition for something coming out of the Real into the revelation of being. . . . But what becomes of that which is not left to be in this *Bejahung*? Freud has told us this at the outset: what the subject has thus repudiated (*verworfen*), let us say from the opening out into being, will not be found in his history, if we give that name to the place where the repressed comes to reappear. For I beg you to note how striking the formula is being without the least ambiguity; the subject will want to "know nothing" about it in the sense of repression. For in order for him to have some awareness of it in this sense, it would have somehow had to come into the light of primordial symbolization. But, once again, what happens to it? What happens to it you can see: what has not come to light in the Symbolic appears in the Real. For this is how the *Einbeziehung ins Ich*, the introduction into the subject, is to be understood, and the *Ausstossung aus dem Ich*, the expulsion from the subject. It is the latter that constitutes the Real, in that it is the domain of what subsists outside of symbolization. [pp. 387–388]

the beginnings of the cinema. An anonymous critic panned the book in a brief review in a daily paper. A few weeks later, the same paper sang the praises, this time signed, of the same author's works in the form of a funeral eulogy: he had jumped from a window. We shall call him Adam.

Was this an honor suicide like that of his father, a career officer in the military, who had shot himself in the heart long ago? The child, away on holiday at the time, learned only much later the circumstances of his father's disappearance. What had remained was the pistol, which constantly aroused his curiosity, since his father had spoken of it as a childhood memory that kept on haunting him. Every day the weapon had been placed threateningly on the family table by the German officers who occupied the house during World War I. His father said that, as a child, he, the father, had expected it to go off at any moment.

Afterward the father and his siblings, themselves the children of an officer, had to leave their home. They lived on the outskirts of Lorraine, the theater of all wars going back at least as far as 1870, and, during the First World War, were deported to a concentration camp with their grandparents, while their father, Adam's grandfather, was at the front. Right after the war, at the instigation of his teacher, the oldest of the children, Adam's uncle, who later would become the director of a large psychiatric hospital, wrote a small book about his deportation to Holzminden, reporting the horrors of the camp in the style of a children's story.

When the analyst first heard Adam telling this story, she corrected him: the words "deportation" and "concentration camp" referred to the history of the *Second* World War, not the First. But he was insistent, arguing that, although he had spoken wildly on this topic in the past, his uncle's text was reliable.

The analyst had to admit she was wrong when other patients from the same province told her about how their own grandparents had been deported under the same, hardly believable, circumstances. One of these patients conducted her own investigation in her native region and found a book of local history, recently written by children in a high school near Verdun together with their history teacher. They had questioned the last survivors of the Great War and established the authenticity of the testimony: there, at the right place, was the photograph of

the "barracks of the Holzminden concentration camp, where a number of citizens of Lorraine were deported" (Delmas 1988, p. 180). Today,
years later, a historian has validated their claim (Becker 1998).

But neither the book of the Lorraine children nor Adam's uncle's
story could prevent the blind repetition of fate. A succession of violent deaths had afflicted the family before carrying away the novel and
its author. What is seeking to be inscribed in this way, at the edge of
the impossible, at the risk of one's life?

Psychoanalysis seemed unequal to the task. Discredited, the analyst wanted to stop her practice then and there. She still reproaches
herself for having let the patient go so far away in order to write, despite
all his good reasons for getting the necessary background. Unrealistically,
she is sorry that she was not there *with* him, in the borderlands of the
wilderness, and that she could not deal with criticism. As though the
frame of the novel had been unable to contain the anonymous lethal
violence at issue in the plot, the hero, whose true adventure had made
generations dream, had let himself starve to death, abandoned. It was
as though the analyst had been unable to contain the war, the camps,
and the deportation within the frame of their mutual work; the hunger of which the hero of the book dies had swallowed everything up:
the book, its author, and the analysis.

For what the analyst had not seen is that the hero of the novel was
dying of hunger almost in a live broadcast, in front of the microphones
and cameras—in spaces that are known and yet stricken with non-
existence, like the camp at Holzminden where Adam's family had died
a thousand deaths. The blending of times and places told a story as com-
pacted as the blocks of snow in an avalanche. Suddenly the mountain
seems to collapse, carrying away and mixing together very different
strata of earth, rocks, ice, and glacial snow.

How to explain such blindness on the analyst's part, if not by a
total blindness to aspects of her own history? The war of 1914 had not
yet come back into fashion, and, at the end of the twentieth century,
the wars of decolonization were casting a certain aura of suspicion on
everything having to do with military matters. This suspicion also fell
on families like Adam's, in which, from father to son, the men had
fought wars as officers, and on an army that had been sullied in the
Dreyfus Affair and wound up fleeing in disarray at the end of the

"funny war" and the "strange defeat" (Bloch 1940).[23] Yes, Adam had deliberately undertaken an investigation of the war fronts and the silences of official history.

Like madness, traumas can cause psychoanalysis to fail. Yet the practical and theoretical solution is indicated by these same patients, though in enigmatic formations that, at first, are too condensed for the analyst. Their unfolding in the transference does, indeed, lead to an initial inscription in which there is a risk of suicide. The suicide of Primo Levi well after the writing of his 1958 book shows that entering these territories entails a risk inherent in the very act of putting them into words.

Yet for a long time ancient wisdom has reflected on the problem and on possible solutions. Thus the treatises of ancient India bear witness to the creative function of sacrifice and its connection to speech (Renou 1978). The original sacrifice proposes as oblation the body of the man who is offering the sacrifice. It is therefore the matrix of those that follow. But the mythical dismemberment of the sacrificer is replaced by the unit of measure, corresponding to the sacrificer's size,

---

23. In the Dreyfus Affair of 1894–1906, a Jewish officer was accused and found guilty of espionage on the basis of forged document written by officers manipulated by the Germans. The anti-Semitic campaign that resulted caused a longstanding division of opinion, in the army, society, and even families, into pro- and anti-Dreyfus factions. Alfred Dreyfus was sent to Guyana for several years. The reversal of the verdict was due to the intervention of Emile Zola, among others, and Dreyfus was pardoned by the president of the Republic. The Maison des Sciences de l'Homme (House of the Human Sciences), where the Ecole des Hautes Etudes en Sciences Sociales (School of Advanced Studies in the Social Sciences) is located, was built on the site of the prison in which Dreyfus was incarcerated and in which his first trial was held in 1894. During World War II, a number of prisoners were tortured there by the Gestapo. The Hotel Lutetia, situated directly across the street, welcomed the return of the deportees in 1945. During the occupation, it served as a luxurious residence for Nazi dignitaries. The derogatory term "funny war" refers to the years 1939–1940, when the French forces were defeated and Marshall Pétain asked Hitler for an armistice. The historian Marc Bloch, who described this period, was, with Lucien Febvre, the founder of the Ecole des Annales, originally the Ecole des Hautes Etudes en Sciences Sociales (EHESS), an institution of higher learning and research at the doctoral level, bringing together the various disciplines of the human sciences. An officer in both world wars, he entered the Resistance, was tortured, and, in 1944, was murdered in a ditch (Bloch 1940).

traced concretely on the ritual area. Thus the sacrificer remains alive to receive the fruits of the symbolic operation.[24]

Lacan (1953) was inspired by this tradition in theorizing the death instinct and the repetition compulsion:

> There is therefore no further need to have recourse to the outworn notion of primordial masochism in order to understand the reason for the repetitive games in which subjectivity brings together mastery of its dereliction and the birth of the symbol. . . . Thus the symbol manifests itself first of all as the murder of the thing, and this death constitutes in the subject the eternalization of his desire.
>
> *The first symbol in which we recognize humanity in its vestigial traces is the sepulture*, and the intermediary of death can be recognized in every relation in which man comes to the life of his history. [pp. 103–104, emphasis added]

But this passage is fraught with danger. Real death is very close to the murder of the thing when the thing is one and the same as the subject to the point of annihilating him as a subject.

This Thing, *das Ding*, is defined by Lacan as that aspect of the Real, of the unnamable and unrepresentable, that can at least be spoken of and imagined. So it is with the monsters that inhabit the forest, that space of the marvelous in which the notion of time is lost. They also appear on maps, on the edge of the *terrae incognitae*, in the space in which extraterrestrials and other aliens proliferate.

In the 1970s, Gisela Pankow (1969) was one of the rare analysts in Paris at that time to venture into the terrain of the psychotic transference. One day in supervision, speaking about the risk of suicide, she said, "Tell the patient that there is something in him to be killed, a monster to be sacrificed, but that this isn't him." She asked her pa-

---

24. "In fact, the sacrificer seeks simultaneously to indicate that he is the victim and that he is other than the victim. In offering the victim, it is himself whom he wants to offer and avoid offering" (Malamoud 1989, p. 214). "The sacrificial operation thus involves two phases: the initial situation in which the sacrificer wants to offer nothing other than himself, then the phase in which this sacrifice is 'extended,' prolonged, spread out: the sacrificer offers a victim that is other than himself but that for this very reason is another 'himself'" (Malamoud 2002, p. 31).

tients to make models: "Bring me monsters. I'm a monster seller." To one patient, who put a leg over her balcony on the seventh floor, she asked straight out, "What am I going to do with your corpse?" He came back into the room to talk about it. She added, "If you're dead, you won't be there anymore for us to think together about the results of your act."

Lacan (1953) ends his paper "Function and Field of Speech and Language in Psychoanalysis" with a quotation from the fifth lesson of the Bhrad-Aranyaka Upanishad about speech as a gift. This is why Pankow's comments are certainly not to be considered simplistic recipes for mastering death. For, if there is something to be sacrificed, this is true on the analyst's side as well.

1.1.5. Gilda: Madness Speaks to the "Leftovers" of the Analyst's History

"After five years of analysis with you," said Gilda, "I've just made a discovery. The goal of my psychosis, for twenty years, was to get me to find a *feeling* to bring back together the separate pieces of what I've been able to understand over the years. A feeling of shame that I couldn't feel, since I'd become catatonic. I'd lost face, literally, because when I was 20 I violated a major taboo of my society, of any society.

"Without feeling anything, I'd turned into my own executioner. A certain scent of childhood in psychosis this week propelled me back to my first years. My parents weren't able to be of any help to me, since, after the war, they too had lost all feeling. This sense arose as though from an electrical outlet connected to you, the analyst. Right at the beginning, you told me, 'Yes, it's possible to get out of madness.' You assured me that my craziness was a search, remember?"

How could anyone forget our first encounter in the main room of the hospital five years earlier. Seeing her sitting there deep in conversation with a patient who declared herself to be the craziest on the service, the analyst took her for an intern.

"Are you a psychologist?" the analyst asked, introducing herself as a psychoanalyst on the service.

"No, I'm psychotic," she replied, smiling at the professional's confusion. "I have frequent stays here. I'd rather come to see you at the clinic,[25] when I get out."

She did so, several months later, at which time the analyst learned that Gilda had actually been a psychologist, and that her thesis had dealt with the "streets of shame" she had entered, without affect, at the urging of a thesis director who was fascinated by the wretched of the earth and by the methods of participant observation. In this context, madness and the asylum were her only possible means of escape.

Like all hospital inmates, who begin by ascertaining who it is they are dealing with, she asked, "And you? What are you doing here?"

"I'm an analyst, and also a researcher at the Ecole des Hautes Etudes en Sciences Sociales."

"What are you working on?"

"Madness and the social link."

The analyst had told her about her institutional affiliation from the outset, as though to ward off the shame that had slipped in between the two of them and that Gilda did not seem to feel. Thus they were both researchers first and foremost, and they were going to take up a postdoctoral investigation in the analysis. And the analytic work did, indeed, consist of an ongoing research process. But, outside of the university setting, this project was able to make use of the powerfully heuristic resources of madness.

Five years later, having emerged from her madness, Gilda reminded the analyst of that "yes" that she had relied on. The analyst had assured her that it was possible to come out of what she later referred to as hell. Gilda then claimed her insanity as her most precious instrument. The "feeling" she recovered was its tangible result. She set about demonstrating it, in her style, with a jester's miming worthy of the Commedia dell'Arte.

As a medieval saying has it, one that could be the motto for this book, "Madness is more a device than a destiny" (Fritz 1992, p. 326).

---

25. At that time, public psychiatry in France was organized in such a way that a hospital service was linked to a geographical sector in which there were one or more clinics providing free external consultations for the residents, especially after they left the hospital. Here, the head of the psychiatry unit, a psychiatrist and analyst, had appointed psychoanalysts to his service and at the clinic.

The device—*engin* in French, *ingenium* in Latin—is genius and inge-
niousness here, a tool. It is a means of leaving the hell of unhappiness,
not the verdict condemning someone to an inexorable repetition.

The disappearance of feelings and the absence of affect are central to
the neurological research of Antonio Damasio (1995). When she met
Gilda, the analyst happened to be reading Damasio's *Descartes' Error*,
which had just been translated into French. There was great uncertainty with regard to Gilda. With each psychotic break, each new hospitalization, the medical team wondered about organic lesions. And
so did the analyst: What if their interviews were of absolutely no use?
This was not the first time that a scientific work has been directly
and transferentially connected to working with madness. We shall
be giving several examples in this book.

1.2. THE ANALYST SPEAKS

1.2.1. The Analyst's Situation

Throughout the twentieth century, a veritable "war of nerves" (Bion
1997, Shephard 2000) has been the battlefield of organicist neurologists
and, on the other side, of psychoanalytically oriented therapists, in
particular when confronted by war traumas. Rationality, rationaliza-
tions, ratiocinations: reason is courted by many discourses. Rationality is held to be acquired in the experimental sciences, and all the more
so in those that employ the language of mathematics. Now, it is precisely this same rationality that is at stake, at the heart of working with
insanity, in the psychoanalytic approach to madness.

For nearly thirty years, our research has taken place in two settings.
One is clinical: at the psychiatric hospital, in the clinic, and in private practice. The other is scientific, at the Ecole des Hautes Etudes
en Sciences Sociales (EHESS). In other words, we have in effect been
go-betweens in the synaptic space that connects and divides these two
domains. As nonmedical psychoanalysts, we do not have to diagnose
or medicate when madness presents itself to us. In any case, like
Melville's Bartleby (1853), we prefer not to. Moreover, as early as the
1920s Harry Stack Sullivan (1974) pointed to another absurdity that

is still current: in learned opinion, if a psychosis is cured thanks to psychoanalysis, this is because it wasn't a psychosis.[26]

As for the scholars at our EHESS, for the most part the historians, anthropologists, linguists, experimental psychologists, sociologists, and economists readily express reservations concerning the scientific validity of the clinical experience. Worse, our analytic training took place in the framework of Jacques Lacan's Ecole Freudienne.[27] Although for years his seminars had been welcomed as "complementary lectures" at EHESS (which was at the time called the Ecole Pratique des Hautes Etudes), nowadays our scientific colleagues still consider his style impenetrable. But this marginal position itself creates a productive dynamic linked to discomfort—indeed, to uncertainty.

In any event, our daily experience has taught us that the only rigorous path leading to meaningful results is first established by the patient. It is from him that theoretical discoveries emerge. He is the PI, the principle investigator, of research, on condition that we consider ourselves his research assistants and act as such. Thus the analytic relation constitutes a laboratory in which clinical impasses give rise to a particular heuristic process.[28]

Paradoxically, research with psychotics reveals cognitive issues, connected with sociohistorical realities and the attendant emotions, that are accessible only via the transference. In this specific field, the classical opposition between cognitive knowledge and unconscious knowl-

---

26. "If the patient recovers, then he couldn't have been schizophrenic: he was obviously misdiagnosed" (Sullivan 1974, p. 23). And, in the same vein: "Again the fundamental characteristics of the schizophrenic process itself are still in doubt. We are but beginning to free ourselves of the many misconceptions concerning a 'dementia praecox,' and the majority still revise diagnoses when the patient recovers" (p. 159). The freedom envisioned by Sullivan is still on the horizon.

27. Lacan decided to dissolve the Ecole Freudienne de Paris right before his death in 1981. We, for our part, have no inclination to participate in the clan wars among his epigones.

28. Helen Swick Perry, the editor of Sullivan's (1974) papers, cites a comment Sullivan made in a 1927 conference in which he was discussing a talk by William Alanson White on "Psychiatry and Its Relation to the Social Sciences": "I should say the studies of groups of two or three came pretty near to giving us for our purposes an understanding of the social forces as they appear in the relation of individuals and as they affect those individuals in relation to each other" (p. 184).

edge is put in question. The change in scale from the individual to the social is no longer valid. Their articulation is precisely what is at stake theoretically and practically when it comes to madness.

Yet it is not our concern to sum up the discourses on madness but rather to find what "it" has to say. This is why we shall not disregard any of the tools it has employed throughout its history, and we shall speak indifferently in terms of psychosis, madness, folly, craziness, insanity, and so forth—everyday words stemming from the oral tradition, literature, and science. Why should we deprive ourselves of the discoveries of Shakespeare, Rabelais, Cervantes, Molière, Erasmus, Faulkner, Feydeau, Pirandello, Musil, Kenzaburo Oe, or Toni Morrison, the great explorers of these regions? Or of researchers like Descartes, Wittgenstein, Auguste Comte, Harry Stack Sullivan,[29] Erwin Schrödinger, Cantor, Gödel, Charlotte Beradt, Hannah Arendt, or John Nash—all these authors, all these scholars, drew their resources from traumatic madness. Each, in his or her own way, responded to the imperious need to write in the wake of social convulsions that tend to eliminate the subject. These authors have guided us from their own researches and have marked the elaboration, year after year, of our seminar "Madness and the Social Link" at EHESS.

---

29. Our longstanding interest in Sullivan's work has focused on several aspects of his research:

1. Early on, he stated the possibility of a transference with psychotic patients.
2. He establishes a relation between his psychotherapeutic practices with schizophrenics at Sheppard Pratt Hospital in Baltimore and the practices described by the anthropologist Edward Sapir (1949) among the Plains Indians (Sullivan 1974).
3. He is obviously in accordance with the theses of Wittgenstein and Lacan regarding the field of speech and language; see especially Sullivan 1945, pp. 198–226. This paper, presented in May 1944, was not published before 1950, since, as Helen Swick Perry (1982) reports, "He is attacking the dignity of the person" (p. 193), a position difficult to support in the period immediately after the war and one that called for new theoretical instruments inspired by the logic of modern physics. Perry was extremely helpful to us when we visited her in Cambridge in 1983. Her book was an outstanding guide for us in the interdisciplinary field explored by Sullivan, an area Lacan referred to as the field of the sciences affine to psychoanalysis.

All of them, in their link to madness, have considered its heuristic potential. Small or large, gentle or furious, madness defines a field, lasting briefly or for a longer time, that reveals not so much the immobile and computerized criteria of the *Diagnostic and Statistical Manual of Mental Illness* (*DSM*) as a psychopathology of everyday psychosis. Between our small acts of craziness and the large-scale madness of asylums, between the most secret insanities and collective ones like those corresponding to the totalitarian perversions analyzed by Hannah Arendt, there extends a continuum.[30] Whatever the scale, domestic, public, or political, madness traces the field of the Real, which breaks the social contract on a point that cannot be symbolized, at the same time offering us tools for its exploration, its naming.

Obviously, we are also referring to the work of the many analysts who have given precise accounts of the evolution of their patients, often diagnosed as psychotic or going through a psychotic episode in the course of a classical analysis or at the end of one. Each time, the analytic work comes up against an irreducible Real and necessitates a theoretical and technical change. The psychoanalytic work of Harold Searles (1965) at Chestnut Lodge, for example, conducted as joint research with his schizophrenic patients, confirmed for us, as soon as it was translated into French, that, "yes," madness can really find a way out of its impasses and sufferings through psychoanalysis without losing its heuristic force in the process, even if it takes time, even if treatment is limited to few patients in comparison to the masses handled by public health services.

1.2.2. After Some Others

This position, of course, gives rise to doubt, even to hostility, on the part of "armchairs"[31] who declare that madness is unanalyzable. *Eppur*

---

30. "The field of mental disorders seems to be a continual gradation, in which little of discrete types is to be found" (Sullivan 1974, p. 159).

31. "[T]here will continue to be plenty of armchairs philosophizing about 'brain diseases' and 'lesions' (with the 'neurologizing tautology' criticized by Meyer")" (Sullivan 1974, p. 248). One of the characteristics bringing Lacan close to Sullivan is their common impertinence and their taste for provocation when it comes to the self-importance of the establishment.

si muove: many patients, rich or poor, emerge from what is medically termed psychosis. Ever since the 1920s, numerous books devoted to the psychoanalytic treatment of psychosis in adults and children have described the exact moments in which a new creativity germinates from catastrophic symptoms, moments in which the subject emerges despite the psychiatric diagnosis and prognosis. In these books and papers the psychoanalysis of the psychoses is set forth in styles that vary greatly from one author to the next but with many common features that any practitioner in this area can recognize and explain.

What are these common features? The uselessness of recourse to anamnesis, the failure of neutrality, the violence of negativity, and the horizon of hospitalization reveal the impasses of classical analytic technique. These features outline situations in which theoretical concepts about the subject, desire, and the repression of desire must give way to the characteristics of another field: the one in which Lacan locates the return of the Real, Sullivan "the dreadful not-me,"[32] Bion "the nameless dread,"[33] and Freud (1907) an unconscious that has nothing to do with repression: "Everything that is repressed is unconscious, but not everything that is unconscious is repressed" (p. 48).[34]

---

32. From a dynamic perspective, we may compare the Lacanian field of the Real with Freud's uncanny, which Sullivan (1945) describes as follows: "The dreadful not-me [is] associated with . . . what I call uncanny emotion, chilly crawling sensations, and the like, often meant by the words 'awe, dread, loathing, and horror'" (p. 249).

33. "If the dream-work capacity is destroyed," Bion (1959) writes, "the patient feels dreads which is particularly terrifying, because it is nameless, and because the nameless itself springs from the destruction of the patient's capacity for dream-work, which is the mechanism responsible for naming" (p. 45).

34. Similarly, in connection with a distinction between "the uncanny that we actually experience [e.g., that "the dead do live"] and "the uncanny that we merely picture or think about," proceeding in the latter case "from repressed infantile complexes" and in the former case "from actual experiences in real life," Freud (1919) states: "[W]e might say that in the one case what has been repressed is a particular ideational content, and in the other the belief in its (material) reality. But the last phrase no doubt extends the term 'repression' beyond its legitimate meaning. It would be more correct . . . to say that the animistic beliefs of civilised people are in a state of having been . . . *surmounted* rather than repressed" (pp. 248–249). Likewise: "Here I am not using the term 'the repressed' in its proper sense. What is in question is something in a people's life which is past, lost to view, superseded and which we venture to compare with the repressed in the mental life of an individual" (1939, p. 132).

In these zones where the process of symbolization turns out to be impossible, it therefore makes no sense to bring up the past, even in terms of a repetition. The future, the grammatical tense of desire, is likewise impossible to envisage. The analyst is faced with a veritable symptom of time. It is of no use for him to evoke the patient's memories or echo obvious signifiers; the patient inevitably replies, "Don't wear yourself out. Everything is present. The only thing that matters for me is the here and now." In this *hic et nunc* we posit the existence of a real traumatic experience that has volatilized spatiotemporal reference points, sometimes for several generations. The suspension of the flow of time here does not refer to a mechanical causality of the symptom but to a task of inquiry into the specific temporality of this death zone (Benedetti 1980) that had dropped out of history.

1.2.3. The Analyst as "Annalist" of Inaudible Histories

Auguste's experience, and also, as we shall see, Gilda's, teach us that the political themes that pervade most of the insanities expressed on the public square are often relevant with regard to the history of lineages and societies. Pieces of history hitherto cut off from transmission thus burst into daylight in forms that may be extravagant or minimalist but are always shocking until they find the "annalist," the chronicler who keeps the records of a gesture that has been silenced. The medieval *geste* owes its name to the deeds it recounts but also to the gestures employed by the *jongleurs*, the fools or jesters of long ago, ancestors of the madmen of today (Schmitt 1990).

Here the theorem formulated by Winnicott (1974) in his last paper, "Fear of Breakdown," holds true in its efficacy with such patients: "The underlying agony is unthinkable. . . . The unconscious here is not exactly the repressed unconscious of psychoneurosis. . . . The patient needs to 'remember' this, but it is not possible to remember something that has not yet happened, and this thing of the past has not happened yet because the patient was not there for it to happen to" (pp. 104–105).

The imminent catastrophe, the announced end of the world, has already happened but could not be inscribed in the past as past, since in this respect the subject of speech was not there. Nothing in the other was given him, no speech to name what happened there. Totally cut off, ignored, but also well known to everyone, sometimes uttered in history books and even advocated by the duty to remember though that made no difference, the truth was unable to be transmitted. The information has remained a dead letter, outside the field of speech.[35]

How, then, to approach these regions where our patients have been before and toward which they are, paradoxically, seeking to guide us? In the tragedy *Oedipus at Colonus*, first performed in 401 B.C., Sophocles explains the rules of the game for us. The blind wanderer Oedipus, led by his daughter Antigone, asks a local man what place it is that they have come to. The latter replies that they are approaching the suburb of Colonus, near Athens, and mentions the proximity of an area that is taboo. This is a space that allows for "no gaze, no voice, no word" (*aderktos, aphonos, alogos*) (l. 131, translation modified). The words, uttered by the Chorus Leader in the terror of this sacred wood where Oedipus will literally disappear, perhaps express the most impressive poetic description of the domain of the Real.

The transferential relation at first consists of such a crossroads close to zones like these. There, in the simple dialogue of tragedy or transference, an initial orientation, an initial adjustment, takes place. As the passerby questioned by Oedipus says, "That is this country, stranger: honored less/ In histories than in the hearts of the people" (ll. 62–63).

1.3. EXITING MADNESS: A DEMAND FOR TRUTH

1.3.1. Gilda: On the Threshold of Time

One day, after fifteen years of madness and periodic hospital admissions, Gilda said to her analyst, "Now I've discovered the light of morning. I was the daughter of night and the moon. Today I get up at seven A.M. I discover that my body lives in three dimensions; I feel the air

---

35. "For the function of language is not to inform but to evoke. What I seek in speech is the response of the other. What constitutes me as subject is my question. In order to be recognized by the other, I utter what was only in view of what will be. In order to find him, I call him by a name that he must assume or refuse in order to reply to me. . . . *Speech is in fact a gift of language*, and language is not immaterial. It is a subtle body, but a body it is" (Lacan 1953, p. 86, emphasis added).

caressing my face, my breath in my chest. I have a place in the world among other people. I see life in colors, in relief.

"Now I'm entering time. Let this hour be, let June be, full as a month, not like an abstraction! Before, I was running after time; I lived in a non-time. I had no rest, never. I kept on wandering endlessly in the streets.

"The world of madness was flat. Everything was in black and white. I never stopped thinking. My only constant was cogitation. Words ran on without stopping, while I remained, flat, behind the windowpane. Cut off, with no contact with the world. My perceptions were considerably distorted.

"Really, I was the goddess: Isis, Kali, Lilith. I was the devil, the fallen angel Lucifer. Let no one say that this experience was nothing. Let no one erase this experience with medication. I got more out of it than I could bear. And I drank, to stimulate myself. I was a zombie, but I never changed my name, Gilda. They all thought it was a false name. I always kept that last shred of identity. In the streets, so little of me was left. In fact, there was no me anymore. Only my wanderings across the ages. I was the Great Mother, the Earth, ready to kill her creation, this humanity condemned forever.

"Now I realize that this was a journey. Like Dante's with Virgil, if that doesn't sound too pompous. Since I've known you. . . . In fact, our six years were a journey into and out of the hell of the streets, of madness, of alcohol and medications.

"After having said 'yes' to me, one day you said 'no.' No to the streets, to alcohol. I stopped everything, right away, including drugs. Your 'no' wasn't a condemnation.

"Do you remember?"

The analyst had only a faint memory of this "no," no to the practices stemming from the lethal ideologies so frankly depicted in the films *Salo* (Pasolini 1975)[36] and *The Damned* (Visconti 1969).

On the other hand, she vividly recalled that her own history as an analyst touched on that of this patient, during the war, on opposite

---

36. Salo is the name of a place near Lago di Garda, where, in 1943, Mussolini agreed to be placed by Hitler at the head of a fascist government, the Italian Social Republic.

sides of the same border. And she recalled how this historical commotion had precisely "awakened the dead" who, for both of them, were signposts on one part of the road.

In their third meeting, the analyst had asked Gilda about her accent: she was Italian.

"And you? Where are you from?" the patient asked in return. The mirror in which Gilda had lost her face and her social image was already broken enough, so the analyst replied straightforwardly:

"From Savoy, on the other side of the border. We were Italians a little over a century ago.[37] How old are you?"

"Forty. And you?"

"Fifty."

"You were born during the war. Was your father a soldier?"

"Yes."

"Mine too. He was in the mountain troops, the *bersaglieri*."

This name had a familiar ring to the analyst's ears. This was the part of the Italian army that had occupied the valley where she was born in 1942, just before the Germans arrived. She replied, without thinking:

"Perhaps they fought with one another?"

"I'd be surprised," Gilda said. "Besides, I have a detail that might be of interest in your research on madness and the social link. At the last minute, my father was sent to Libya. He was the sole survivor of his section, which was massacred during one of the battles of El Alamein,[38] which the English considered a victory. He wasn't on duty that day. He found all his buddies dead. Back home, he had to tell the relatives, family after family, how their boy had died. Sometimes I wonder if I'm not one of them. My father considered me his little soldier. We were poor; he wanted me to be first in school, and I was."

This was too much. The analyst was very careful not to tell Gilda that her own father had barely escaped the massacre of twenty-one hostages by the Germans at the Col du Petit Saint-Bernard, exactly on the frontier with Italy. Shortly after this interview, she found Gilda in

37. Savoy, until then a province of the Kingdom of Piedmont-Sardinia, became part of France only in 1860, by a plebiscite, at the time when Italy became unified.

38. This famous battle, in which Montgomery defeated General Rommel, took place on October 23, 1942, in North Africa.

the hospital. A real Fury, the patient was once again the goddess of the inferno, repeating imperiously that she would prefer to see the analyst outside, in the clinic, when she was discharged.

By an odd coincidence, their appointment time, the first session in the morning, fell on a day when there was a transportation strike. The two of them met in front of the closed door of the clinic. The sun was shining. By silent agreement, they sat side by side on a public bench in the deserted street and worked for the entire time of the session, which went very pleasantly.

1.3.2. The Army of the Dead

Never, until that day, had the analyst recognized the extent of the silence surrounding the taking of hostages and the massacre, though this event had often been recounted as one of the many episodes of day-to-day warfare in the valley where she was born.[39] But, without her noticing it, almost every summer she found herself walking up to this pass, as though on a pilgrimage. Quite recently a marble plaque had recorded the massacre of the twenty-one who should have been twenty-two. Were they part of the army of the dead (Schmitt 1994), the raging army of young men killed in combat, led by the Great Goddess? Since that time we have learned that, in the regions adjacent to the Alpine Arc, which joined Gilda and the analyst on either side of the mountain, these ancestral cults had led to witch trials undertaken by the Inquisition in the sixteenth century. The historian Carlo Ginzburg (1980, 1989) has detected here the traces of cults of a Mother Goddess and shamanistic practices coming from Asia.

---

39. This is the valley of La Tarentaise. After the Normandy Invasion on D-Day (June 6, 1944), the Germans pulled back toward the Alpine passes, protecting their retreat with the help of Italian troops. Parachute drops of weapons on the part of the Allies came to the aid of the various sectors of the Resistance. The Alpine Division, reunified as a regular army unit under the command of Colonel de Galbert and the Alpine Hunter officers, fought on the mountain ridges between France and Italy during an icy winter, while the inhabitants of the valley were subject to atrocities by the enemy under a rain of shellfire from the mountain passes.

Well before she read the works of this historian of microhistory, the analyst was obliged by Gilda's analysis to revisit her own history. When, on a walk on the Col, she actually read, carved on the plaque, the date of the event, August 13, 1944, two months after the Normandy Invasion, she realized, fifty years after, that apparently she had already been born at that moment. She too, then, had been a contemporary, on the scene, of various episodes of the battle of the Alps (Gaide et al. 1996) that had constantly been spoken of by her relatives. But, described outside of any chronology in which she could have been able to situate herself, only images survived, without connection to each other (cf. Steinberg 1995).

She saw herself once again, on the balcony, alongside flags that had been set up in an atmosphere of rejoicing and then suddenly taken down. Or, all alone in a car, at night, in the snow, she was gulping a jar of honey on her father's secret visits to Lieutenant de France. This young man from the shadow army would be assassinated shortly before the end of the war. She was told of streets crossed under gunfire when her family sought refuge in the villages of the foothills. It was there that a kind lady gave her a book. She called it her "bada," a made-up name, and never let go of it.

She knew nothing about it except this name. After checking recently, she learned that this famous book was not a work of literature and was neither for children nor for adults, but was a telephone book dragged around everywhere by the 2-year-old kid when the phone lines had been cut. Since then, for her as for Don Quixote, books have remained a final rampart against the blows of fate. This interpretation seems more accurate to her than one that would see repressed oedipal wishes in the repeated dreams in which she was fleeing in mortal danger before armed soldiers. She gradually came to understand that she and her family owed their lives, from before the time she was born, to such adventures.

These materials—bizarre objects, repeated dreams—waiting to enter history can serve as transitional objects (Fromm and Smith 1989, Winnicott 1971) and can also provide the makings of traumatic dreams. They could also take their place as neologisms in delusional constructions seeking a way out in order to survive. Who, nowadays, would dare to consider as such a neologism the very word *sociology*?

1.3.3. Auguste Comte: An Excess of Subjectivity to Confront a "Superpositivity"[40]

Paradoxically, it is the inventor of this discipline, Auguste Comte, the leading figure of scientific positivism, who provides the most rigorous account of the heuristic use of madness.

Thirty years ago, after a classical literary training, we entered a sociology laboratory in the Ecole des Hautes Etudes en Sciences Sociales (EHESS). We knew that the main office of this research center, at 10 rue Monsieur le Prince, Paris V, was in the very house where Comte had lived and taught. But at the time we did not know that the famous occupant had experienced an intense attack of madness in 1826, when he was 28 years old (Capurro 1999, Gouhier 1931).

We were even more ignorant of the fact that, in this temple of the foundation of the human sciences, the father of sociology, who invented the name of that discipline, had claimed throughout his life that this crisis was one of the foundations of his theory. Committed as a mental patient in the home of Esquirol[41] for several months, then released against medical advice, he gradually recovered from his elation at the cost of a serious despondency. One year later, he threw himself into the Seine, was rescued in the nick of time, and then, before a happy few, resumed his teaching of positive philosophy. He had just begun it in 1826, at the time of his crisis.

His madness bore a family resemblance[42] to Gilda's, since she, too, had traversed all the ages of humanity. Successively, and not without uproar, she had identified with the mother goddesses of the entire world. Each time, the police would bring the goddess back to the hos-

---

40. "Would not a methodologically subjective positivity, without giving up the indispensable control of the outside, open onto an expanded positivity, freed from the limitations of the object, a regenerated positivity, *a kind of superpositivity, a sort of surrealism*? This is the entire project of subjective positivism, of which the *Subjective Synthesis* of 1857 represents a first stage. *The integration of subjectivity to positivity here can seem to be a pact with madness.* Nothing allows us to think that Comte was the dupe and the victim of the pact" (Arbousse Bastide 1972, p. 52, emphasis added).

41. Jean-Etienne Dominique Esquirol, the famous psychiatrist, later came to follow Comte's courses at the same address.

42. "I can think of no better expression to characterize these similarities (between games, language games) than family resemblances" (Wittgenstein 1945–1949, § 67.179).

pital. Going beyond the research she had used for her thesis, she had become these sacred figures, reenacting them in a fusion of identity[43] but without a ritual to protect her.

The Positivist school underwent splits that challenged these critical episodes with embarrassment before spreading into Latin America.[44] As for Auguste Comte, despite the return twenty years later of attacks that he was better able to overcome, he never denied the knowledge gained during these episodes. Let us cite a passage from his "Personal Preface" to Volume 6 of the *Course in Positive Philosophy*, dated 1842, in which he mentions his crisis in the spring of 1826:

> Wisely given over to its spontaneous course, this crisis would undoubtedly soon have reestablished the normal state. But thanks to the disastrous intervention of an empirical medication, in the establishment of the famous Esquirol, the most absurd of treatments led me rapidly to a very pronounced alienation. After medicine had finally, and fortunately, declared me incurable, the intrinsic power of my organization, assisted by affectionate care at home,[45] triumphed naturally in a few weeks, at the beginning of winter, over the illness and, especially, the remedies. Eighteen months later, the success, essentially spontaneous, was so consolidated that, in August of 1828, making use of Broussais' famous work, *Irritation and Madness*, I was already making philosophical use of the personal enlightenment that that sad experience had just afforded me at such great cost with regard to this large subject. . . . I thought that, with this frank statement, I had to protect myself in advance against the base insinuations secretly brought about by the various animosities arising more and more from the growing popularity of my new philosophy. [quoted in Gouhier 1931, p. 48]

What was new in this philosophy, when applied to madness, is not the triumph of the study of the brain, as one might expect from a logical-positivist approach. Comte's theory defines madness as the "excess of

---

43. "Within the sacred space, the young girl to be initiated becomes identified with the goddess Changing Woman" (Nagy 1996, p. 89). "I must insist that this kind of 'acting' in the context of archaic Greek poetry is not a matter of pretending: it is rather a merger of the performer's identity with an identity patterned on an archetype—a merger repeated every time the ritual occasion recurs" (p. 97).

44. The Brazilian flag bears the positivist motto "Order and Progress."

45. His wife, Caroline, was a former prostitute.

subjectivity" that was the primary characteristic of alienation. It recognizes "the insurrectional emergence" of the subject excluded by anatomical research and, above all, banished by "the political commotions that sever the bond between the living and the dead. . . . The word alienation, in the etymological sense, is never more appropriate than in this sad case, in which all objective populations together were brutally mistaken about this noble yoke of the past, even in dreaming about the future" (Arbousse Bastide 1972, pp. 59–60).

Defying the certitudes of the dominant discipline of anatomical pathology, Comte, in "A Sociological Definition of the Brain," posits this organ as a "device by which the dead act on the living."[46] Hence one can consider "illness in the West as a continual insurrection of the living against the dead" (Arbousse Bastide 1972, p. 68).

The subject of madness, in his experience as a patient, is trying to tie together the traumas of his individual history and those of history writ large, in an inscription to which Comte's philosophical work bears witness. Comte criticizes "the sterility of works relating to brain physiology." In contrast to the materialistic and doctrinal vertigo into which such research can sink, he advises the reading of Cervantes' *Don Quixote*,[47] which, for him, reveals an exemplary lesson: "Cervantes' admirable composition profoundly describes the way in which our emotions modify our sensations, sketching out the true theory of madness before any biologist" (Arbousse Bastide 1972, p. 52).

Auguste Comte surely had reason to recognize himself in the Knight of the Sad Countenance. Like Cervantes, he had been caught up in the convulsions of his time. He was born in 1798, under the Directory, toward the end of the French Revolution, into a rather modest family attached to the Ancien Régime and to their religion. He lost a little sister at an early age; she had been baptized in secret, as he and his other

---

46. This powerful definition, which has nothing to do with a morbid imagination, accords with the very paradigm of the symbolic order (Lacan 1953). Cf. also the dialogue in Sophocles' *Antigone*, in which Antigone says to her sister, Ismene: "Take heart. You live. My life [*psyche*] died long ago./ And that has made me fit to help the dead." Creon, their uncle, replies: "One of these girls has shown her lack of sense/ just now. The other had it from her birth" (ll. 559–562).

47. This novel was recently the basis of two years of our seminar at EHESS, devoted to the madness of war and political results of trauma.

siblings had been. Shortly before his attack of madness, he himself lost a little daughter, the fruit of an affair with a married woman, a child loved in secret whom he visited on the sly. We may wonder whether the importance that funerary rites took on for him after the death, in 1846, of Clotilde de Vaux, the Lady of his thoughts, is connected with mournings such as these in the face of massive disturbances in the register of the Symbolic. It was then, in 1849, that he founded the Religion of Humanity and the Positivist Church, which led a number of his disciples to distance themselves from him.

But a second order of facts brings him close to Cervantes. Accepted at a very young age at the Ecole Polytechnique, soon after this institute was created during the Revolution, he was one of its most brilliant students. Trained in the scientific disciplines, its students today still hold the rank of officer. In 1814, along with his classmates, Comte was ready to fight and to give his life for the defense of Paris when the coalition of European armies, opposed to the return of Napoleon, threatened the capital.

After Waterloo, at the time of the restoration of the monarchy, Comte, deemed too subversive and too much of an agitator, was summarily expelled from his school. He never recovered, either morally or materially, from the trauma that, from Achilles to present-day soldiers, shatters whoever is betrayed by his own commander (Shay 1995). Throughout his life he was in a precarious state financially and, apart from the lessons he gave at 10 rue Monsieur le Prince to a few students, had to depend on the help of John Stuard Mill,[48] who, with some of his English students, provided him with a stipend for some time.

Comte was able to overcome his crises several times thanks to Clotilde de Vaux, who, like Dulcinea for Don Quixote, was Comte's

---

48. Mill played a large role in the rescue of traumatized geniuses. One was the celebrated naturalist Jean-Henri Fabre, "Monsieur Fabre" (1823–1914). A primary-school teacher, he pursued his entomological research, alone, in the Vaucluse. There he met Mill, who was living in Avignon and accompanied him on his walks. When, in 1871, having come up against harassment from his colleagues, ill, without resources, and fearing that he was about to die, he wrote to Mill in London and described his serious condition. Mill replied immediately, sending him 120 pounds so that he could break all his ties with the teaching profession. Afterwards, Fabre wrote an immense work that earned him the title "the Homer of insects" (see Fabre 1979).

near and distant Lady of courtly love in life and death. Indeed, she was the Other par excellence to whom he addressed his thoughts, the guarantor who made it possible for him to think and who did not betray him.

Here, too, we come very close to Descartes, for Auguste Comte was not the only one to bear witness to the powerful link between scientific genius and quasi-delusional enthusiasms. Having experienced such an episode in 1619, Descartes did not fail to write them down and even to justify them. For they are the very foundation of his famous Method, the keystone of his entire philosophy including his scientific discoveries.

2

From the Principle of Objectivation to the Birth of a Subject

2.1. FROM THE LESION IN THE BRAIN TO THE LESION IN THE OTHER

2.1.1. Neurology and Psychoanalysis: A Contemporary Issue

No more than Auguste Comte, we shall not get involved in making a simplistic contrast between biology and psychoanalysis. A field of research defines its rigor in delimiting its investigations, leaving aside a number of phenomena sacrificed in order to establish the boundaries of its validity. Impressed by books like those of Oliver Sacks (1973, 1985, 1995) and Antonio Damasio (1995, 1999), we have even found ourselves speaking directly to certain patients, not without transferential effect, about symptoms similar to those described by neurology. But, in those cases, there was not the slightest connection with any lesion.

For the most part, the neurosciences make reference, in the laboratory, to a notion of consciousness subject to the principle of objectivation. They must therefore neglect the unconscious processes that are, indeed, impossible to apprehend rigorously outside the dimension of the transference. Among physicians, however, certain investigators like Sacks constantly reveal, in their descriptions, that this dimension is familiar to them. For our part, we know our own limits when it comes to the hard sciences. What we are doing here is not so much contrasting scientific training with literary or philosophical studies as using our daily practice to sketch out a region of particular kinds of knowledge, explored by madness and its analysts.

Winnicott had warned us that these patients, familiar with the borderlands between life and death,[1] oblige their analysts to mobilize wide domains of knowledge and culture. This includes contemporary scientific culture, accessible through scientists who, like the physicist Erwin Schrödinger,[2] consider it their duty to inform the general public when their discoveries give rise to scientific revolutions.

The fact that the discoverer of the canonic equations of quantum mechanics believes it will take fifty years for epistemological upheavals to reach the public is remarkable. For, in connection with the Civil War, William Faulkner (1936) makes the same observation about the delay in the transmission of the major upheavals of our societies.[3] His

---

1. "Psychotic patients who are all the time hovering between living and not living force us to look at this problem, one that really belongs not to psychoneurotics but to all living beings. I am claiming that these same phenomena that are life and death to our schizoid or borderline patients appear in our cultural experiences. It is these cultural experiences that provide the continuity in the human race that transcends personal existence. I am assuming that cultural experiences are in direct continuity with play, the play of those who have not yet heard of games" (Winnicott 1971, p. 117).

2. "The fabulous *material* development led to a *materialistic* outlook allegedly derived from the new scientific discoveries. These occurrences have, I think, contributed to the deliberate neglect of science in many quarters during the half century that followed—the one that is just drawing to a close. For there is always a certain time-lag between the views held by learned men and the views held by the general public about the views of those learned men. I do not think fifty years is an excessive estimate for the average length of that time-lag" (Schrödinger 1956, p. 114).

3. The temporal framework of *Absalom, Absalom* is the immobilization of the half century (1860–1910) between the suffocating South of the narrator and the freezing room at Harvard in which he talks about the war to his roommate (who will become a medic in the world war). The reenactment that takes place in this space-time is described as follows:

> The room was indeed tomblike: a quality stale and static and moribund beyond any mere vivid and living cold. . . . They did not retreat from cold. They both bore it as though in deliberate flagellant exaltation of physical misery transmogrified into the spirit's travail of these two young men during that time *fifty years ago, or forty-eight, rather forty-seven, and then forty-six, since it was 64 and then 65* and the starved and ragged remnant of an army having retreated, swept onward not by a victorious army behind it but rather by a mounting tide of the names of lost battles from either side. [pp. 275-276, emphasis added]

literary oeuvre draws its inspiration from this vanished time. We, too, regularly observe the same time lag, in the work that our patients lead us to do with them, for the historical catastrophes of the twentieth century. This book, in turn, is being written some fifty years after the end of the Second World War. How—that is ultimately to say: to whom—did we begin to write it?

The neurologist Antonio Damasio (1995) says that his book is his "side of a conversation with a curious, intelligent and wise imaginary friend who knew little about neuroscience but much about life" (p. xviii). We have chosen to sit in the precious armchair of this conversation. That chair might, to be sure, unexpectedly turn into the "siege perilous," the empty chair at the Round Table,[4] in the quest for the Real that unites us with our patients and with our scientific colleagues. For the latter are, like us and our patients during the analytic work, challenged to produce transmissible forms and formulas by way of exploration of the Real: for them, in nature; for us, among men.

Thus we too are engaged, as the neurologist says, in a conversation with an imaginary friend who knows little about the psychoanalytic treatment of madness but is aware of risks taken by each discoverer of the unexplored worlds of our world.

2.1.2. Objectivation/Positivity: A New Paradigm for Psychoanalysis

In his Tarner Lectures at Cambridge, Schrödinger, who won the Nobel Prize in 1939, emphasized the impasses of the objectivation principle on the subatomic scale and hence the need to replace it with the study of the interactions with the mechanism of observation.[5] He suggested

---

4. In Arthurian legend, Merlin predicted that no one would sit there without incurring the greatest danger, until, one day, the greatest knight in the world would come, marking the end of the adventures of the kingdom of Logres: that knight would sit there and remain unharmed. This was Galahad, son of Lancelot.

5. In *Mind and Matter*, Schrödinger (1956) notes:

The first of these antinomies is the astonishment at finding our world picture "colourless, cold, mute." Colour and sound, hot and cold are our immediate sensations; small wonder that they are lacking in a world model from

that the study of the psyche also ran into such impasses and that there was no reason to place an impenetrable wall between the two fields of knowledge (Schrödinger 1954).

Schrödinger directly called on psychologists to "reconsider the initial gambit" of the exile of the subject. Around the fifth century B.C., in Greece, this maneuver had established the objectivation principle that makes classical science possible. Of course, Schrödinger assures us, the whole of science will not have to begin over again.

An enthusiast of biology, he liked to cite his friend Sherrington, who won the Nobel Prize in 1932 and prophesied the scientific trends that would reduce the encephalon to a telephone switchboard (nowadays, we would say: to a computer), confusing the fibers of the electronic machinery with the messages they convey. Schrödinger also mentions a student of Sherrington's, Sir John Eccles, winner of the Nobel Prize in 1963. In *How the Self Controls Its Brain* (1994), Eccles defies his materialist critics.

These critics maintain that insurmountable difficulties stand in the way of the hypothesis that nonmaterial mental events like a thought can in any way act on material structures like the neurons of the cerebral cortex. Eccles proposes that it is possible to avoid this impasse,

---

which we have removed our own mental person. The second is our fruitless quest for the place where minds act on matter or vice versa, so well known from Sir Sherrington. . . . The material world has only been constructed at the price of taking the self, that is, mind, out of it, removing it. Mind is not part of it; obviously, therefore, it can neither act on it nor be acted on by any of its parts. . . . Yet I would say that a rapid withdrawal from the position held for over 2000 years is dangerous. We may lose everything. . . . But here the problem is set. *The relatively new science of psychology imperatively demands living space; it makes it unavoidable to reconsider the initial gambit.* [pp. 128–129, emphasis added]

Moore (1989) describes Schrödinger's meeting with Jung in 1946: "[He] proceeded to Ascona to take part in an Eranos Tagung, one of a series of annual conferences founded by Jung. The topic of the meeting was 'The Spirit and Nature.' Schrödinger's lecture was on 'The Spirit of Science.' Its theme was that the spirit is to an eminent degree subjective and thus evades objective examination. He quoted an Indian philosopher's commentary on the Vedanta Sutras" (p. 429).

since the dimensions of the structures serving synaptic transmission are so tiny that they can be made to function similarly to the fields of probability of quantum physics. Thus it appears that the juncture between cerebral functioning and quantum physics is part of certain theoretical advances in neurology.

We can bear witness to how urgent it is to "reconsider the initial gambit" when approaching the shores of madness. Omnipresent nowadays and omnipotent socially, the objectivation principle compels submission. We have already seen that, reduced to passivity, psychiatric patients go as far as to make themselves the object of this science. Here is where the tragic borders on the absurd and can also arouse comic verve, as in the fierce satire *Mount Misery* (Schem 1997). But what is at stake is the subject's freeing himself from objectivation.

Giving up the objectivation principle certainly does not mean that arbitrariness rules in the field opened up by this new paradigm. Nor does it mean that nothing rigorous is produced. Auguste Comte, drawing the scientific lessons from his madness, spoke of a positivity, indeed, a superpositivity, just as, in 1917, Apollinaire invented the words *surrealism* and *surreality* (Nadeau 1944, Sass 1992). The poet marked by a bloody star then recovered from a war injury to his head.

Madness, small or large, is perceived by way of the gaps in which the interlocutor necessarily finds himself situated in the unpredictability of the analyst–patient relationship. In these moments, when what cannot be said is shown, only the analysis of these interferences, registered unbeknownst to analyst and patient, is able to produce the subject of the investigation and thus gradually to determine the Real that is involved.

Singularities and fleeting, stealthy impressions on the analyst's part are clearly part of the field and process of investigation, on condition that he is capable, later on, of working them out and, still later, of giving the patient an account of them. Likewise, the patient's exceptional gifts of observation, his ability to interpret facial expressions and expressions of the landscape, of the atmosphere, of the tone of voice, and of objects themselves are an integral part of the investigation. He knows how to distinguish between a sincere smile and the smile imitated on command.[6] He differentiates between the times when the shrink is asking him genuine questions and the times when he is only pretending to do so in order to extract supposedly objective information.

2.1.3. The "Superpositivity" of Madness

This positivity, at issue in research in analytic work with madness and trauma, borders on the domain of the Real. One of the ways of representing it, though it is by nature unrepresentable, is to approach it in its connection with the two other orders, the Symbolic and the Imaginary. Thus the famous Lacanian acronym RSI takes the form of the Borromean knot, which Lacan adopted from the coat of arms of the Borromeo family. It is composed of three interlocking rings, somewhat like the emblem of the Olympic Games. But the knotting is such that, "if you cut one, all three are set free" (Lacan 1972–1973, p. 124). For Lacan, this is the very figure of madness.

What we want to do here is compare this sophisticated image—which, while Lacan was elaborating it, called for contributions from mathematicians of knot theory (Soury 1986)—to the formulations of Harry Stack Sullivan (1945) in a paper written at the end of the war. Just after this confrontation with the Real, when the tool of names and speech was broken by the mass murders, Sullivan speaks of "the string of words" without which nothing can be transmitted to our children. He then comes up with a word that especially pleases him: nexus, knot, "the place where things get together and are snarled or tangled":

> The nexus of all this experience by which we form views of the world, the universe, our place in it, and so on, is always in the experience of me-and-my-mind, or you-and-your-mind if you feel very separate from me. And in this you-and-your-mind there are some things which are fairly clearly capable of being named which go on experiencing and formulating. . . . We symbolize and formulate the present—and by symbolize I mean we relate it to things, form thoughts, words, and so on, which will stand for it. [pp. 201–202]

---

6. Damasio (1995) describes the laboratory experiment showing that the newborn infant, already dwelling in language, is able to distinguish the two facial expressions.

In emphasizing what Lacan calls the signifying chain, in this paper Sullivan, like Lacan, is setting out to distinguish the subject, "I," from the "me" and "the dreadful not-me" that has to do with the uncanny (p. 249). "The coming of 'I,' as a term that was not there when it was 'me,' is great stuff" (p. 215).

Knotted to the two other orders, the Symbolic and the Imaginary, the register of the Real will be retained here in connection with its effects of unlinking:

—Rupture of the Symbolic, of the place in which alliance,[7] the guarantee of promises and treaties, and hence the social bond, is founded. It is thus the foundation of the subject of speech and of history.
—Disorganization of the orientation points of the Imaginary (Lacan 1949) and hence of the function that allows for relations of specular identification: the body image, which presides over the boundaries of the "me."

Let us sum up some of the formulas already mentioned. The Real is first defined negatively as what is impossible to name and represent (Ch. 1.1.3 and Lacan 1969–1970), that which "doesn't stop not being written" (Lacan 1972–1973, p. 59). This is why it always returns to the same place as the uncanny: in a surreality, a superpositivity, outside the field of speech and beyond the mirror, imposing the presence of

---

7. Lacan (1953) acknowledges his debt to the anthropologist Claude Lévi-Strauss, director of studies at EHESS and professor at the Collège de France, for this definition of the symbolic order:

Thus it is the virtue of the Word that perpetuates the movement of the Great Debt whose economy Rabelais, in a famous metaphor, extended to the stars themselves. And we shall not be surprised that the chapter in which, with the macaronic inversion of kinship names, he presents us with the anticipation of the discoveries of the anthropologists, should reveal in him the substantific definition of the human mystery which I am trying to elucidate here. . . . The inviolable Debt is the guarantee that the voyage on which wives and goods are embarked will bring back to their point of departure in a never-failing cycle other women and other goods, all carrying an identical entity: what Lévi-Strauss calls a "zero symbol," thus reducing the power of Speech to the form of an algebraic sign. [pp. 67-68]

uninscribed catastrophes, breaking the limits of body and soul, escaping history, in time and in oblivion.[8]

2.1.4. The Subject at Stake

With regard to the impossible, Lacan emphasizes paradox: "Yes, I am teaching something positive here. Except that it is expressed by a negation. But why shouldn't it be as positive as anything else?" (1972–1973, p. 59). One hundred years after Comte's superpositivity, this positivity of the Real was at the center of the investigations of the surrealists, deeply interested in the resources of language games at the borders of language: found objects, readymades, objective chance, psychoanalysis, infatuation, madness, dreams, and automatic writing appear as attempts to bring about the return of the subject after the mass destructions of the First World War.

The day after the armistice of 1918, the Surrealist Group established a social bond of insurrection. Far from being, at the outset, that new artistic school producing works that would be the glory of museums, the group thought of itself primarily as a means of knowledge. On the basis of the new scientific and psychological paradigms discovered by Einstein, Heisenberg, Broglie, and Freud and calling for a new way of looking, they felt "invited to fertile and passionate researches" (Nadeau 1944, p. 42). Jacques Lacan, like André Breton a psychiatrist in those years, was for a time a member of the Surrealist Group that decided to "open the sluice gates of the unconscious" (p. 148).

The controversial id, the "it" (Groddeck 1917–1934, 1923), had just made its appearance in the psychoanalytic epic. "This is not an 'I' but an 'it,' and yet the 'I' may be subjugated and enslaved by the 'it.' The two forms of medicine must be joined, as body and soul" (Sacks 1973, p. 313). "Where id was," Freud (1933) writes, "there ego shall be" (p. 80). It is in these terms that Sacks (1973) describes the return from such blind forces in the case of patients who, ever since the 1920s, had been buried in the immobility of an epidemic of lethargic encephalitis. They were able to be "awakened" in 1969 thanks to a recently discov-

---

8. For a penetrating analysis of these themes, see Muller 1995.

ered drug, L-dopa, though they were affected by other uncontrollable symptoms.

With a consummate art of transference and its analysis, whatever the hazards, Sacks sets out to enable subjects whose psychic faculties had remained intact to regain a foothold in their history and in the community of the living. The transferential relationships woven with each one are the sole framework of the subject's awakening from uncanny experiences representing figures of the Real—to the extent that the Real can be imagined.

Regaining a foothold in history, obviously, is not reducible to adaptation or social conformity. It involves the inscription of a dissociate truth, an "unthought known" (Bollas 1987), known through impressions that have been split off (*retranchées*, literally, "cut off"), and the awakening of a subject of history (having nothing to do with his desubjectivized homonym of historical materialism). This is even the condition of the emergence of the subject of desire.

These cases of trauma or madness are a challenge hurled at clinical treatment, since the analyst comes up against a piece of the Real. Because signifying speech was lacking, nothing could be inscribed, on this point, in the unconscious. The customary tools of treatment are thwarted, since, in this regard, the subject of speech, even repressed speech, has not been constituted. What is at stake, then, is precisely the coming into being of the subject, the subject of a history not so much censored as erased, reduced to nothing, and yet somehow existing. We use the term *dissociated unconscious* to refer to the unconscious that is at work in such moments and that is "distinct from the repressed" (Lacan 1955–1956, p. 200).

2.1.5. The Logic of Catastrophic Zones: Lesions in Otherness

Approaching the Real, at mortal risk, thus overturns customary identifications. Under these conditions, at the very least normal symbiotic relations[9] are required in order to face the danger. For, paradoxically,

---

9. Cf. the well-known words of Madame de Sévigné (1660–1696) to her daughter, Madame de Grignan, in the context of an acute analysis of French aristocratic society in the seventeenth century: "The north wind of Grignan hurts me in your

the limits of the body are ruptured so as to extend its capacity for survival. The unconscious, heightened wakefulness of baby-nurses when they are asleep next to infants is an example. Activated in extreme situations, this lowering of the threshold of the self's boundaries is sometimes actually a condition of survival.

It should also be noted that, in exactly opposite situations, where the issue is not escaping a death zone but making individuals or masses of people enter one, a rupture of the self-boundaries is actively brought about by techniques of manipulation aimed at submission to the leader or the ideology (Grossman 1995, Milgram 1974).

The boundary between these two impulses seems thin. And there is a fluctuating tilt toward one or the other of these pools of attraction, making a sudden transition from actions of liberation to those of servitude. Madness can very often be considered a normal mode of survival in the face of actual manipulations on the part of the environment, from a prior moment that has dropped out of time. What we are dealing with in that case is a normal craziness that bears witness to a normality that is crazy, trivialized, dehistoricized, and denied: "What happened didn't happen." From that time on, the place vanishes with the past: there is no place, no past. It has become impossible to trust one's own emotions and sensations.

To express this state of things, the philosopher Ludwig Wittgenstein (1933–1934) offers stimulating aphorisms concerning the seat of the emotions: "An innumerable variety of cases can be thought of in which we should say that someone has pains in another person's body, or, say, in a piece of furniture, or in any empty spot" (p. 50). Did he suffer from the "empty spot" left by his three older brothers when they committed suicide or by his dear friend Pinsent, who died in an airplane accident in July 1918 while investigating the causes of a previous accident (Monk 1990)?

"The idea of an ego inhabiting a body ought to be abolished," Wittgenstein says (1914–1916, p. 22). This does not mean that he defends the dualist conception of mind and body revisited by the disputes

chest" (p. 321), she writes on December 29, 1688, when her daughter is ill in her castle in Provence. Nowadays these words would imply a fusional relationship, quite suspect by our new criteria!

of present-day neurobiologists. The issue is not pitting neurons and the psyche against each other but rather exploring traumatic situations in which bodily sensations are anesthetized by fear to the point, for example, where the philosopher adds, "I turn into stone and my pain goes on" (1918, § 288). In this context, Wittgenstein explains, "Pain behaviour can point to a painful place, but the subject of pain is the person who gives it expression" (§ 302). "The man who cries out with pain," he writes, "or says that he has pain, does not choose the mouth that says it" (1933–1934, p. 68; cf. 1914–1916, p. 61).

This gap that opens up is precisely the place into which there slips a transference that can name the pain—demonstrated, perhaps not even felt—on behalf of the other.

We are thinking of the direct application of this proposition in Sacks's *Awakenings* (1973), since it would be reductive to ascribe the awakening of soul and body solely to the miracle drug. The author emphasizes a third crucial factor in the experience of awakening and its disappointments, and this depends on the intelligence, the sensitivity, the music and rhythm of the body, and the words of the neurologist, those who are working with him, and all those with whom the patients are connected: their families, of course, but above all the community of mutual care that they alone can provide among themselves.

Children, too, are very quick to detect the zones of petrification, even transient ones, of those who are supposed to be caring for them. They may express this in sometimes bizarre statements that are worth questioning, with an acute perception of the blanks in the other that is perhaps registered by what Damasio (1995) calls "somatic markers."

Thus there are circumstances in which awareness is altered not by brain damage but by the damage that wrecks the dimension of otherness to the point of one's paradoxically becoming the subject of the other's suffering, especially when this other is unable to feel anything.

2.1.6. The "Children" of Phineas Gage

For neurobiology, one clinical case is well on the way to becoming as famous as the Schreber case (Freud 1911) is for the psychoanalysis of the psychoses. In the nineteenth century, Phineas Gage's frontal brain was half destroyed in a mining accident (Damasio 1995). Afterward he presented strangely: he seemed perfectly normal, with his capacity for reasoning intact, but he performed disastrously in some aspects of daily life. Such frontal lesions have even given rise to a diagnosis that has become popular: today I can call my neighbor frontal, that is, incapable of expressing his emotions and incoherent in his decisions, just as he could call me paranoid, hysterical, or perverted.

Our clinical work brings us into contact with some of Phineas Gage's descendants, as it were—people whose cortex was not necessarily mutilated but whose emotions were nevertheless disrupted and anesthetized, leading to horrific decisions regarding, for example, their own children. Without there being any lesion whatsoever, the same distortions in the expression of feelings have made them unable to transmit their position as subject affectively with regard to certain elementary oppositions such as danger and safety, right and wrong, shame and pride, happiness and unhappiness, and the like.

Their cognitive functioning often disguises this deficit as hypernormality: indifference passes for wisdom, insensitivity to those close to them as devotion to distant causes, rhetorical skill for intelligence. A self-centered and deceptive sentimentality, well observed by Damasio, reduces the color of the world to a monochrome vision, depriving their families of essential information along with the sensations and feelings that convey this information.

Our patients are perpetuating such a hell, one that continues on in the anesthesia of several generations. This major distortion characterizes the transmission of traumas: an insensitivity marks everything reminiscent of the catastrophe, while a pseudo-normality reigns in the family. Only one of its members persists in showing that something is wrong, that there is a history of devastated social bonds but that its expression is threatened with extinction.

If they manage to get to an analyst, these descendants may manifest only an omnipresent shame, unalloyed misfortune, a sense of radical injustice, and a global sadness, all these being signs of an imminent catastrophe that they can neither name nor dispel. For some time, the initial diagnosis of depression prevails, and ad hoc antidepressants are prescribed. Prescribed for life, they are increasingly accompanied by periodic shocks, trivialized with the acronym ECT[10] and said to be "for symptomatic relief." For, today, certain patients present as very cool at first meeting, like zombies with a fixed gaze, doleful voice, and a face either dull or widened by a fake smile that clashes with the rest of their appearance.

When questioning them about the environmental dimension, as Damasio calls it, we must not ignore the fact that the individual present here is not limited to his brain case and the neurons it encloses. We must take into account all the people with whom he is connected[11] by means of various language games and even, in this very case, by the absence of all language of words and emotions (MacDougall 1989). It often happens that, in the past, his family has crossed through spaces beyond good and evil, coinciding with the historical, political, and social upheavals of the century, and has partly come to a halt there.

Where and when? This is just what a representative of the unfortunate family line has come to find out, in the name of others, of his relatives, when he has run out of resources. This forever looming catastrophe has broken through the imaginary frontiers separating inside from outside, future from past, one person from the other, endangering the patient up to the symbolic dimension of otherness: the trustworthiness of the other has become problematical.

2.1.7. "A Death in the Family"[12]: The Neurologist Comes to the Aid of the Psychoanalyst

What follows is a case history in which the analyst has made use of the story of Phineas Gage. Here, however, there is no organic lesion; what had been injured is the very dimension of otherness.

Tristan is a man in his forties, acknowledged as a master in the craft that is his job. He comes to the analyst's office on the brink of failure,

---

10. Electroconvulsive therapy, in which what used to be called electroshock can be recognized, has been back in favor for several years.

11. "All my relatives," say the Sioux of South Dakota in their ceremonies.

12. *A Death in the Family*, James Agee's 1938 novel, lets us hear the voice of a child in the aftermath of misfortune.

professional and familial. A series of bad decisions has transformed his talents into nightmares, and here he is, referred by his doctor, who no longer has confidence in psychotropic drugs in his case. Questioned about previous catastrophes, he mentions—though with skepticism, "because all that is so far away; what are you going to look for there?"— the death of his sister, who was two years his senior. Reluctantly, he describes the circumstances of the accident, which, he repeats, has nothing to do with his current disaster and distress. From then on, he speaks in the present tense.

He is 4 years old, standing with his sister in a safety zone in the middle of the street. His mother has already crossed with another little sister in a stroller, and their father is on the sidewalk behind them, looking elsewhere while he waits to cross. A streetcar appears, sounding its horn loudly. The little girl drops her brother's hand and runs across the street to her mother. A speeding car knocks her down; she is hurled to the side of the road, where the boy sees her huddled like a rag doll.

Forty years later, he realizes that he is the only one who, second by second, can rerun the film that neither of his parents has seen. Today he is, as it were, still in the middle of the street and, later, in the middle of a room in which he sees his sister on a bed with a big bruise on her cheek and forehead. It is probably then that he is told that she is dead.

The analyst nods without saying a word. Tristan immediately protests: "That doesn't mean anything. It goes too far back in the past."

"Yes," the analyst replies, "but that moment wasn't registered as past. It's still suspended like a present without time."

He doesn't understand: "I'm like a groggy boxer. I keep on getting hit in the head, and each time I get up, without thinking, and keep on fighting. I've never been able to defend myself."

This story preoccupied the analyst well beyond the framework of the sessions. She could not stop thinking about it, without knowing what to make of this invasion. Just as she is writing these lines, she remembers that she had an older sister of about the same age, who ran under the wheels of a motorbike at the beach, under similar circumstances, but without great harm.

At the time of the sessions, since she was rereading the works of Damasio (1995, 1999) on frontal lesions, she had the opportunity to use these books as transitional objects. Could it be, she asks the patient, that the blow to the little girl's temple had a similar effect on his own forehead, resulting in his inability to feel the instinct of self-preservation, as he says? At the age Tristan and his sister were at the time of the accident, small children can be connected by what is called transitivism: one of them may begin to cry when the other is hit.

For the first time, this man, who up to then had maintained a gentle and polite distance, seemed overcome by a strong emotion. He described a strange experience:

"When I find myself in the state of strong concentration required by my work, I have a very clear flash: I see myself struck on the head by the explosion of my machine. This image is very sharp—too sharp, I should say."

The following sessions were spent in working out major decisions that he quickly thought up to ensure his survival and to get out of the difficulty that had gone on for years. For, although he had golden fingers and exceptional intelligence, he had never been able to anticipate the dangers and risks of reality.

But the analytic work was just beginning. How did it happen that, for the first time, he felt that he was an actor, no longer a spectator, in this dramatic sequence? Dread now reached him, but only on the basis of the analyst's impression; until then, his words as a child had counted for nothing. The official versions, collected in the local press, told a very different story and told it in different ways: now the little girl was holding her father's hand, now her mother's. But only Tristan knew that she was holding his. He alone had seen the accident that the adults, from their geometric vantage points, could not see. Ever since that time, he had kept on pursuing his sylph, a beautiful, immortal girl, like the fairy of the mist, like a specter.

The scene took place on a beach of the Normandy Invasion, in which his grandfather had played a heroic role. His grandmother had joined up as a war nurse. Both had seen more than they could bear. Twenty or so years later, Tristan's family was on vacation at their house at the seashore. The terror that had manifested itself on the day of the accident was not, therefore, just the terror that had descended upon the protagonists of that drama. It pervaded the place where his parents and grandparents had seen so many young people fall. The little boy had been left alone in the face of what he, in turn, had seen.

The death of his sister as the last little soldier to die there was not conceivable. They tried to make a good impression, to harden themselves, as they sadly covered up the truth. The fall of the child was abandoned. Tristan had never even gone there. Besides, it was of no importance as far as he was concerned. Didn't he have the power to bring her back to life through his craft, through his own life? Ever since he was a teenager he had always been able to revive his girlfriends, whom he chose when they were, in fact, crushed by the burden of life.

Speaking of him in terms of a lesion in alterity means that, despite his extraordinary gifts, on such occasions no trustworthy other had been able to hold his hand. The analyst had to win that place "for real," as children say, not just formally. The leitmotiv of his lack of instinct for self-preservation was the goal of their joint investigation of the time and space of the trauma. Yet are we entitled to say that, for this man, the accident functions as the "cause" of a lack of self-consciousness?

2.2. WAR AND PEACE IN PSYCHOANALYSIS

2.2.1. A Problematic Causality

In line with this determinism, which seems to be obvious, it would have been easy to predict that the life of this family was going to be turned upside down; there is clearly no way to change the past. Destiny appears to prevail; disaster keeps on striking a little girl full force in an implacable repetition. How is it possible to erase self-destruction, to tame fate and free up creative energy? Yet the causalist model must be suspended here—and subverted.

As though the death of a child were not enough, belittling diagnoses pounce on family troubles. The genetic causality of depression, bipolar disorder, schizophrenia, and suicidality are so many blows inflicted on the relatives, just as the mining bar struck Phineas Gage. What could be more normal, we are told, than a child's weak psyche if an aunt was an inmate in an asylum? Nowadays the ancient magical belief in hereditary transmission unto the seventh generation seeks the backing of genetics instead of teaching us how to put into a story the foreclosed parts of history.

How can we think of exceptions to the iron law of statistics, which arouse in the public the sacred terror of a curse according to a schema that Sullivan pointed out as early as the 1920s but that goes back to the dawn of time?[13] Patients with madness in their families all ask us the same question: "Do you really think it's possible to resist *La Forza del Destino* [Verdi's opera of 1862]"?[14] If the analyst replies, "Yes," he at first seems to be a quack; if he says, "No," he becomes the instrument of the same fate. This aporia is one of the challenges hurled by the patients who haunt these catastrophic zones.

2.2.2. Transference in Neurologists

Here we come up against one of the logical impasses familiar from the field of madness and trauma. The way out is shown by Wittgenstein's formula that "language is not a cage" (1945–1949, § 26).[15] Wittgenstein is warning us when he asks whether naming is simply attaching a label to a thing. Tristan certainly did not lack words to attach to what he had seen; what he lacked was someone "else" to authenticate them. What remained were forms, detached from the accident and living off a quasi-autonomous life. To his amazement, he recognized them, scattered in his creations, in the gesture of showing these to the analyst.

---

13. "It can be accepted, it seems, that the empirical psychiatry of today includes magical notions" (Sullivan 1946, p. 140).

14. Here destiny is incarnated by the goddess of Fate, Até, whose name, in Greek, comes from a verb, *ao, meaning "to make crazy." Similarly, in Latin, *quos vult perdere, Jupiter dementat*: those whom Jupiter wants to destroy, he drives mad.

15. "One thinks that learning language consists in giving names to objects. . . . To repeat: naming is something like attaching a label to a thing. One can say that it is preparatory to the use of a word. But what is it a preparation for?" (1918, § 26). "Excalibur is the name of an object; this object no longer exists when Excalibur is broken into pieces, and as no object would then correspond to the name, it would have no meaning" (§ 39). "We said that the sentence 'Excalibur has no sharp blade' made sense even when Excalibur was broken in pieces. Now this is so because, in the language game, a name is also used in the absence of its bearer" (§ 44). "Now suppose that the tool with the name is broken. We could also imagine a convention whereby B has to shake his head in reply if A gives him the sign belonging to a tool that is broken" (§ 41).

The main issue in psychoanalysis from the *Project for a Scientific Psychology* (Freud 1895) to *Beyond the Pleasure Principle* (Freud 1920) is the exposition of how the language function arises (Lacan 1959–1960), passing through successive filters, after traumas in which the afflux of stimulation exceeds the capacities of the subject:

> If we may assume that the experience acquires its traumatic character only as a result of a quantitative factor—that is to say, that in every case *it is an excess in demand* that is responsible for an experience evoking unusual pathological reactions—then we can easily arrive at the expedient of saying that something acts as a trauma in the case of one constitution but in the case of another would have no such effect. [Freud 1939, p. 84, emphasis added]

What was demanded of the child in excess, in addition to seeing the accident, which remained as though glued to his retina, was the total aloneness in which he was left by the maddened adults. This aloneness was intensified by the fabrication of contradictory versions of what had happened, aimed at diminishing the family's unbearable guilt. No reliable linguistic filter was placed between him and the event. All that remained were spectral silhouettes of beautiful girls appearing and disappearing in his creations, along with splendid images of explosions.

In the transitional use of Damasio's book a language game was being played, in which the analyst, without at first noticing what was going on, authenticated the fact that the accident happened to *him*, the little boy, and that he too could have disappeared in the same collision if he had not stood still. What if he had followed his older sister? The stalled film, broken at the moment of the shock, now got started up again: What if . . . ? Yet he was surprised that he still felt no terror, not even that famous survivor guilt that is so much talked about. What if his repeated failures and his devotion to those unfortunate women were returning to him like the mark of that tragic flaw?[16]

In the transference, the horror of the scene came to affect the analyst: "Well, I feel it, for the moment, in your place."

But as for the neurologist, his conception of language, presented as pure internal translation of images into words, seems to us to be

---

16. The tragic flaw is not limited by individual responsibility but extends to all those touched by the irruption of the Real (Saïd 1978).

prejudicial to reflection. The inability to say what is happening in the case of a traumatic experience is usually described as a lack of words in the internal reservoir. In the face of such a neurobiological short circuit, all one would have to do is use the famous camera to observe which areas of the brain are activated. Every week, this new mascot of the media offers us colored lobes like circus freaks: this chess champion, or child genius, or horrid criminal, or mystic on the threshold of levitation. God himself is said to reside in a corner of our convolutions, if not detected then at least detectable. Given such scoops, psychoanalysis comes out the loser; it has a lot of trouble exploring human madness with the eminently shaky and intersubjective camera of the transference.

And yet it happens that the neurologist himself tries it out. Right in his laboratory setting, Damasio (1995) honestly vouches for a transferential moment in his experience. Here is how he presents the case of Elliot, a Phineas Gage of today, who had become unable to feel emotions after the removal of part of his frontal lobes damaged by a tumor:

> He was, as I said earlier, an emotionally contained sort, but many illustrious and socially exemplary people have been emotionally contained. He certainly was not overemotional; he did not laugh or cry inappropriately and seemed neither sad nor joyful. He was not facetious, just quietly humorous. . . . On a more probing analysis, however, something was missing, and I had overlooked much of the prime evidence for this. Elliot was able to recount the tragedy of his life with a detachment that was out of step with the magnitude of the events. He was always controlled, always describing scenes as a dispassionate, uninvolved spectator. Nowhere was there a sense of his own suffering, even though he was the protagonist.
>
> Mind you, restraint of this sort is most welcome from the point of view of a physician listener, since it does not reduce one's emotional expense. But, as I talked to Elliot again for hours on end, it became clear that the magnitude of his distance was unusual. Elliot was exerting no restraint whatsoever on his affect. He was calm. He was relaxed. His narratives evolved effortlessly. He was not inhibiting the expression of internal emotional resonance or hushing inner turmoil. He simply did not have any turmoil to hush. This was not a culturally acquired stiff upper lip. In some curious, unwittingly protective way, he was not pained by his tragedy. I found myself suffering more

when listening to Elliot's stories than Elliot himself seemed to be suffering. In fact, *I felt that I suffered more than he did just by thinking of those stories.* [p. 44, emphasis added]

Here the neurologist describes a familiar moment in a psychoanalyst's experience when neutrality is challenged: the observer "feels" instead of staying objective, in this very context of the patient's inability to feel.

2.2.3. The Horrified Other[17]

This point of transference is the heart of what happens not only with traumatized patients but also in the case of madness. The role of what Arendt calls a "horrified other" is not a fault affecting the objectivity of the observer but a threshold that must be crossed in order to make contact with a world that is otherwise unreachable. It is also a tool that can change the course of a destiny. The analyst does not rest content with registering the impression but must find a way to state it in the session, in the form of a language game. For this impression does not belong to him; it is the result of conjoint work.

We share with other clinicians this touchstone of the "possible" (Lacan 1955–1956) psychoanalysis of the catastrophic zones in which madness and trauma are mingled. Clinicians agree that, in such cases, neutrality not only is contrary to ethics but also destroys all scientific relevance. Wittgenstein (1929–1930) notes that, at the end of his lecture on ethics, he found it absolutely necessary to speak in the first person, since, on that level, nothing can any longer be the object of a statement; all he can do is come forth as a person saying "I," not as a sociological description but speaking from his own resources.

It is clear that some organic lesions cannot be repaired. But, as Oliver Sacks (1973) so remarkably demonstrates in *Awakenings*, it is still pos-

---

17. The phrase is Arendt's (1951). Arendt observes that "[o]nly the fearful imagination of those who have been aroused by such reports, but have not actually been smitten in their own flesh, of those who are consequently free from the bestial, desperate terror which, when confronted by real, present horror, inexorably paralyzes everything that is not mere reaction, can afford to keep thinking about horrors" (p. 441). Cf. Conrad 1902.

sible to change the nature of the relationship so as to carry through all the way the expression, not necessarily verbal, of a language game with a subject. Throughout his book, Sacks shows that he is speaking from his own resources.[18]

We are not trying, in these pages, to celebrate the undeniable miracles of love and empathy. For love is not enough. When it comes to drastic human experiences, rage and apathy are also language games.

2.2.4. On the Borders of Language: The Analyst's Dissociated Impressions

Sometimes the analyst does not have conscious access to his own impressions, even within the session. When the impossible arises, it is not surprising that awareness, and even the unconscious of repression, prove faulty (Freud 1907, 1919, 1939, Lacan 1966). At this outer edge, as Wittgenstein (1918) would say, "a whole cloud of philosophy may be condensed into a drop of grammar" (§ 222). Now, if the grammar of naming on the edge of the Real surely does not operate with labels, it is all the more inoperative with the images of interiority. When the boundaries of inside and outside have been breached, it is only in between that it is possible for anything to be shown.

This grammar thus sets other processes going, and these are to be explored with the patient. In societies in which art is medicine,[19]

---

18. "It is the function of scientific medicine to rectify the 'it.' It is the function of art, of living contact, of existential medicine to call upon the latent will, the agent, the 'I,' to call on its commanding and coordinating powers so that it may regain its hegemony and rule once again. For the ruler is not a measuring rod or clock but rule and measure of the personal I" (Sacks 1973, p. 285).

19. "Perhaps one day it will be known that there was no art, only medicine," states J. M. G. Le Clézio (1971). He continues:

Illness, madness, mortal dangers appear, from time to time, and they are not accidents. They are signs of the need to express oneself. The Indian peoples have learned to recognize these signs; they know that the need for language, painting, and music is in these crises. It is not a question of amusing oneself (to distract from what boredom?) or of externalizing one's inner states. But when one of these signs appears, by chance, in the body of a man, child, or woman, it is because the whole society is threatened. Language—that

multiple traditions, ceremonial and artistic, bring onstage what cannot be said. We shall give an example taken from our practice, an example for which, paradoxically, Damasio (1999) provides an introduction, this time in his second book, *The Feeling of What Happens*:

> For the purpose of the investigation, I separate three stages of processing along a continuum: *a state of emotion*, which can be triggered and executed non-consciously, *a state of feeling*, which can be represented non-consciously, and *a state of feeling made conscious*, i.e., known to the organism having both emotion and feeling. I believe these distinctions are helpful as we try to imagine the neural underpinnings of this chain of events in humans. Moreover, I suspect that some non-human creatures that exhibit emotions but are unlikely to have the sort of consciousness that we have may well form the representations we call feelings without knowing they do so. Someone may suggest that perhaps we should have another word for "feelings that are not conscious," but there isn't one. The closest alternative is to explain what we mean. [p. 37]

Damasio begins by defining the concepts he will be using: state of emotion, state of feeling, and, finally, state of feeling made conscious. But a word seems to be missing. Oddly, the neurologist is trying to approach another important human experience not covered by these three concepts; for lack of a better term, he calls this "feelings that are not conscious." He circles around this phenomenon that has no referent in language and ultimately has to fall back on a reference to domestic animals.

Yet, though these animals do not speak, they still inhabit our language (Hearne 1986).[20] We know nothing of their feelings if these do not reveal themselves in one way or another, in a game with those of us who interact with them. As Wittgenstein (1933–1934) says, "There is a kind of general disease of thinking which looks for (and finds) what would be called a mental state from which all our acts spring as if from

---

language one had taken into one's body, that power of the hand to draw circles, triangles, and crosses, that power of the voice to modulate animal cries—all that had been kept thwarted must speak so that it can free itself, emit these vibrations, plow its furrows on the world. Slow explosion of art. [p. 57]

20. Hearne was a trainer of dogs and horses, a theoretician of her work according to her reading of Wittgenstein, and assistant professor of English at Yale.

a reservoir" (p. 143).[21] This chronic problem takes hold of the analyst as it does anyone else.

In the following case history, we have given a name to these "feelings that are not conscious," without asking the opinion of cats or dogs. Besides, it is the analyst who plays the role of the guinea pig, with enough unawareness to validate the experiment rigorously. Here, these feelings are shown through what the analyst reveals involuntarily, what the patient observes and questions, and what we have called *cut-out impressions*.

2.2.5. Henry: *Casus Belli* in Analysis

For Henry, the analyst's office was probably the last chance before hospitalization. He was subject to periodic fits of clastic rage during which he broke precious art objects belonging to his family. He had never taken medication, although this situation had gone on since he had left the university, in which he was brilliant, a few years earlier.

For a very long time he found it hard to speak about his daily life and seemed to be in a permanent state of humiliation over unfortunate decisions and broken relationships. What he basically did in talking to the analyst was relate his dreams, the liveliness and aesthetic sparkle of which contrasted with the monotony and emptiness of his days.

Late in the afternoon one Friday, his tone of voice changed abruptly. "You're gray," he told the analyst point-blank. Surprised by this unusually direct and uncanny judgment, she said nothing. Several times he came back to his comment: "You're gray." The analyst said she was tired at the end of the week and, to herself, thought about some form of projection. Henry really had nothing more to say. He reluctantly filled the rest of his session with trivia and long silences.

The following Tuesday, he had hardly sat down when he declared that this was their last meeting. As a well brought up man, he thanked the analyst for her goodwill and her efforts; he no longer wished to

---

21. Cf. Wittgenstein 1933–1934, p. 41: "I have been trying in all this to remove the temptation to think that there 'must be' what is called a mental process of thinking, hoping, wishing, believing, etc. . . . , independent of the process of expressing a thought, a hope, a wish, etc."

impose on them. He was about to leave the room when, in an instant, she recalled the grayness he had seen in her face. When he was practically on the threshold, she managed to say,

"Friday, you saw something that I couldn't feel when you noticed that shadow on my face. That morning, I had attended the burial of a friend,[22] and by the afternoon I had completely forgotten it. But this erasure wasn't proof of my indifference. On the contrary, I'd been shocked that he was put in the ground without a word from anyone, without a proper ritual. I'd come away with my mind blank, empty. What you saw on my face was the color of an impression that was not so much repressed as cut off, impossible to put in an image or a word."

Henry stared at her intently and sat back down. The two of them had come up against the experience of "feelings that are not conscious," and he had set in motion the process of their naming.[23] Henry's lethargy corresponded to an intense concentration focused on details that were annulled by those around him. This kind of erasure could drive him mad, to the point of unceremoniously destroying things in his family home. For once, he had not had to go that far, to the point of destroying his analysis, but the imminence of the rupture had prompted the analyst to speak.

In the drop of negation, which might be called judgment of refusal of attribution,[24] instilled in the analyst's first reply, a whole cloud of confusion was concentrated, a typhoon of social movements from which his family had escaped thanks to this particular use of the grammar of negation.

As in Wittgenstein's family, some of his ancestors were Jews in the Austro-Hungarian Empire who had converted to Christianity so as to be able to occupy the best social positions. But when the Nazis came

---

22. See Davoine 1992, where this friend is given the name of Paul. For another *casus belli*, see Davoine 1990.

23. "But has for instance a name which has never been used for a tool, also got a meaning in that game? Let us assume that X [here, *gray*] is such a sign, and that A [here, Henry] gives this sign to B [here, the analyst]—well, even such signs could be given a place in the language game, and B might have, say, to answer them with a shake of the head. . . . The meaning of a word is its use in the language" (Wittgenstein 1945-1949, §§ 42–43).

24. See Lacan 1955–1956, pp. 200-210, Freud 1925, and this volume, Chapter 1, note 12.

they were arrested as Jews nonetheless, then arrested yet again as capitalists by the Stalinists who were pressing forward with their conquest. Some escaped to Israel, but they could not settle there because they were considered Christians. Thus he had finally spent his childhood in Latin America, where his family managed to live through other dictatorships and other revolutions. They survived, and even did so successfully, on condition that they did not look back.

In a certain sense, Henry's own way of looking back was to destroy art objects: something then had to be said about the broken pieces of their former history. The masterpieces were the mute witnesses to revolutions, disasters, pillaging, and massacres. He saw them as ghosts, as it were, and he defied them in order to get them to tell their saga.

He had forced the analyst to report such an episode, one that was haunting her face. As though she had worn a mask invisible to her own eyes, he had received a funereal impression, which he had detected with an entirely scientific acuity.

As Wittgenstein (1933–1934) notes, when we say, "'this face has a particular expression' . . . what has to be explained is this: why do we talk to our impressions? . . . Something peculiar happens undoubtedly" p. 177).[25] Thus Henry was speaking to the gray in the analyst's face, detecting there something that he could not name as "funereal." For that to be possible, the analyst, placed before this mirror, had to do more than mention the Friday burial: she had to analyze—aloud, speaking to Henry—the effect that the strange absence of a rite had had on her (Wittgenstein 1934–1936).

If she had continued in a position of neutrality, he would have "broken" her as an incompetent who was interfering with his research into the traces of a vanished history. This rupture between them would obviously have pushed him toward a state of aloneness periodically marked by fits of rage. Conversely, the challenging of the analyst's professional ethos had resulted in a sort of confession, referring to a wordless burial, similar to the burial of the history of Henry's lineage.

---

25. Cf. "What makes human sacrifice something deep and sinister anyway? . . . [T]his deep and sinister aspect is not obvious, just from learning the history of the external action, but *we* impute it from an experience in ourselves" (Wittgenstein 1930–1933, p. 16e).

Here, too, the patient urges the analyst to produce a new concept in the place where, even in the specialized vocabulary of psychoanalysis, language comes up short. When the analyst told colleagues this story, some of them mentioned similar experiences, in which they had had to reveal a piece of their so-called private life contrary to the rule of benevolent neutrality. But what does "private life" mean in such a case?[26]

The name given to this unfelt feeling remained: cut-out impression. One should not, of course, unload one's problems onto one's patients. Quite the contrary: what is being done is unloading strange, uncanny impressions from *them*, impressions received through their acute sense of alertness and survival. If the analyst had remained silent, the psychoanalytic work would have simply stopped there. Or worse.[27]

2.2.6. Genesis of the *Symbolon* against the Background of War

Every catastrophe in the social order, domestic or organic, sets in motion a loss of trust, limited or radical, in the safety of the laws governing men, the universe, or the body. Otherness undergoes an abrupt change of status. From guarantor of the good faith from which issue speech and the permanence of physical laws, the other becomes a surface of signs and forms to be deciphered against a background of devalued words.

---

26. "Whence the idea of the privacy of sense data? " (Wittgenstein 1914–1916, p. 19). Sullivan (1946) writes as follows:

That there are particular human lives, each with a unique career line, I no more deny than I do the fact that I am a particular person who has a particular dog. I act in two modes, in my public mode and in the private mode in which I feel my inviolable isolation from my fellows. So, doubtless, does my dog. . . . I seek to stress the central fact that the true or absolute individuality of a person is always beyond scientific grasp and invariably much less significant in the person's living than he has been taught to believe. [p. xii]

27. . . . *Or Worse* (. . . *Ou pire*) is the disturbing title of Lacan's seminar for the year 1971–1972.

On the other hand, whether or not it has a neurological origin, the impossibility of feeling anything blurs the mirror that connects us to ourselves and to others. For the game of language also involves tone of voice, facial expressions, and the theater of emotions.

Profound disorders in the functions and articulations of these two domains, the Symbolic and the Imaginary, open the field to the unlinkings proper to the Real and come close to what has no name, no boundary, no other. In the case of cerebral lesions, traumas, or madness, patients are dealing with the same field of the Real: a major breakdown has destroyed trust in speech, contact with other people's feelings, the reliability and continuity of microcosm and macrocosm. But at issue here is saying, wanting to say (*vouloir dire*), and not just talking about something.

Wittgenstein (1918) writes of the ambiguity of the French *je veux dire*, which means both "I mean" and "I want to say." He notes that this *vouloir* says more about the subject of the act of saying than one might think. But the revelation of what the subject does not know about himself occurs, in this case, less through self-observation than by way of the expected reply. For this "wanting to say"/"meaning" is addressed to someone (§§ 657, 659).[28]

Thus the Symbolic is not a metalanguage calmly containing all human significations past, present, and future.[29] There is no Other of the Other, as Lacan says aphoristically. This is why the Other, in the

---

28. Compare the following from Lacan's 1953:

The form in which language is expressed itself defines subjectivity. Language says: "You will go here, and when you see this, you will turn off there." In other words, it refers itself to the discourse of the other. . . . [S]peech commits its author by investing the person to whom it is addressed with a new reality, as, for example, when by a "You are my wife," a subject marks himself with the seal of wedlock. . . . Human language (according to one of my most acute listeners) constitutes a communication in which the sender receives his own message back from the receiver in an inverted form. [p. 85]

29. "Which is what I mean when I say that no metalanguage can be spoken, or, more aphoristically, that there is no Other of the Other. And when the Legislator (he who claims to lay down the Law) presents himself to fill the gap, he does so as an impostor" (Lacan 1960, pp. 310–311). Cf. Wittgenstein 1945–1949:

dimension of the Symbolic, necessarily involves a constitutive lack without which no one would be able to speak or to speak to someone.[30]

Thus the horizon of the Symbolic is not the totality, the totalization, or indeed the "totalitarianization" of all form of knowledge. Quite the contrary: it is made necessary by current situations of rupture, departure, or confrontation. The etymological metaphor of the *symbolon* emphasizes the signifying gesture in which two new allies exchange the two pieces of a broken shard, in such a way that their being fitted together later on[31] is a pledge of mutual hospitality for them and their descendants. These humble bits and pieces, broken for the occasion, take the place of one's word given as a guarantee. Of no intrinsic value, they are the basis of value and the foundation of the social tie, at the same time as they are the possibility of language itself.

When he goes outside the limits of his field of expertise, the neurologist, like everyone, makes use of the common language to make himself understood. Like all other discourses, his conveys various ideologies, for example the ideology that conceives of the self as private property, protecting its interior behind the barricades of an intimacy reduced to making utilitarian decisions, minimizing the costs and maximizing the profits. Analytic experience teaches us that, under the shock of sociohistorical ruptures, such a construction collapses in families

---

The results of philosophy are the uncovering of one or another piece of plain nonsense and of bumps that understanding has got by running its head up against the limits of language. These bumps make us see the value of the discovery. When I talk about language (words, sentences, etc.) I must speak the language of everyday. Is this language somehow too coarse and material for what we want to say? Then how is another one to be constructed? And how strange that we should be able to do anything at all with the one we have. [§§ 119–120; cf. 1934–1936, p. 43]

Similarly, Sullivan (1945) says, "I have to ask you to realize that in talking about speech I am using speech" (p. 207).

30. This is why, when he writes, Lacan represents this Other with a bar on the O (in French, on the A of *Autre*).

31. The action of reuniting is, precisely, *symballein* in Greek. Its opposite is *diaballein*, meaning disunite or slander: indeed, the work of the devil (*diabolos*).

through the generations, whatever their social status, and entails an exorbitant cost for the symbolic patrimony.

In refraining from replying to Henry, when he asked her about her gray color, the analyst did not understand that her silence was noisy and confirmed the impression, registered on her face, of a disappearance without word or trace. This silence, even considered as a consequence of her private grief, did not belong to her (Wittgenstein 1945–1949, § 398). On the contrary, it was the common property of the field of death that they shared that day, with the result that a bit of confidence, like a small piece of terra cotta, could be produced, creating the possibility of a *subject* between them, what Benedetti (1971) calls a transitional subject, in a symbolic exchange for which there had never been room.[32]

Henry had the habit of saying, "I'm no one." After the analyst's recognition of his acute sense of observation, he could trust his body and his speech, gradually giving body and voice to many keen perceptions annulled by the absence of response on the part of those who had watched him grow up.

This process of subjectivation began a second phase of his analysis. When he regained his place in the social world, he took up a career as an interpreter.

---

32. According to Benedetti,

in psychotherapeutic practice, the transitional subject, formed by elements of the therapist and elements of the patient, is essentially positive. . . . But it also comes about through the appearance of a negative transitional subject. . . . This psychotherapeutic dialogue . . . limited, in its determinations, to the encounter between therapist and patient, . . . rests on an attitude that not only guarantees the patient that nothing harmful to him will be undertaken but also presupposes that one is acting independently of psychogenetic theories of illness. [pp. 105–106]

He goes on to speak "of introjection by the patient of the therapist's words and introjection by the therapist of the patient's suffering" (p. 107). In other words, we speak of this encounter as a tying together, at the edge of the symbolic, of unlinked elements, proceeding from forms and images on the border of the Real, for the analyst and for the patient.

2.3. SHOWING WHAT CANNOT BE SAID

2.3.1. The Festival of the Mad Rises from the Ashes

It is our human condition to be unable to escape the dimension of the Symbolic. The inexorable performances of machines and the profusion of screens lead us to believe that, one day, we shall be able to do without this cumbersome peculiarity—without which, however, these same technical feats could not exist. How much easier life would seem if we could mechanically suppress diseases, insanities, anxieties, and mood swings, and make the dead simply disappear without poisoning our lives! Unfortunately, no machine, even that of a totally rational party or perfect organization, has ever succeeded in replacing the need to say.

"Wanting to say"/"meaning," when one loses one's reason, is to sing like Cherubino in Act 1, Scene 5 of *The Marriage of Figaro* (Mozart 1786). "Poor Cherubino, are you crazy?" Susanna asks. "I no longer know what I am, what I'm doing," he replies. "I speak of love to the water, the shadow, the mountains, the flowers, the plants, the springs, the echo, the air, the wind. . . . And if there is no one to hear me, I speak to myself of love" (p. 69). The French Revolution would soon cause more than one person to lose his head, as the song put it. Hummed in the very depths of an asylum to her analyst, the tune sung at the same time as Mozart's opera—"For the Love of My Lizzie I'm Losing My Head"— greeted the return to speech of a mute patient. As we shall see in the discussion of the case of Blue Flower (7.1.2.), she felt that her throat had been cut as happened during the Revolution.

At time of persecution, the madness of "talking to yourself when no one hears you" (Wittgenstein 1914–1916, p. 15) has always sought refuge in literature, oral or written. In the speech he gave when he received the Nobel Prize, Gao Xingjian (2000) confirms this: "If I undertook the writing of my novel *Soul Mountain* at a time when, despite self-censorship, my works were forbidden, it was simply to give vent to my inner aloneness, for myself, without counting on being published one day."[33] Gao Xingjian is now writing in Paris, as Descartes wrote in

---

33. He continues as follows:

If an individual wanted to keep his thinking independent, he could only talk to himself and did so in the greatest secrecy. I must say that it was at this very

Holland and, during the Nazi period, Wittgenstein wrote in Cambridge and Schrödinger in Dublin. Da Ponte, the librettist of *The Marriage of Figaro*, also wound up emigrating to the United States.[34]

Sometimes the loneliness described by Frieda Fromm-Reichmann (1946) in the last paper she wrote before her death (cf. Silver 1989, 1996) reaches the point where one can no longer refer to it or even say it. The subject's exile is even more radical then. Escape is impossible, even by talking to oneself, since words do not mean or *want to say* anything to anybody anymore. All that remains is to show.

In the Middle Ages and the Renaissance, the court fools, or those onstage in the public square, were paid to show one and all, including the king, what cannot be said. Risks were involved. The Festival of the Mad, also called the Feast of the Innocents or of the Children, was banned by the Church several times, as well as by the state, which relentlessly persecuted this kind of theater (Heers 1983, Zumthor 1978).

In 1529, Berquin, who was a great admirer of Erasmus and had translated *The Praise of Folly* into French, mounted the stake in Paris, under the rule of the very humanistic Francis the First. In 1535, Thomas More, to whom the book was dedicated and who was always so merry, according to his friend, "that one might think telling jokes was the main object of his life," was beheaded on the order of his protector, Henry the Eighth, in an England that passed for the most civilized country in Europe and the one most eager for knowledge (Van Damme n.d., p. 79). What common dimension is there, then, between fools, innocents, scholars, and children?

Curiosity, scientific by nature, is doubtless present even in babies, on condition that the adult cooperates in the investigation. It is well

---

time, when there could be no literature, that I became aware of how necessary it is: it is literature that enables the human being to preserve his human awareness. It could be said that speaking to oneself is where literature begins; communicating by means of language comes second. When man injects his feelings and reflections into language, since he turns to literature, literature is born. When, afterward, with no utilitarian aim and without even thinking of being disseminated, he nevertheless continues to write and receives pleasure thanks to literature, and even some recompense, this is in itself a reward. [emphasis added]

34. He taught Italian literature at the newly founded Columbia University and died in 1838 at the age of 90.

known that an infant at the breast will immediately stop suckling when his mother receives an alarming telegram. The child has observed and registered through bodily markers that his mother's facial expression, odor, and heartbeat have changed. He is especially sensitive to variations. Shall we insult his intelligence by saying that this is a mere mechanical reflex, or shall we instead recognize, in addition, a silent way of asking a question?

From the outset, this question will be validated by the response that confirms or disconfirms his experience. The cognitive stakes are considerable, a prelude to the opening or the closing of the field of *logos*. A disingenuous reply or an embarrassed silence, when adamantly repeated, sends the subject into nonexistence on this point. He exiles himself, falls silent, goes crazy. Instead of speaking to him, people speak of him, as an aberration (see 5.3.1, The Mother of Vinegar). Grammar has suddenly changed direction: subject and object have changed sides. The observer has become the observed. The budding child scientist remains bewildered, on the edge of the exploration that is refused to him; he is made into a fool, a madman, an innocent—until he manages to find someone else who accepts the challenge of reopening the question.

The U-turn of the observed observer can veer off into tragedy, to be sure, but it may also have a comic aspect. This is the plot of *L'Arroseur Arrosé*,[35] the film Louis Lumière made in 1894, at the very beginning of the film era. The eye of the filmmaker, behind the camera, substitutes for the inquisitive eye of the gardener, fastened on the opening of a hose that has suddenly dried up. When the mischievous little boy who is keeping his foot on the hose releases the pressure, he releases laughter along with the spurt of water: the gardener's eye is splashed, and the first spectators laughed until they cried, leaving the theater wiping their eyes. All comedians, heirs of the *jongleurs*, know that they are balancing on the edge of catastrophe and tears. Likewise, patients in a manic state show—amid laughter and tears, in the excitement of verbal virtuosity—the death zone that no one wants to see.

An abrupt interruption in a continuity is such a catastrophe, in the sense in which the mathematician René Thom (1977, 1983, 1990, 1991)

---

35. Translator's note: Literally, "the sprinkler sprinkled," this term is equivalent to "hoist on one's own petard."

describes it in his catastrophe theory.[36] The connotation is not necessarily negative. This discontinuity is of interest to us, since it is at the origin of the need for the symbol within reach of everyone: adults, children, and innocents. For the etymological meaning of *symbolon*—a means of reuniting—in fact comes from such a rupture. A piece of terra cotta is broken at the very time of a separation. Later, in the next generation, when the descendants meet, the other piece of terra cotta will fit, more or less, in the break of this discontinuity, to symbolize alliance at the time of the catastrophe of a departure or a conflict.

This very fact, we want to point out, vouches for the actual existence of a rupture. The subject of speech, which is also the giving of one's word, emerges from this gesture. He is reborn toward and against all the attempts to annul him along with what happened. We shall not dwell on the criteria of the good-enough mother (Winnicott 1971), which also implies a good-enough Name of the Father (Lacan 1953) as guarantor of the alliance and the surname of the lineage.[37] We wish only to emphasize the formidable collapse of the universe for children, or infantilized adults, on the false pretext that "they can't understand." When that happens, the thread of speech may be radically cut. In this regard the Name of the Father, guarantor of giving one's word, can no longer function.

We are referring here to an approach to language that has its source in the Other, intrinsically stricken with incompleteness, and not in a translation machine inside the brain case. Yes, speech proceeds from images, colors, odors, and gestures, but only insofar as these are authenticated in the dimension of the symbolic pact. If, for example, the

---

36. "For me, any discontinuity in phenomena is a catastrophe. The edge of this table, where the wood becomes air: this is a surface of separation, a locus of catastrophe" (Thom 1991, p. 28). "The action of the saw on the wood is the realization of an elementary catastrophe. . . . This static catastrophe is the memory of a dynamic catastrophe that took place at the time this plank was made. Solids, then, retain the memory of all the catastrophes they have undergone (p. 49).

37. "Even when in fact it is represented by a single person, the paternal function concentrates in itself both imaginary and real relations, always more or less inadequate to the symbolic relation that essentially constitutes it. It is in the *name of the father* that we must recognize the support of the symbolic function which, from the dawn of history, has identified this person with the figure of the law" (Lacan 1953, p. 67).

mother distressed by the telegram is able, despite her uneasiness, to say a few words to calm her child, the tone of her voice will convey, in effect: "Something serious has happened, but you are not responsible for this sudden upheaval. Trust us."

In general, when the world becomes nonsense, children tend to think that they are the cause of the catastrophe, since this is the only way they can make sense of it to themselves. Later, still patching together their reasoning, as soon as the constitution of the ego and imaginary, mirrored relations make projections possible they will learn to blame their neighbor. When the symbolic, which provides a third other as a locus of trust, cannot be evoked in the face of absurdity and denial, one has to make do with two dimensions of logical stop-gap: it is better to assume that one is oneself the cause of an inexplicable event, or to unload it onto the other, than to confront an event without a reason. This is one of the most effective survival strategies in the face of the uncanny, the strange and disturbing field of the Real.

2.3.2. Canton, China, July 1985: The Silence of an Admirable Mother

These situations are not unusual. In the psychopathology of everyday madness, we have had occasion to experience just such a "catastrophic" moment, and we have been able to mention it, on occasion, to some of our patients. This was during a trip to China, in 1985, with our two young children. In this account, we shall appear under our two first names.

Right on the first leg of the trip, a rupture appeared in the continuity of the vacation. At the edge of a pool, we discover that Françoise has a slight growth, painless but disquieting nevertheless, on the surface of her stomach. Despite the fear of cancer that immediately arises, to preserve the serenity of the trip we decide to put off seeing a doctor until we get back, a month later, and to act as though nothing were wrong, saying nothing to the children.

Three days later, we are visiting the Canton zoo, where a space closed off by cloths covered with characters that are Chinese to us (and to the Chinese as well) draws our attention. After paying a very modest additional sum, we plunge in together, not knowing what kind of curious beast awaits us there.

As in the good old days of fairs in the previous century, we find shelves displaying jars, of various sizes, containing a collection of human monsters, Siamese fetuses (if such a diagnosis can be made in Canton), the hands and feet of acromegalics, photographs of androgynes, hydrocephalics, microcephalics, and other freaks in formalin. Before the children's wide eyes, Jean-Max quickly changes into a professor of natural sciences, not to mention the philosophical touch that explains to them the presence here of these lifeless bodies for pedagogical purposes and general edification: "Nature knows what it is doing, and as a rule it does not allow its errors to come to term." (In such cases, one does what one can with what one has.)

The remainder of the visit and the evening finish with no further surprises and with no questions about this rather exotic display. But at bedtime the older child, who, wherever he is, usually falls asleep immediately and peacefully, calls us, crying, from the adjoining room. He can't get to sleep. His anxiety is resistant to all the classical tools mobilized in such circumstances: rational explanation with reference to the time lag, to the heat, to fatigue, to the change in food, and so forth. On the contrary: seated on the edge of his bed, the child screams that he is now seeing monsters all over his room.

The parents, psychoanalysts, immediately make the connection with the monsters of the afternoon. Relieved, they explain to him that he was very struck by these striking creatures, that this isn't serious, that it's like a nightmare, and that it will all disappear, especially if he goes to sleep as soon as possible.

The child screams even louder: this time, he is really hallucinating. The parents even turn around to see whether strange forms, in this bizarre country, could be made out on the walls or the curtains. Finally, the father and mother look at one another over the miserable child. In a very different tone, a bit ashamed, Françoise, admits to the boy that, indeed, something wrong is happening in her stomach: "It's not you who should be afraid but me. I found a little lump in my stomach, and that made Daddy and me worried. We've decided to go on with our trip, because I'm not sick. When we get back, I'll see a doctor and get it taken care of."

The child calms down at once, saying, "Well, I was looking for something to be scared of." It is almost three in the morning. He falls asleep as he is finishing his sentence. His young brother, who had first been curious about all this disorder, has been asleep for a long time, leaving it to his older sibling to do the job,

It was a fine trip. During our visit to the many tombs of deceased emperors, sometimes filled with strange terra cotta groups accompanying the ruler to the afterlife, the children, laughing, often said to their mother, "Don't you worry; we'll pour *eau-de-vie* on your grave." This "water of life" is the name given, in the French countryside, to various fruit distillations that—to judge by the amount of alcohol they contain—may really be able to wake the dead. When they returned, Françoise underwent an operation for the removal of a large ovarian cyst, fortunately benign.

Situations like this are repeated in the course of symptoms that appear psychotic: like the mad, former babies who grew up too fast in order to be able to face problems beyond measure seek out partners who can do justice to their investigation. Their questions, impossible to articulate, are revealed with the help of nonverbal images until they find the Other who is able to meet these obvious though unarticulated questions. There is no dictionary or machine to translate these images.

On the other hand, the dimension of speech can be deliberately perverted in the techniques of mass manipulation—slogans, subliminal messages—to prevent thought. This is the basis for the effectiveness of what Arendt (1951) calls the "fictitious world" of totalitarianisms,[38] in which human beings have become superfluous abstractions in the service of the Cause or the Movement. On the individual scale, this could have been the outcome of our anecdote, if the child had submitted to his parents' first official doctrine.

Let us imagine, for a moment, the following catastrophic scenario: continuing to play the admirable mother, Françoise keeps the secret. The child would find himself burdened with the cut-out truth of the story. Rushing into a hyperactive exploration, or barricaded in a hyperpassive withdrawal, nowadays he might have been quickly diagnosed and chemically brought back to reason. In such a fictitious

---

38. "In a totally fictitious world, failures need not be recorded, admitted, and remembered. Factuality itself depends for its continued existence upon the existence of the nontotalitarian world" (p. 388).

world, his legitimate anxieties, too, would have seemed superfluous. Later on he might have become addicted to his mother's mute sufferings or to other equally hollow and violent causes.

Many small children have not received the words that would have allowed them to keep at bay the disasters experienced by their parents and ancestors. Rather, like the children of Oedipus or Medea, they were abandoned, sacrificed on the battlefront of hatred, wars, and civil wars; they were armed with rifles, real or psychic, to be sent as human shields to protect the adults who remain in the rear.

2.3.3. The Analyst in Clown Costume

But, in a context like this, in which truth seeks to come back to life through analysis, the transference is not unidirectional. Here, passing back and forth from the patient's place to the therapist's, is where we see that insensitivity, for example, is not exclusively caused by brain lesions. Damasio (1995) explains that it is readily observable in what he calls sick social systems, those that aim at the annihilation of all the subjects that resist them, to the point of inflicting psychic death and brainwashing. The scale can extend from a single family to the entire nation.

Patients who come from such totalitarian environments find it difficult to interpret what Damasio calls the somatic markers on others, and even on themselves. A deliberately instilled confusion maintains them in a state of constant doubt about what they are feeling. This doubt is depicted in Ingmar Bergman's film *The Serpent's Egg* (1977), in which the hero, inquiring about his brother's suicide in Germany in the 1920s, encounters the early signs of the human experimentation that would begin to be perpetrated on a large scale ten years later. The director shows how the protagonists' sensations are constantly refuted by the discourses that influence them. Sometimes the contradiction is so unbearable that the sensory apparatus itself finds itself under attack. The hero is apathetic and, as it were, embodies the negation of his own inner awareness. We, the viewers, can very well imagine that we are looking at the delusional ideas of the negation of one's own organs, one's own brain.

Now this is not a "Cotard's syndrome,"[39] which, besides, is rarely seen today, since modern medicines have achieved the feat of rendering mute an absence of organs. To account for such phenomena, we have to find words other than *individual*, *subjectivity*, and *interiority*, in which images polarized by the dichotomy inside/outside get in the way of reflection. We prefer, in these extreme cases, to represent the subject as essentially divided, but divided between a patient who is unable to feel and a therapist who, like a photographic plate, receives the impressions of what is shown there.

For here the therapist is confronted by a situation in which he must trust his own impressions to detect the violence and terror that are borne by the patient, although the latter does not feel them. The therapist is on the alert at these times, as though he himself were penetrating into the zone of real danger. But he can formulate this only on the basis of representations drawn from analogous zones in his own experience.

At this crossroads, at the risk of appearing like a clown the therapist must describe his impressions and, so to speak, animate a character who entered the session disaffected and reified. What we say on these occasions is that we are feeling, imagining, and dreaming in the patient's place, and that we have to tell him about it; otherwise we would be experimentally continuing the excision of otherness that was perpetrated on him.[40]

---

39. "Cotard's syndrome (the idea of damnation, immortality, and negation) is rarely complete in these acute melancholias, but certain delusional ideas that make it up are observed quite often, especially the ideas of negation of organs" (Ey et al. 1967, p. 249).

40. "The 'detached' observer of humanity is comfortable 'in his mind,' and, I surmise, pleasantly 'objective' in his verbal formulations—he doesn't 'have' any 'funny ideas'; more accurately, he doesn't become acquainted with any of his 'funny ideas'; they work themselves out in his sleep, in the 'non-sense' of his dreams! Query: Why not a study of psychiatrists' dreams?" (Sullivan 1946, p. 259). (We would add: Why not indeed—and psychoanalysts' dreams, too.) "In the psychoanalysis of the psychoses, there is something more than in neurosis: there is the fact that the very movement of the unconscious can be manifested only via the therapist's response" (Benedetti 1980, p. 259). "Significantly, therapists who dream about their patients are always dreaming for their patients; these are 'therapeutic dreams'" (p. 305).

2.3.4. Truce, Truth, Trust: "Join the Dance"[41]

The stability of space and time in the human race is rooted not only in biological programs and in the extraordinary homeostasis of our bodily boundaries. It also depends on the dimension of promise and the law, much more fragile in humans than natural laws are for other animal species.

In his own field of observation, Damasio (1995) necessarily puts this dimension in parentheses. Nevertheless, the neurologist leaves it to the human being, who plays a role in him alongside the scientist, to philosophize.[42] In so doing, he constructs the "model of being human" that underlies his hypotheses and experiments: "The picture I am drawing for humans is that of an organism that comes to life designed with automatic survival mechanisms, and to which education and acculturation add a set of socially permissible and desirable decision-making strategies that, in turn, enhance survival, remarkably improve the quality of that survival, and serve as the basis for constructing a person" (p. 126).

Let us join in celebrating the filling in of the ditch between daily life and the vegetative system. In the "Universal Studio" of abstraction, we see sparkling, well-educated egos, in full possession of their private lives and mental images, skillfully handling these very images drawn from the stock of their memories and, as a result, making the right decisions—of course, in the best of worlds. Our patients, however, who do not present these ideal profiles for employment agencies, surely have something else to teach us about the missing link between

---

41. Traditional French nursery song:

Join the dance,
See how we dance,
Jump, dance,
Kiss anyone you want.

42. "Does this mean that love, generosity, compassion, and other commendable human characteristics are nothing but the result of conscious but survival-oriented neurobiological regulations? . . . No, that is definitely not the case" (Domasio 1995, p. 114).

the machine man (La Mettrie 1746), his neurological mechanism, and the happy actors of success stories. Above all, what they teach the analyst is another way of considering their symptoms: as instruments of research adapted to a truly bizarre world.

In that way, most of them give evidence of a strange modification of the arrow of time, whose course sometimes seems to go backward or to stand still without past or future. This anomaly could be described as the destruction of an "autobiographic consciousness" that is, in certain cases, indeed caused by specific neurological lesions (Damasio 1999, pp. 43, 113). But what the destruction actually affects in these patients is the very precarious Other of good faith. Thus the dimension of a broken, petrified time persists in the catastrophic zones of several generations earlier, which remain present for certain descendants even, as it happens, in the middle of success stories.

In such a situation of despair, in which trust is undone, there must be recourse to a truce[43] to guarantee truth once again.[44] A new language game becomes possible to the extent that an other proves capable of entering the game. But not any other, and not any other game. This other has usually been through a parallel experience: he is the buddy, quick to detect the least detail in the other's bodily manifestations so as to get out of the quagmire with him. A silent language is then estab-

---

43. Hearne (1986) associates the two words *truce* and *trust*, to which we add *truth*. She emphasizes that this connection is sustained "by means of a curious etymology, that ought to be in the Oxford English Dictionary but is not" (p. 134).

44. See Lacan (1957):

> If I have said that the unconscious is the discourse of the Other (with a capital O), it is in order *to indicate the beyond* in which the recognition of desire is bound up with the desire for recognition. In other words, this other is the Other that even my lie invokes as a guarantor of *the truth* in which it subsists. By which we can also see that it is with the appearance of language that the dimension of truth emerges. . . . For I can lure my adversary by means of a movement contrary to my actual plan of battle . . . . But in the propositions with which I open *peace negotiations* [we would say: undertake a *truce*] with him, what my negotiations propose to him is situated *in a third locus* which is neither my speech nor my interlocutor. This locus is none other than *the locus of signifying convention* . . . in relation to the Other who is the guarantor of *Good Faith* [we would say: *trust*]. [pp. 172–173, emphasis added]

lished, one that is based on images that are shown rather than said, showing what cannot be said.

2.3.5. "Whereof One Cannot Speak . . ."

Wittgenstein made this delicate point the transition from his first to his second philosophy in the period between the two world wars, when his mental health was of concern to those around him. The last sentence of the *Tractatus* (1918), "Whereof one cannot speak, thereof one must be silent," became what might be formulated as "thereof one cannot be silent and cannot help showing what cannot be said." He called this showing an *ostensive definition* that holds true solely in the dimension of the transference to someone else, the other, who is able to receive the impression of this showing and to show how he received it by the use he makes of it.[45]

It should be noted that Wittgenstein worked on the *Tractatus* during the First World War, on the eastern front, in a situation of extreme solitude in which he had to deal with the total absence of anyone to talk to (Wittgenstein 1914–1916). What is more, his only friend, the Englishman David Pinsent, was on the side of the enemy. Wittgenstein would never see him again: Pinsent was killed in an airplane accident in 1918. Only his philosophical work, conceived in the midst of real, hellish agonies, bound him to an intellectual community. His second philosophy, which took him out of the silence, was elaborated after his return to Cambridge in 1929, when he finally found, once again, the small group of his interlocutors.

---

45. "Now one can 'ostensively' define a proper name, the name of a colour, of a material . . . . The definition of the number two, 'That is called two,' pointing to two nuts . . . . But how can two be defined like that? . . . An ostensive definition can be variously interpreted in every case" (Wittgenstein 1918, § 28). "Whether the word 'number' is necessary in the ostensive definition depends on whether without it the other person takes the definition otherwise than I wish. And that will depend on the circumstances under which it is given and on the person I give it to. And how he takes the definition is seen in the use that he makes of the word defined" (§ 29). "Philosophical problems arise when language goes on holiday" (§ 38).

Wittgenstein would have liked to be a psychiatrist, indeed, a psychoanalyst. He encouraged one of his philosophy students, the Irishman Maurice O'Drury, in this path and sent him Freud's *The Interpretation of Dreams* in 1935, on the occasion of his graduation as a psychiatrist (Monk 1990, O'Drury 1981). Two years later, in the year of the Anschluss, Wittgenstein was in bad shape and came to visit O'Drury in Dublin. He asked to be introduced on the latter's ward at St. Patrick's Hospital in order to talk with some chronic patients. He met with them several times (O'Drury 1981). At this very moment, the political situation in his native Austria was tearing him apart. In *The Danger of Words* (1973), O'Drury describes the lessons he received from Wittgenstein on the interface of scientific, philosophical, and psychoanalytic research.[46]

Here we can see that a period that did not know it was between two wars gave rise to scientific and psychoanalytic investigations after and about the crumbling of a world that our patients are constantly asking us to face.

---

46. When *La Folie Wittgenstein* (Davoine 1992) was written, we did not know of this biographical anecdote. But, on the basis of our reading of the "Notes for Lectures on 'Private Experience' and 'Sense Data'" (1934–1936) and the *Philosophical Investigations* (1945–1949), we assigned Ludwig Wittgenstein this fictional role when we were with our patients. When we met Wittgenstein's biographer, Brian McGuiness, at a conference on the philosopher and asked him whether our fiction was plausible, he kindly referred us to O'Drury's 1981 work. O'Drury was also the psychiatrist of Schrödinger's wife, Anny, during their exile in Ireland. He ordered heavy courses of treatment and electroshocks for her, which, as he later said (1973), he regretted.

3

Conclusion of Part I: From Scientific Revolutions[1] to Therapeutic Revolutions

3.1. WHAT SCIENTISTS ARE RISKING

The edges of the Real in the physical, psychic, and social world are woven through with silent matter. It makes itself felt, through our bodies and our emotions, each time there is an inscription in the domain of the Symbolic—in the form of equations, of course, but also as signifying formulations.

Let us make no mistake: madness and delusion do not correspond to the inadequate representation of a world of which there might exist, elsewhere, a rational conception acceptable to everyone. Madness marks the moment and the dynamics of the passage in which one subject tries to exist by inscribing a Real that is not transmissible. And this is also the way science proceeds.

Thus it has been possible to be in a delusional state and, at the same time, carry on scientific investigations leading to paradigm changes. It is as though the research resulting in the inscription of something hitherto unheard-of, and to the birth of a subject recognized by his peers, were being simultaneously conducted on two levels at the point where the symbolic chain is broken in the presence of the unknown: on the one hand, in the world of matter, and on the other, between people in the death zones into which the subject of speech may have disappeared.

Newton locked in a trunk, opened in 1936 (Keynes 1947, Verlet 1993),[2] just as Saussure locked in a chest in Switzerland (Starobinski

---

1. The term *scientific revolutions* is taken from Kuhn 1970.
2. "Newton's trunk was kept for over two hundred years by his descendants. In 1936, the trunk was opened and its contents offered for sale. . . . J. M. Keynes learned

1971)[3] writings that, at first glance, could pass for crazy, though at the same time these men produced discoveries that made their names famous. These writings were concealed and withheld from publication by their authors.

Others, like Auguste Comte or Emmanuel Swedenborg, an encyclopedic scientific mind before his "illumination"[4] at the age of 57 (Swedenborg 1749–1756), were diagnosed as mad or even committed to an asylum. Thus Georg Cantor became delusional and was hospitalized several times, even as he pursued his work on set theory. He claimed, among other things, that the philosopher Francis Bacon was the author of the works of Shakespeare (Cantor 1960). Kurt Gödel became delusional, especially after the death of Einstein, with whom he used to converse while the two of them walked around the Institute for Advanced Studies at Princeton. Terrified of being poisoned, he died of starvation in a Princeton hospital not long ago (Wang 1987).[5] To a

---

of this and, to his amazement, discovered the hidden side of the founding hero. . . . [There were] writings devoted to theology and alchemy . . . . The first physicist had also been the last of the magicians" (Verlet 1993, p. 27). Cf. Westfall 1993.

3. In studying the saturnian verses, Saussure intends to demonstrate that the words of the poetic work came from other, prior words and were not directly chosen by the creative awareness. These investigations, which remained secret, are contemporary with Saussure's *Course in General Linguistics* of 1915.

4. Swedenborg abandoned worldly science in 1745 after a visionary experience. Kant's (1766) attentive examination of his voluminous writings is one of the starting points for his critical philosophy.

5. Wang recalls how he visited Gödel at home on December 17, 1977, a month before the latter's death:

> His mind remained nimble and he did not appear very sick. He said, "I've lost the faculty for making positive decisions. I can only make negative decisions." A day or two later, he was persuaded to enter Princeton Hospital. . . . I phoned him on January 11; he was polite but sounded remote. It was said that Gödel's weight was down to sixty-five pounds before his death. His paranoia conformed to a classic syndrome: fear of food poisoning, leading to self-starvation; reportedly he died, in the foetal position, of malnutrition and inanition caused by personality disturbance. [p. 133]

Of Gödel's theory of mind Wang writes as follows:

> Unlike certain ignorant philosophers, Gödel realizes that his incompleteness theorem does not by itself imply that the human mind surpasses all machines.

colleague who was horrified that he could believe that extraterrestrials were sending him messages and recruiting him to save the world, John Nash, as a patient in 1959 in McLean Hospital near Boston, calmly replied that these ideas about supernatural beings came to him in the same way as his mathematical ideas; he therefore took them seriously (Nasar 1998; cf. Howard 2001).

To different degrees, the same peculiarities can accompany many other changes in scientific paradigms. The findings of these scientists, later published in books and journals, are less cold and insensitive in style than the accounts of them. They were preceded by intense periods of anxiety and enthusiasm. When, in 1927, he discovered the uncertainty principle on the Isle of Heligoland, where he was being treated for a severe asthma attack, Heisenberg (1971) thought he was going crazy.[6] His colleague Erwin Schrödinger (1956) likewise states that "a mathematical truth is timeless; it does not come into being when we discover it. Yet its discovery is a very real event. It may be an emotion like a great gift from a fairy" (p. 154). He was no doubt recalling the fairy gift he received at Arosa, in the winter of 1925–1926, when he produced his famous equations.

Let us venture the converse: what Real is approached by symptoms of madness manifested by the patients we shall be meeting here? The change of vertex (as Bion might put it) that makes us consider patients as researchers even as we acknowledge their suffering, suffering that is so close to the agonies of scientists, differs from the so-called scientific method that considers them as objects of experimentation. Accordingly, Wittgenstein (1945–1949) was surprised at the alleged neutrality of the researcher in this domain:

Some additional premise is needed: 1. It is sufficient to accept what he calls a rationalistic optimism. 2. Mind is not static but constantly developing. 3. He believes that there is mind separate from matter, and that this will be proved scientifically (perhaps by the fact that there aren't enough nerve cells to perform the observable operations of the mind). . . . More generally, Gödel believes that mechanism in biology will be disproved. [p. 139]

Another "beautiful mind" (cf. Nasar 1998).

6. In this same work, he mentions the anxiety, almost to the point of vertigo, that he felt when he contemplated the strange inner beauty of atomic processes.

Misleading parallel: psychology treats of processes in the psychical sphere, as does physics in the physical sphere. Seeing, hearing, feeling, willing are not the subject of psychology in the same sense as that in which the movements of bodies, the phenomena of electricity, etc. are the subject of physics. You can see this from the fact that the physicist sees, hears, thinks about, and informs us of these phenomena, and the psychologist observes the external reactions (the behaviour) of the subject. [§ 571]

Schrödinger was especially attentive to this when, after the war, he warned his colleagues against the barbarity that erects a wall in the sciences between research protocols and the emotions and anxieties of the researchers. It is as though the interference of the latter with the "elided subject" (Bitbol 1990) of research had to be considered suspect from the point of view of scientific rigor. Schrödinger clearly believed that the objectivation principle necessary for the existence of classical science had broken loose there, destroying everything in its path.

He had had a direct experience of this during the rise of Nazism, when he nearly came to blows with the Hitler Youth and was rescued just in time by one of his students. He was the only non-Jewish German physicist to leave his professorship—he held the Max Planck Chair in Berlin—without a word in 1938, going into exile in Ireland (Moore 1989). More recently, Patrick Tierney's *Darkness in El Dorado* (2000) tells us about certain sinister avatars of this same process of objectivation, this time in connection with the study of the Yanomani people of the Amazon region, decimated and mistreated by all kinds of experiments for the greater glory of so-called researchers.

3.2. DESCARTES' ERROR?

Where should we place the origin of this disjunction, with its dreadful ethical consequences? Do we have to go back to the dawn of the modern era, when Descartes, in effect repeating the initial gambit of objectivation, made a watertight division between the domains of extension (the body and other objects) and the different register of thought and the soul? Would a revival of his famous dualism anticipate the opposition of biological science and psychoanalysis? The quarrel of God and the Devil, mind and body, is fought all the more strongly between the defenders of the pan-psychic and those of the pan-neuronal.

Echoing the words of the song, "I have fallen in the gutter:/it's the fault of Voltaire./My nose is down below:/it's the fault of Rousseau" (Hugo 1862, p. 395),[7] is it really Descartes' fault, what Damasio (1995) refers to as his error? We want to underscore here that dualism is often used as a mere rhetorical foil, ascribing to the author of *Discourse on the Method* (1637) an error that is not his.

The approach conducted according to methical doubt is, to be sure, the basis of Cartesian philosophy and of modern science. But, mischievously, it brings us back to the field of our experience in the mental hospital. When Descartes comes to doubt the sensations of his own body, isn't he a cousin of Elliot as described by Damasio (1995), as well as of a number of discouraging patients? Some of these patients apparently forget that they have a body, as we shall see in the story of Joseph (6.2.1.). The issues involved in Descartes' foundational theory overlap exactly with those of the actual work of madness.

Reason is pushed to the point where it conceives of a body that can no longer be trusted—to the point where it can challenge the body's very existence. But what is really at stake is the foundation of a trustworthiness that cannot be impeached. Only then, only from that fixed point, can the reliability of sensations be put to the test.

"Damasio's error" consists in his interpreting Descartes' text as a programmatic methodology aimed at future neurologists and psychologists. In reality, however, the philosopher is establishing the elements of a new "discourse" that essentially seeks to assert the guarantees of speech.[8] This reliability is also what allows sensations to be expressed.

---

7. Gavroche's song in the musical *Les Miserables* (Schönberg and Boublil 1987) occurs in a scene featuring one of the most famous child warriors, of whom there are so many today. The last stanza is interrupted by the death of the child, who is targeted, after a terrible game of hide and seek, by a National Guardsman.

8. Damasio is wrong about "discourse" in the sense in which Lacan (1969–1970) distinguishes among the effects of utterances that may be identical, depending on whether they are caught up in discursive configurations aimed at governing (the master's discourse), teaching (university discourse), challenging the master's discourse to produce his repressed knowledge (the discourse of the hysteric and of science), or giving words to what is left over from the other discourses (analytic discourse).

The analyst thereby comes to recognize that the subject was able to leave his body and seek refuge entirely in thinking when the validity of his sensations was annihilated by the maneuvers of a deceptive Other, the very Other whom Descartes calls the evil genius. In the same vein, in order to become capable of expression, sensations were even able to take refuge in hallucinations, including negative ones. Damasio (1995) cites Descartes:

> From that I knew that I was a substance, the whole essence or nature of which is to think, and that for its existence, there is no need of any place; nor does it depend on any material thing, so that this "me,"[9] that is to say, the soul by which I am what I am, is entirely distinct from body and is even more easy to know than is the latter; and even if body were not, the soul would not cease to be what it is. [p. 249]

The neurologist is well aware that Descartes was seeking a logical foundation for his philosophy, what, with Lacan, we call the guarantee of the Symbolic. As Descartes clearly observes, "[R]emarking that this truth, 'I think, therefore I am,' was so certain and so assured that all the most extravagant suppositions brought forward by the skeptics were incapable of shaking me, I came to the conclusion that I would receive it without scruple as the first principle of the philosophy for which I was seeking" (cited in Damasio 1995, p. 249).

Diverted from its trajectory, the experience of Cartesian thought is thus reduced by Damasio to "the suggestion that reasoning and moral judgment, and the suffering that comes from physical pain or emotional upheaval, might exist separately from the body" (p. 250).

Now, when a patient assures us that he has lost his brain, he is not seeking to verify that his thinking functions without his body. When he says he has lost his heart, his face, or his lungs, he is obviously not asking us to schedule him for an X ray of his thorax or to hold a pocket mirror up to him. What he wants is for us to work together to find a principle that will guarantee the validity of his speech, his speech and ours—that is, the symbolic validity of the exchange.

---

9. It is important to note that, with his own French translation of the Latin *subjectus*, Descartes made the term *subject*, the "I" instead of the "me," available to psychology and psychoanalysis.

That being the case, if taking "as a general rule that the things that we conceive very clearly and very distinctly are all true" is an assured principle, "there is only some difficulty in correctly recognizing which are the things that we conceive distinctly" (Descartes 1637, p. 53).

The philosopher even opens the path of clinical treatment: "For it is quite a remarkable thing that there are no men at all so dull and stupid, not excluding even the insane, that they not be capable of arranging various words together and of composing of them a discourse by means of which they make their thoughts understood" (p. 81). The only compass is what "in truth" guarantees the exchange of words: "For finally, whether we be awake or asleep, we ought never let ourselves be persuaded except by the evidence of our reason. For reason does not at all dictate to us that that which we see or imagine be true. But it does very well dictate that all our ideas or notions must have some foundation in truth" (p. 59). In all the stories we are telling in this book, we are trying to let ourselves be persuaded by the evidence of our reason how this foundation of truth is established on the basis of the most extravagant symptoms.

Although there is no handy metaphor for the experience, we have sometimes managed to bring about the link between holes in the head and the mutism of ancestors; between a vanished heart and the collapse of all courage; between a lost face and repeated, humiliating assaults. We shall return to these examples to show that, by departing from strict neutrality, we played our part there.

It follows that using words as though they were things, showing them concretely with unfathomable psychic suffering, is not a deficit of thought but the only possible means of entering into the dimension of speech when trustworthiness has wholly collapsed. Under these conditions, doubt that destroys all guarantees is an obligatory step on the way toward establishing in the transference a place that is the guarantor of truth. Only then can words and thoughts stop being things[10] and finally reach the path of metaphor (Loraux 1990). This doubt about the permanence of the body and the cosmos can affect the most articulate minds.

---

10. Until this moment when a possible reliability is founded again, "thoughts are things, things are thoughts, and they have personality" (Bion 1963, p. 22).

3.3. *PROFERAM*[11]: FROM THE REAL TO INSCRIPTION

Ernest was a young scientist who was referred to the analyst by one of his friends. He had left home suddenly and was wandering the streets. During his first visit, he explained that he had left after being betrayed by a certain Virginie—and that was all. He said no more about it, since he hated to talk about himself. Still, he came back in order to please his friend. The sessions consisted of exchanges of small talk, except for a single occasion on which he announced, as though it were a matter of great importance, that he had taken with him into the street three objects that never left him: a worn-out scarf, a broken pair of glasses, and a used-up fountain pen. He refused to say more.

A year later, he came to his session in an unrecognizable state. In no way eccentric up to then, he now appeared like an alien, wearing, in the middle of summer, a discolored yellow wool scarf around his neck and broken eyeglasses on his nose, with his hand in his pocket no doubt holding the pen.

"What's with that scarf?" asked the analyst, taken aback and, without thinking, opening the conversation.

"It's holding my head on my neck."

"Whatever for?"

"Because I have a girl's head on a boy's body," he replied, as though this were obvious.

The analyst was astonished. She had never suspected the least delusion in this young man, and she asked him on impulse: "What's this girl's name?"

"Virginie."

"The Virginie who left you?"

"No. I was 10 years old, the age when I wore the scarf and glasses that you see and used that fountain pen at school. Rummaging around in a dresser drawer, I found the photo of a baby. I asked my grandmother, 'Is that me?' 'No,' she said, 'it's your sister Virginie, who was born right before you and didn't live long. She's dead.' 'What from?' 'A malformation of the spine. Your parents never wanted that to be

---

11. *Proferam* is first-person future indicative or present subjunctive of *profero*, "bring forth" or "expose publicly."

known. Besides, after you were born another baby, a boy this time, died under the same conditions.' That's all."

"How terrible for your parents!"

"Maybe in a soap opera. They never showed any reaction. My grandmother either. I'm going now. I've decided to kill myself. It'll look like an accident. I've got a piece of paper on me that will give my body to science. It has nothing to do with you."

"I consider myself responsible. It's your sister and brother, not you, who should rest in peace in a grave."

"I don't understand anything you're saying. But thank you for doing your best. That's all I have to say."

"I'll expect you at your next session. Even if you can't say anything, bring me something, a drawing, an object, whatever you want."

The analyst was clutching at straws. Time went by in terrible suspense. At the next meeting, Ernest announced that he was going to live. He had come to this decision while scrawling an anatomical diagram, though he had not brought it to the session. On the paper, he had drawn an exchange of brains in a sawed-through skull. Then he had had a dream that, he said, should interest the analyst, since she had a major role in it:

"You're a schoolteacher. In the schoolyard, I'm playing at the head of a column of girls, while a girl is at the head of a column of boys."

"So the fatal spinal column became the column in a children's game?"

"That's not all. You make us go into the classroom and write the Latin word *proferam*. What does that mean?"

"Remember your Latin. I can certainly play the schoolteacher, since I taught Latin when I was young. So, tell me, what tense, what mode, what person?"

He hesitated, and the analyst whispered to him, "First person, subject 'I,' in the subjunctive of wish or the future indicative: 'May I proclaim before the world.' You have a whole program for a tragedy that must not be spoken of."

To continue the grammar lesson: the real column has risen to the rank of metaphor,[12] and, from now on, can be spoken before the world

---

12. With the utmost linguistic rigor, this metaphor demonstrates the passage from the thing, the real spinal column, the instrument of fate, to the signifier of a playtime column: the sacrificial moment when the Thing, *das Ding*, that must be destroyed in

by a subject who is open to the future and borne by the subjunctive of desire.

The crisis had passed. The symbolic play of metaphor, in the transference with the analyst, had been able to lend speech to the strange, mute forms that had appeared in the Imaginary, on the edge of the Real.

This sacrificial moment recurs each time that a new signifier, hitherto impossible, comes into being and is put in circulation (Lacan 1953, Wittgenstein 1945–1949). In this way, what Cocteau (1934) calls the Infernal Machine can be jammed and thwarted, the machine of destiny "that never stops not being written" until an Other, the analyst, takes the place of the monster, the master of fate, which can then be defied and tamed. From that time, the young man's analysis propelled him toward the future, ending a period that had become frozen in the wanderings of homeless beings. The little wandering souls had, in some way, found peace.

What made the analyst so sure that she could, for a moment, play the monstrous role of the mistress of death, only to turn around, acknowledge her flaws, and claim responsibility for the announced suicide? Her admission of failure established good faith, as opposed to a faultless otherness, the otherness of Moloch exacting his tribute of children to be devoured. This instance of good faith took the form of the schoolmistress who teaches children to speak and write.

What was the analyst claiming responsibility for? Afterward, Ernest made fun of her, saying she was a warmonger who made him fight instead of letting him die. And in fact, she had temporarily taken the guilt on herself, like the leader emerging in battle from a leaderless group (Bion 1946a,b). These terms sounded odd to Ernest in the context of the wars of decolonization into which his father had been drafted at the very moment of his babies' births and deaths. For, until recently, these "events" did not even have the right to be called war.[13] Everyone felt guilty, no one felt responsible.

---

order to be named, nearly claimed this patient's very life when, with bits and pieces, he embodied as well as he could, on the verge of the Real, the thing impossible to say, in order to show it to the analyst (cf. Lacan 1953).

13. Throughout the Algerian War (1954–1962), military operations were officially described as "operations for maintaining order" by successive governments, and this "war that dared not speak its name" was conventionally called "the events."

Many years later, when she met Gilda, the analyst would learn that she, like this woman, had been recruited early on, in her distant province of Savoy, on the Italian border, to face the army of the dead.[14] These transference stories place us before the following alternatives: either this raging band continues its course, constantly receiving new ghosts into its ranks, or it manages to open out, laterally, toward practices of inscription and symbolization.

3.4. DESCARTES' DREAMS

When he was about the same age as Ernest, Descartes passed through a similar phase of emptiness and near-madness. While sleeping, he was overcome by the terrifying experience of a band of ghosts hotly pursuing him, while strong gusts of wind from the beyond prevented him from moving forward and made him fall with every step. It is with these dreams, these visions, that, at the age of 25, on the night of November 11, 1619, St. Martin's Eve, he founded his philosophical approach some seventeen years before the publishing of the *Discourse on the Method*. For, after this experience, we see him making the decision to quit the army and work as a philosopher and a scientist.

This episode, while hardly "Cartesian,"[15] was the starting point of Descartes' career and provided him with an unexpected resource: messages emanating from the unconscious. After his brilliant studies with the Jesuits, he became a freelance fighter, without the status of a mercenary, in the army of the Duke of Bavaria during the Thirty Years War. His biographer, Samuel de Sacy (1985), describes him as one of the last

---

14. This is the so-called raging army, also known as Mesnie Hellequin (Ginzburg 1989, Schmitt 1994) from the name of the king of the dead, the Erl-King, who gave his name to Harlequin, the main character of the Commedia dell'Arte, who is masked in brown leather.

15. "All too often, in French, over the course of centuries a word comes to mean its opposite, . . . so that the word *Cartesian* has only a slight, and entirely formal, connection with Descartes We do not have to summon up much erudition to discover how alien Descartes is to his Cartesian renown: all we have to do is read him" (Sacy 1985, p. 5).

knights, in love with life and independence,[16] just as absolute monarchy was about to suppress for good and all these quixotic remnants of another era.

We know of only a few episodes from this period of war. The first has to do with the famous mathematics contest posted on the wall of the University of Breda in Holland. A very young soldier, Descartes bet a man who was reading it alongside him that he could solve the problem. He won the prize and, in this way, also won the friendship of the unknown man, who turned out to be Isaac Beeckman, a renowned scholar of the time, a physician and mathematician who was much older than Descartes.

At the end of 1618, Descartes dedicated a small treatise on music to him. "Written in haste, among ignorant soldiers, by an idle man subjected to a way of life very different from his thoughts" (Sacy 1985, p. 68). Descartes' transference to Beeckman is similar to Wittgenstein's to Bertrand Russell during World War I, when Wittgenstein, isolated among ignorant soldiers, was able to write the *Tractatus* in the midst of battle. This link is therapeutic, in the precise etymological sense we shall be examining later. Before making the journey that would lead him to Germany and the army of the Duke of Bavaria, a grateful Descartes wrote to Beeckman in April 1619: "In reality, you are truly the only one who shook me out of my lethargy; you alone reminded me of things that I knew but that had escaped my mind, which was

---

16. In Descartes' (1637) own words:

For it seemed to me that I could find much more truth in the reasoning that each one performs concerning the affairs that are important to him and the consequences of which must punish him soon afterward, if he had judged badly, than in those reasonings in which a man of letters engages in his study concerning speculations that do not produce any effect, and which are of no other consequence for him but that, perhaps, the more they are removed from common sense, the more vanity he will derive from them, because he will have had to employ so much more ingenuity and artifice in trying to render them plausible. And I always had an extreme desire to learn to distinguish the true from the false in order to see clearly in my actions and to proceed with assurance in this life. [p. 23]

drifting away from any serious preoccupation."[17] He then started out on a journey to join the Bavarian army.

It is in Ulm that we find him eight months later, this expert fencer and tireless traveler, returning from the coronation of Emperor Ferdinand. The second episode known to us from this period is the famous image of Descartes in the room with the stove,[18] during the period of inactivity when hostilities were suspended for the winter. On November 10, 1619, exactly one year after the first encounter with Beeckman, after a day of intense philosophical meditation that filled him with enthusiasm, he went through a period of great agitation. For three days and nights he hardly closed his eyes. Two nightmares took him to the edge of madness, to the brink of hallucinations and a complete breakdown, until a third dream showed him the path his life should follow. On that day, he discovered "the foundations of a wonderful science." We know of this from another biography, this one contemporary with Descartes, by Father Baillet (1691, cited in Descartes 1618–1637). Baillet mentions the original texts written by the dreamer of Ulm under the title *Olympica*; though Leibniz was still able to read them, they have since been lost.

There were, then, two terrifying nightmares. In the first, ghosts stir up whirlwinds and infernal spirits bent on his downfall. In the second, there is a horrendous noise followed by sparks of fire dancing around his room. A pain he felt upon wakening made him fear that some evil demon was at work, trying to seduce him. He overcame his terror in a third dream, thanks to the visit of the Spirit of Truth, who presented

---

17. He continues:

For it is not yet certain that the movements of the war will summon me to Germany, where I suspect that there will be many armed men but no combat. If this is the case, I will walk around in Denmark, Poland, and Hungary until I find, in Germany, either safer roads no longer occupied by pillaging soldiers or the certainty that we are at war. If I stop somewhere, as I hope to do, I promise that I will immediately set about reorganizing the *Mechanics* or the *Geometry*, and I will credit you as the mentor of my studies and their first author. [1618–1637, p. 41]

18. In that part of the country, this was a room heated by a large tile stove. There was a bench on which one could sleep during the winter.

him with books containing all the knowledge in the world: the sciences, but also the poets.

Two poems, one, "Est et Non" ("Yes and No"), referring to Pythagoras, and the other, "Quod Vitae Sectabor Iter" ("What Way of Life Shall I Follow?") by the Latin poet Ausonius persuade him to turn to research once again. To help him remain standing in life and keep his place in the world of knowledge, he thus accords a privileged place to poets, "whose capacities for enthusiasms linked to divinity have a much greater effect than those of men shut up in their studies."[19] It is easy to understand the pleasure with which we have so often come across such a man in our own path.

Here we can see that the evil genius who plays a major part in his *Discourse* is not an abstraction to be used in scholarly papers. As Descartes (1637) himself states, the *Discourse on the Method*[20] will appear, seventeen years later, as the tangible result of that night: "But like a man who walks alone and in the shadows, I resolved to go so slowly and to use such circumspection in all things, that if I did advance but very little, I would at least guard against falling" (p. 33).

3.5. FROM MADNESS TO THE *METHOD*

For our purposes here, the lesson to be drawn from this episode is that scientific revolutions, in Kuhn's sense, also touch on the resources of the unconscious. Concerned about the health of his readers and corre-

---

19. The account of the *Olympica* continues:

For he did not think it very surprising that poets, even those who say only silly things, were full of opinions that are more serious, more sensible, and better expressed than those to be found in the writings of the philosophers. He attributed this marvel to the divinity of enthusiasm and to the power of imagination, which brings forth the seeds of wisdom (which are found in all men, like the sparks of fire in pebbles) much more easily, and even much more brilliantly, than reason in the philosophers. [1618–1637, p. 56]

20. This work was published in Leyden, Holland, in 1637, anonymously and, at first, in French, not in Latin as was the custom at that time for this type of writing (e.g., the *Philosophical Meditations*, written in Latin in 1641). Descartes said that his Discourse could thus be read by women as well, since women are half of the world.

spondents, Descartes ultimately seemed to take little interest in the dualism between soma and psyche and more eager to take what might be called a psychotherapeutic position. He returns to this at several points, for example in the following recommendation, written in 1646, to Elizabeth of Bavaria[21]: "Just as the health of the body and the presence of agreeable objects are of great help to the mind in expelling all the passions involved in sadness and affording entry to those involved in joy, so, conversely, when the mind is full of joy this is of great use in making the body feel better and objects seem more agreeable" (cited in Sacy 1985, p. 145). This princess had good reason to be sad. After her father lost his throne in Bohemia, her homeland was devastated, and her people, the Czechs, lost their sovereignty for three hundred years.

Each time, the impact of the Real is brought to bear on a subject who then, in his own eyes and those of others, loses his very consistency as a subject. He becomes a schizo or a depressive, a victim or a refugee, or, better, an acronym of incomprehensible initials, like PTSD (posttraumatic stress disorder), as though these generic names had absorbed all one's singularities. He has, in fact, entered the zones of chaos in which the feeling of being oneself and "the feeling of what happens" (Damasio 1999) are compromised on account of a social, political, or natural disaster, or a familial, relational one—or a physical, indeed, neurological one.

Thus the convergence of these clinical, philosophical, and neurological inquiries has shown us how science in the making and the production of madness come together in processes the criteria for the analysis of which are, in reality, strictly the same. Descartes, a man of science, a man of thought, a man of passion, is the subject par excellence of these

---

21. Elizabeth was the daughter of the sovereign Palatine elector of Bohemia, Frederick V, called the king for one winter. After the decisive battle of the White Mountain, Descartes is able to follow, with his own eyes, a historical catastrophe. The emperor retakes Prague, the city in which John Dee, Kepler, Commenius, and Giordano Bruno had stayed, and the Czechs, terribly repressed, lose their civil, political, and religious freedoms for three centuries. The Thirty Years War begins, libraries burn, carnage lays waste Bohemia and the Palatinate. The elector will not recover from his failure; his daughter Elizabeth will live in Holland (Glucksman 1987). Elizabeth certainly had reasons to be depressed, as we would say today.

processes. His genius brings us all the words and all the rigor of reasoning necessary to account for what happens at these crucial moments. But we have also seen that his approach is sometimes strengthened by a confrontation, or even a simple conversation, with the community of his equals. He has taught us that the practice of his method often calls for long journeys to put preconceived ideas to the test of criticism and to meet those who sometimes enable him to take a further step.

In quest of such lessons, even at the front of his own wars, Descartes (1637) continues to open out a path for us:

> And inasmuch as I hoped to be able to achieve this goal better by conversing with men than by staying any longer shut up in the stove-heated room where I had had these thoughts, the winter had not been over for very long when I set out to travel. And, in the nine years following, I did nothing but roam here and there in the world, trying to be more a spectator than an actor in all the comedies that are played out there, and engaging particularly in reflections, in every matter, on that which could render it suspect and give us occasion to make mistakes, I meanwhile eradicated from my mind all these errors which had previously been able to slip into it. [pp. 117–118]

II
Lessons from the Front

4
"On the Road"[1]

4.1. GEOGRAPHICAL TRANSFERS: FINDING SOMEONE TO SPEAK TO

4.1.1. Transfers, Journeys, Exiles

On our modest scale, and as the beginners we were in the 1970s, in France, we were onlookers at a general skepticism surrounding the psychoanalysis of the psychoses. With a few exceptions (Pankow 1969), this topic was confined to theoretical comments, case presentations, or cases serving to support the theory as opposed to the transference. In his rereading of Freud, Jacques Lacan (1955–1956) states:

> For the time being I will leave this question that is preliminary to any possible treatment of the psychoses—a question that introduces, as we see, the conception to be formed of the handling, in this treatment, of the transferences. To say that on this terrain we can do anything would be premature, because it would now be to go "beyond Freud," and there can be no question of going beyond Freud when post-Freud psychoanalysis has, as I have said, gone back to an earlier stage. [p. 221]

From the beginning of our practice,[2] which took place in a psychiatric hospital, we therefore set out to travel. On our way, we met remarkable analysts in England and then in the United States, analysts who,

---

1. The title of Jack Kerouac's novel (1957) is also a French song from the postwar period.

2. But, some thirty years later, the publication of this book in the United States is part of the same approach, "on the road again."

not stopping at these preconceived ideas, devoted themselves to the psychoanalytic psychotherapy of the psychoses and its conceptualization. We were all the more aware of their ability to teach us by describing their clinical experience. It was thus that, in 1978, we arrived at the Austen Riggs Center in Stockbridge, Massachusetts, where patients were admitted to undertake intensive analytic work far from shock treatments and heavy medication.

4.1.2. Austen Riggs Center, Winter 1978–Summer 1979

Against the backdrop of the Berkshires,[3] which change color according to the seasons, and surrounded by huge trees, the Austen Riggs Center stands out, white and portly, against the lawn on the edge of Main Street. The absence of walls is striking. It is the month of August. In October, tourists will be pouring into the small town of Stockbridge to admire the foliage. Today we are sitting in green (or red?) leather armchairs in the office of Martin Cooperman, the medical director. He calls us the French Connection, after the film (Friedkin 1971).

We are slumped down in the chairs; despite the air conditioning, it is very hot. Martin is drowsy, as usual, unless this is a sign that he is concentrating. He is trying to communicate his experience in terse formulas. For him, an analysis of psychosis is very simple and, at the same time, very complicated. He describes the transference as a battle in search of a flaw, up to the brief moment of confrontation: "Look out the window at that young man who's making incoherent gestures. Now, if you shift your position with regard to the frame of this same window, you see that he's fighting an opponent who had been invisible before. But that's the snag: you've hardly seen this when the opponent is none other than you, and all you can do is admit this to your partner: OK, it's me you're fighting with."

Cooperman had already described these principles in an article (1983), but here he was simply telling us about his experience. It was often condensed into aphorisms, since concision was his style: "If you say something, it's in order to be silent about the opposite. Otherwise, why say

---

3. For the setting, see Patricia Highsmith's 1957 thriller, *Deep Water*, where the plot turns around a psychiatric clinic.

it? For example, 'Things are going well today.' If things were going all that well, you wouldn't even mention it to anyone. Conversely, if you state, 'I'm fed up with life,' you're more attached to it than you think."

We rose to take our leave. Cooperman bent over to open the bottom drawer of his desk and took out a framed photo. A bit surprised to recognize the analyst in an officer's uniform, we nevertheless listened to the brief summary of the time he spent in France: he wanted to testify before the French Connection that he had indeed served during World War II; cruised along our coasts; landed in Paris; lodged, if you please, in the Hotel de Crillon. But why was he taking us back to the war in this way?

At that time we were not able to understand the ostensive definition (Wittgenstein 1945–1949) he was giving us: what cannot be said necessarily leads to showing. The "Paris by night" of his stay in France made a beautiful picture whose ambivalent negative lay in his drawer. It was not until twenty years later, at an October 1998 conference at Riggs, that Martin Cooperman would decide to tell us that he had originally been the thirty-seventh flight surgeon in the U.S. Navy. In fact, it took us twenty years before we could ask him about this. By that time, Martin was in retirement. We met with him and his wife, Lee, one evening in 1998, at the home in Lenox of Gerard Fromm, his colleague at Riggs, who today is the director of the Erikson Institute for Education and Research there.

After dinner, we went for a walk in the nearby woods. It was Halloween, and the path was spooky, with carved and illuminated pumpkins all around. As we walked, Martin told us that he had been on the Wasp at Guadalcanal when the aircraft carrier sank. He could see the wreck and his drowning buddies before his eyes, shining with tears by the light of the jack o'lanterns. It took him and us twenty years to show us the corpses on the other side of the picture that lay in his drawer. Twenty years to finally ask the question that Percival did not ask King Méhaigné in Chrétien de Troyes' grail legend.[4]

---

4. The scene is the king's castle during a banquet. Percival, fascinated, watches a procession of young people carrying the bleeding spear and the grail. The following day he finds that the castle is empty. As he leaves, he meets a maiden, who says, "Oh unfortunate Percival, what sad adventure is yours that you asked nothing, since you could so easily have cured the good king who is disabled, so that he might recover the full use of his limbs and preserve his lands" (Chrétien de Troyes 1181, p. 263).

We then recalled our meetings with Otto Will, Martin's late colleague at Austen Riggs, when he was in retirement in California. Sitting beside his wife, Beulah Parker,[5] he had told us about the shipwreck
of two destroyers in the Pacific (cf. Thompson and Thompson 1998).
The only doctor to survive on his boat, he had had to operate hastily
on makeshift tables. He also told us the story of a soldier he had brought
out of marasmus, lying as a mute, neglected form under his sheet. Otto
was in his ward as a medical doctor, recovering from an operation. He
got in the habit of sitting beside him every day and speaking aloud his
thoughts and concerns to himself and to the living-dead figure. This
patient at St. Elizabeth's Hospital made a psychoanalyst of him by coming back to speech and to life.

4.1.3. The Ghost Road[6]

Later we kept finding the same reference to war among the pioneers
of the psychoanalysis of the psychoses. In the First World War,
Wilfred Bion (1982, 1997) had been a tank officer, and the famous
English anthropologist William Rivers (1918, 1922) had also served.[7]
When he returned to his neurology practice at the military hospital
of Craiglockhart, he invented an analytic psychotherapy of trauma.
In the opposite camp were Sandor Ferenczi (1919) and Frieda Fromm-
Reichmann (1946), the first woman granted a degree in psychiatry in
Germany. A young major in the Prussian army, she had treated sol-
diers with head injuries alongside Kurt Goldstein; much later, after
World War II, she would influence the style of intensive psychoana-
lytic treatment of psychosis at Chestnut Lodge.

    Going back to the time of our first visit, Ess White, director of
admissions at Austen Riggs, who came from the south, and Richard

---

5. Also a psychoanalyst, on this occasion Parker gave us her book, *The Mingled
Yarn* (1972), in which she relates the tragedy of a family touched by schizophrenia—
a family, she told us, that she knew well.

6. This is the title of the third book in Pat Barker's *Regeneration* trilogy (1992,
1994, 1995).

7. Rivers's socioanthropological works in funeral rites in the Solomon Islands
helped him face the ghosts haunting the dreadful nights in Craiglockhart War Hospital, near Edinburgh, where traumatized British soldiers were admitted.

Noland, chair of the English Department at Amherst College, had recommended that we read Faulkner's *Absalom, Absalom* (1936) in connection with the Civil War. Faulkner, a great specialist in human madness, had volunteered for military service in 1917 and trained as a pilot in Canada in the hope of being sent to France. The armistice of November 1918 put an end to his hopes. Something similar was true of Harry Stack Sullivan, who was discharged after volunteering to go to France but nevertheless continued as a liaison officer at St. Elizabeth's military hospital, where he trained under its director, William Alanson White, the "great encourager" (Swick Perry 1982, p. 167).

Psychotherapeutic experience on the battlefield led to a renewal of the paradigm of psychoanalysis itself, discovered simultaneously by those described rather abstractly by the military as "psychic casualties" and by their therapists, who were drafted to stem the decrease in the operational forces. Some of these, though only a few, quickly noted that the important clinical fact, apart from the duly diagnosed psychic or neurological symptoms, was the disturbed relationship to an other, human or nonhuman, expressed through a language game, verbal or nonverbal (Shephard 2000).[8]

For, as in classical psychoanalysis, the symptom is always a message addressed to the other. The difference is, in a way, the expansion of the spectrum of otherness. Even in cases where all contact seems impossible, this "nothing" is still being addressed. As Fromm-Reichmann kept repeating during supervisions, when we say that there is no transference, this means that, in fact, everything is transference.[9]

This fundamental principle, stated during the two world wars, was periodically forgotten during the years of peace that Robert Graves (1929) called the long weekend between two wars, only to be rediscovered each time disaster returned. It entails a radical critique of the objectivation principle and thus echoes the scientific discoveries of the same period.

---

8. These few therapists, hardly any of whom occupied high institutional positions, nevertheless had a decisive influence on the psychoanalysis of traumas and madness.

9. "The technique we use in our work [at Chestnut Lodge] is different from our approach to psychoneurotics. This is not a result of the schizophrenic's inability to build up a consistent personal relationship with the therapist but is due to his extremely intense and sensitive transference reactions" (Fromm-Reichmann 1946, p. 117).

Without even mentioning the theaters of war in which this practice and its theory were formed, the entire history of the psychoanalysis of the psychoses emerges as a battle to be sustained on multiple
fronts: war itself, present or past; confrontations with mass treatments
(electrical, chemical, or institutional); and, finally, the patient–therapist relationship, which promised neither a rose garden (cf. Greenberg
1964).

4.2. THE SOLDIER'S TALE[10]

4.2.1. Symptoms as Old as the War

Nowadays we are less surprised to discover, on this front of the Real,
analysts who were doctors on the actual battlefront. In our discussions
with some of them, people influenced by their experience in combat
during the Second World War (to which they often refer), we found
several recurrent features in their clinical work: they concentrated on
the here-and-now material in the sessions; took hold of it firmly in the
transference; and connected it up with points of history that might
touch them personally, telling us about these in a direct, unaffected
style.

This way of working certainly contrasted with the customary approach oriented toward anamnesis, strict neutrality, and sophisticated,
abstract commentaries. But, above all, these analysts' references to their
own military experience seemed peculiar and outdated. We would come
to learn how routine, forgetfulness, and disdain quickly covered up
these advances that had been made in and out of necessity.

In 1994 we were the guests of The Washington School of Psychiatry, founded by Sullivan in 1930. As we presented our work with the
psychoanalysis of madness, the portraits of the two ancestors, Fromm-
Reichmann and Sullivan, looked down uneasily from the walls, marking the end of an era: the psychoanalysis of the psychoses was no longer

---

10. As a refugee on the shores of Lake Leman in Switzerland, Igor Stravinsky
(1918) wrote this work with his friends, the Swiss writer C. F. Ramuz and the conduc-
tor of the Orchestre de la Suisse Romande, Ernest Ansermet. The soldier trudges along:
"Been marching, marching a lot, marching for a long time."

of much interest to anybody in the land of managed care, the *DSM*, and statistics.

The writings of the pioneers, which we mentioned in our talks, were apparently sleeping in the caves of the building. In any case, one of the participants, Nancy L. Balakar, M.D., came up to introduce herself as we were saying good-bye. She pointed out to us that the frequent reference to war made by the analysts we had met clearly went back to the Salmon principles. Who was this Salmon, anyway? We hadn't the slightest idea. Dr. Balakar promised to send us articles and books on this topic, and, soon thereafter, she kept her word.

This is how we learned that, as they were about to intervene in the war in 1917 and were wondering about the huge proportion of psychic casualties in the allied forces—one-seventh of the fighters were discharged for disability—the Americans sent an observatory commission to Europe. Thomas W. Salmon (1917) was the consultant for the American expeditionary force, his task being to offer a synthesis of the British and French experiences and design an overall program for the prevention and treatment of shell shock, rebaptized "war neuroses" for the occasion.[11]

The psychic role in war traumas has always been acknowledged, as far back as Herodotus in the fifth century B.C.[12] and the myth of Er in Book X of Plato's *Republic*. It perhaps involves not so much a mental defect consequent to shock as the human ability to produce living paradoxes: Epizelus, mentioned by Herodotus, is partly dead to our world after his companion in arms was killed beside him; Plato's Er is a soldier left

---

11. On the history of the multiple changes in the diagnostic terminology used to describe war traumas, see Shephard 2000.

12. According to Herodotus,

[a] strange prodigy likewise happened [at the Battle of Marathon]. Epizelus, the son of Cuphagoras, an Athenian, was in the thick of the fray, and behaving himself as a brave man should, when suddenly he was stricken with blindness, without blow of sword or dart; and this blindness continued thenceforth during the whole of his after life. The following is the account which he himself, as I have heard, gave of the matter: he said that a gigantic warrior, with a huge beard, which shaded all his shield, stood over against him; but the ghostly semblance passed him by and slew the man at his side. Such, as I understand, was the tale which Epizelus told. [p. 346]

for dead on the battlefield, who, cast out of the normal cycle of time and metempsychosis, returns in his own form as a living dead man. This myth points to a rupture in temporality, one that has had various names at various times. The terms *nostalgia*, used during the Civil War in the United States, and *Swiss disease*, said to afflict mercenaries purchased as teenagers from poor Swiss families, describe the irrepressible sadness that came over these men when they heard music from their native land. Jean-Jacques Rousseau writes that, when they heard the strains of "Le Ranz des Vaches" (still sung in Switzerland today), the Swiss threw down their weapons and wanted to go back home (cited in Rouget 1980).

In the year 2 of the French Republic, during the revolution, the soldiers were hardly older than the young Swiss when they, too, broke down. Shortly thereafter, Baron Larray, chief surgeon to Napoleon, who was aware of the widespread psychological problems affecting the recruits, ordered occupational therapy to distract them. Considered signs of cowardice, these symptoms could lead to courts-martial.

4.2.2. From Shell Shock to Traumatic Neurosis: "God Only Knows"

These problems were found on such a large scale that, in 1917, some psychiatrists effected a real revolution in the treatment of psychic casualties. We realized that this movement contained the roots of psychoanalytic techniques confronted with the imminence of destruction— destruction of the self and the world—that madness shares with war traumas. Who would have imagined that a psychoanalysis of madness had begun in the barracks of field hospitals? It was in this way that doctors drafted into the war got trained for their future practice as analysts: in contact with patients driven mad, under greater firepower than had ever been seen before, in the midst of quagmires, with real injuries to the head or the soul, whereas other doctors confined themselves to assuming the presence of invisible brain lesions.[13]

---

13. Shephard (2000) describes the open conflict between Myers, the pupil of Rivers, and the "brain dissector" Mott: "Where Charles Myers had brought to 'shell shock'

After three years of hell, the French and British doctors had already changed diagnoses several times (Briole et al. 1994). Some of them understood that the striking manifestations of aphasia, blindness, deafness, tremors, paralyses, fixed gaze, repeated nightmares, and insomnia were not all due to lesions caused by the violence of explosions. As a result, the diagnosis of "shell shock" was considered insufficient. Similarly, the hallucinations or deep depressions that appeared after the return from the front could no longer be considered classic psychoses. With their pragmatic sense of humor, the British gave these soldiers the diagnosis NYD, "not yet diagnosed," or even GOK, "God only knows." The French equivalent could be DSSQ, *Dieu seul sait quoi* ("God alone knows what this is"), our own variant of the *DSM*.

The public obviously preferred the mechanical certainty that connected clastic disorders or mutism to invisible brain lesions[14] supposedly caused by an all-too-apparent physical concussion. If the brain was materially disturbed, honor was saved; cowardice was not at issue. Even after it was established that no brain lesion was the origin of posttraumatic disorders, the term *shell shock* was retained essentially because it was felt necessary to ascribe men's psychic breakdown to a physiological fact, as it were by the presence of a foreign body. At that time, the good old image of a blow to the head fit in well with the causalist beliefs that are still current, never proven but always on the verge of being so. Sir John Eccles (1994), winner of the Nobel Prize in medicine and student of Sherrington, calls such an attitude, in reality antiscientific, "promissory materialism."[15]

---

a psychologist's alertness to the special senses and workings of the mind, Fred Mott had spent the previous twenty years dissecting the brains of London's lunatics" (p. 30).

14. "A debate about methods of treatment at the Advanced Neurological Hospital between Tom Salmon and his boss back in America, the neurologist Pearce Bailey, came to a head after the latter visited the French in the summer of 1918. Though a friend, Bailey evidently felt that Salmon inclined to a sentimental, introspective condition about such things which is decidedly opposed to satisfactory military operations" (Shephard 2000, p. 130).

15. "This strange postulate of identity is never explained, but it is believed that it will be resolved when we have a more complete scientific understanding of the brain, perhaps in hundreds of years; hence this belief is ironically termed promissory materialism" (Eccles 1994, p. 89).

Replacing "shell shock" with "war neurosis" did not, in fact, make much difference. The causalist representation of a definitive mental illness continued to connect the damage to the model of brain lesions and, conversely, to a treatment obeying the same mechanics. Thus the Electricity Fairy waved her wand, and electrodes were applied directly to the physical site of the symptom. Thus was born faradization, grandmother of ECT[16] and even more magical today, since the same response claims to be equally suited to each case.

But, from the outset, other psychiatrists preferred to base their work on other principles, which would become the Salmon principles. For, whether or not they were treated with electricity, the *poilus*,[17] who, although they later became our mustached grandfathers, were, after all, young men at the time, were resistant to all sedative medications. They seemed old before their time, and some of them would remain invalids for the rest of their lives.

---

16. ECT is electroconvulsive therapy, to give electroshock its complete new name. Its publicity brochure impressively describes its applications nowadays; Loo and colleagues (1994) list the following as "formal indications": melancholia, mania, mixed states, periods of acute hallucination, schizophrenia, pregnancy-related psychoses resistant to neuroleptics and postpartum depression, and depressive pseudo-dementia. As "possible indications" they list schizophrenias, mental confusion, mental anorexia, obsessive-compulsive problems, and resistant double depressions. "New indications" are ECT as consolidation and ECT as continuation. There are, however, some "controversial indications," including malign neuroleptic syndrome (MNS).

Contrary to what one might think, the authors of this article are not Jansenist followers of Deacon Pâris, called the Convulsionaries of Saint-Médard after the Parisian cemetery where they gathered, at the bottom of Rue Mouffetard. But, not far from there, ECT is practiced on the psychiatric service at Sainte-Anne Hospital. Their paper concludes with a lyrical and humanistic peroration:

> The accumulation of knowledge only serves to open new fields of research; while stimulating, these make the task still more difficult. We must continue to be humble while waiting to decipher the mysteries of the mechanisms that elude us and not depart from the aphorism of one of our masters (Deniker), who, thinking of patients who benefit from this treatment, said, "There comes a time to stop wanting to understand and start being able to cure." [Loo et al. 1994, p. 575]

The brave new world (c. Huxley 1932) is thus graciously invited to convulse together in the irrational.

17. "The hairy ones": this was the affectionate name given to French soldiers in the Great War.

4.2.3. "Men Learn from History Only that Men Learn Nothing from History"

This is why "forward psychiatry," like psychoanalysis, has often been contested by military psychiatrists themselves once peace has returned.[18] On this model, everything begins all over again when a new war breaks out. As a result, each conflict in the twentieth century has seen a great increase in the number of psychiatrists on the battlefront, a number reduced to just a few in times of peace. The next conflict always finds itself confronted with the same lack of resources as the one before.

If, today, war psychiatry looms so large in our eyes, this is so particularly because we have ignored its existence for so long, and for the same reason. Conversely, the sociohistorical and psychic reorganizations that take place in the midst of conflicts, in hatred and irrationality, are also the crucible in which psychiatrists became analysts of traumas and madness (Shephard 2000).[19]

When the United States entered World War II, Francis Braceland (1946) had to coordinate psychiatry in the navy on an emergency basis. He states:

> When the final history of World War II is written, and like all history is entombed in large volumes, to the student who reads it carefully, it will reveal the same lessons which are learned so painfully

---

18. "At the time of the outbreak of the war, there were approximately only 25 medical officers assigned to neurologic and psychiatric duties in the Navy" (Braceland 1946, p. 588). Speaking of the Falklands war, O'Connell (1985), after claiming that his is a very personal account, says as follows (not without a touch of Irish wit):

> Just because a man feels strongly about an issue is no reason why he should not support it. . . . My story really begins with the announcement, on 2 April, immediately following the invasion of the Falkland Islands by the Argentinian forces, that a task force was to be deployed. . . . Bearing in mind that a figure between 150 and 800 casualties could be expected, to meet this number there was deployed a task force: a psychiatrist, myself, without any support in the form of skilled nursing personnel specifically designated as mental-health-team personnel . . . . [pp. 1–2]

19. Fairbairn, for example, took his "creative step" during the Second World War (Sutherland 1989, p. 96).

and at such great cost in all wars. Each successive war necessarily brings with it new problems, but the old ones crop up repeatedly, and, as we encounter them again and again, we wonder why man is so slow to profit by experience and history. Perhaps the cynic expressed it best of all, when he said, "Men learn from history only that men learn nothing from history." [p. 587]

This saying is especially true with regard to the specific problem of trauma and war craziness. But it applies perfectly to the treatment of madness itself, which resembles combat and must be begun over and over again. Each time, history must be inscribed in the actualization of blood and tears. And the lessons of history remain buried, in effect, in large tomes, because the same knowledge is not being mobilized. Sixty years after his war, and shortly before his disappearance, Bion (1975, 1982) writes bluntly that he died at Cambrai in 1917 and at Amiens in 1918. Here again, our patients have taught us that this is not a metaphor, an error, or a symptom of Alzheimer's.

4.2.4. The Half-Pay Veterans[20] of War Psychiatry

The experience of these veterans is inseparable from the writings they signed or inspired. Cranky old children, soon out of date, they can say, with Bion (1982) at the end of the 1914 war, "I was now twenty-one and had not experienced what it was to be an antiquity, a survival from a remote past. . . . Though we did not realize it, we were men who had grown from insignificance to irrelevance in the passage of a few short years" (p. 286). They invoked their identity as soldiers, but their testimony was quickly ridiculed and periodically disparaged, by themselves first of all. Nevertheless, they or their descendants clung to it desperately, sometimes without knowing that they were doing so and sometimes in order not to know this.

It was articles and books like these that Nancy Balakar sent us and that we are citing in the second part of this volume. Written for the

---

20. This scornful name, reflecting the reduction of their pension, was given to veterans of the Napoleonic wars discharged by the Restoration. They were a paradigm of the social, psychic, and economic destitution of these veterans, whom no one even wanted to see after the end of hostilities.

most part in postwar periods, they were thus soon forgotten and, with each new conflict, rediscovered. Their public fate reveals exactly the dynamics of the process of dissociation of traumas, a process echoed in the minor or major madness of their descendants.

For us, reading these works was as precious as was, for Don Quixote, reading books of chivalry in order to be able to speak of the traumas of his father, Cervantes. Speaking of the forger who wrote a sequel to the first part of the novel in order to take illegitimate advantage of its fame, he writes:

> What I couldn't help resenting is that he attacks me for being old and one-handed, as if I had been maimed in some tavern brawl rather than at the greatest battle that past or present ages have ever seen or that future ages can ever hope to see. If my wounds do not shine in the eyes of those who behold them, they are at least honoured in the estimation of those who know where they were received. [Cervantes 1605, 1614, p. 483]

We are quoting Cervantes here as an elite soldier-poet who fought against the Turks for five years, lost the use of his right hand in the great battle of Lepanto in 1571, was captured by Algerian pirates, spent the next five years as a slave in the convict prisons of Algiers,[21] and narrowly escaped death and torture more than once. Ten years later, back in Spain, he was thrown in jail once again, in Seville, after a nobleman for whom he worked (as a tax collector for the next naval expedition) was convicted of embezzlement. It was there, in prison, that he conceived a child, Don Quixote, who inherited the traumas of his father, Cervantes. He wrote this masterpiece later, when he was past 50, after learning of his brother's death on the battlefield in Flanders. From childhood on, his brother had been his companion at arms and in captivity. This may be one of the reasons why, throughout the book, the hero barely escapes death and comes back to life in episodes of traumatic revivals that quickly became world famous. A trifle—a gleam, a noise, some dust—is enough to sent him full tilt against windmills or flocks of sheep.

---

21. For an account of life in this prison, in which European travelers of all social classes spent time for several centuries, see Aranda 1656.

Betrayed once again by a plagiarist, Cervantes then wrote a sequel and, this time, put an end to the adventures and to the life of his odd son. In this second part, Don Quixote will now be waging war in peacetime against the perversions of the social link. In the prologue to the novel, Cervantes identifies himself as a war veteran. He is now over 65 years old. He will have his hero die shortly before he himself dies in 1616.

Don Quixote makes his way through the disasters of the time in the company of his inseparable therapist, Sancho Panza, who dresses his wounds physically and morally, and also thanks to his lady, Dulcinea, to whom he sends his thoughts and poetry, and who (though she exists only as pure fancy) waits for him against all expectations. In fact, *Don Quixote* constantly develops a therapeutic tool, one that is always being damaged by catastrophes and always being revived: an antitotalitarian, antityrannical, antidepressive, antimelancholic tool par excellence.

We can take a lesson from Cervantes as we now set up the spatial and temporal coordinates, as well as the horizon of otherness, that make it possible to find a way out of the death zones in which mirrors and promises are broken.

4.3. PEACE PSYCHOANALYSIS, WAR PSYCHOANALYSIS

4.3.1. Thomas W. Salmon and Some Others

Salmon systematized the fundamentals of this knowledge into four principles that became the core of "forward psychiatry." These principles were particularly inspired by the French and British doctors who had noted that soldiers treated near the battlefront, close enough to hear cannon fire, recovered more quickly than if they had been treated in the rear.

As it happens, we had briefly come across the name of Thomas Salmon twenty years earlier, when we read Lacan's (1947) paper on Bion and British psychiatry during the Second World War. Salmon was apparently well known in the United States, but we had never heard of him, any more than the modern European or American reader has heard of Amadis of Gaul, the hero of a thirteenth-century chivalric novel who was so dear to Don Quixote.

Salmon and his principles were not unconnected with the psycho-analytic movement of his time. Before World War I, he had been a physician on Ellis Island, not a professional soldier or even a trained psychiatrist.[22] Along with William James and Clifford Beers, he founded the mental-health movement in the United States and became director of the National Commission for Mental Hygiene established by Adolf Meyer. Meyer was among those who had welcomed Freud to Clark University in 1909, at the same time as a psychoanalytic orientation was developed at St. Elizabeth's, the military hospital under the direction of William Alanson White.

A number of these pioneers, it must be emphasized, had a direct relationship with madness (Fromm-Reichmann 1946). Meyer's mother; Alice, the sister of the James brothers (Strouse 1981); and Beers and Sullivan themselves had experienced psychiatric hospitalizations. Beers (1908) never concealed this episode, which occurred after his studies at Yale and involved a particularly dreadful treatment. His therapist in the battle of "a mind that found itself" was, incidentally, not a clinician but another patient.

Beers's book, admired and supported by William James, shows exactly how his madness motivated his deliberate investigations of the closed wards, public and private, where he was confined, as well as the ferment of his later undertakings. We may recall the same situation in the case of Auguste Comte. As for Sullivan, he never mentioned the crisis of his youth, except to Helen Swick Perry, his editor and biographer.[23]

---

22. This "was probably just as well," according to Ben Shephard (2000), since Ellis Island, "the teeming gateway to the American continent, . . . was no place in the 1900s for academic theorizers. It was the university of life" (p. 127).

23. "One day," Swick Perry (1982) reports, "when I had been driving Sullivan home after a meeting at St. Elizabeth's Hospital in southeast Washington, he told me he was glad that no electric shock or lobotomy had been prevalent at the time he was growing up; he had been ill and hospitalized with schizophrenia, he said, and his case might have been treated so drastically that he would have ended his life as a vegetable" (p. 3).

4.3.2. Getting Out of Hell

And so we are setting forth these principles here. For, ever since we came to know them, we have acknowledged them in our own work with our patients, to whom we sometimes mention them directly. They will be our guide as this book progresses, and we shall show how they work clinically and dynamically for all analysts faced with the urgency of traumas and madness.

Two basic requirements are set down in advance: do not diagnose, and (except for the temporary use of sedatives) do not medicate.[24] As for the principles themselves, they are summed up in four words that provide secure landmarks in a country ruled by chaos: proximity, immediacy, expectancy, and simplicity.

Beneath their apparent abstraction, these terms are in fact coordinates broaching the possibility of a transferential relationship in the context of world collapse. The cosmos is no longer safe: the soldier, sometimes betrayed by his own side, has seen all his hopes and certainties crumble, to the point where, when he returns from hell, he lives like a living corpse. These principles seemed to us to characterize the practices of analysts in contact with human dread.[25]

The film *Human Dread* (Barrois and Andro 1991) brings together the testimony of survivors in a chiasmus: the memory of hell and the hell of memory. The underlying mythological reference is the story of Orpheus (Barrois 1988, 1993, Dodds 1959[26]). Back from the land of the dead, the poet is no longer inclined to sing. Whatever their age, origin, profession, sex, or condition; whatever the circumstances of the trauma (attack, airplane hijacking, wars, accidents, natural disasters);

---

24. We had no trouble taking this position from the beginnings of our clinical practices, since neither of us is a physician.

25. *Human Dread* (*L'effroi des hommes*) is the title of a film made by Claude Barrois and J. P. Andro (1991) for French television. Barrois, now retired, was the medical director at the military teaching hospital of Val-de-Grâce in Paris. We invited him to give a seminar as part of the complementary lectures at EHESS. The title he chose was "The Memory of Hell and the Hell of Memory." We are indebted to his profound clinical experience and to his teaching.

26. Dodds discusses Orphism and the role of dreams and visions among the ancient Greeks in troubled times, especially during war.

whatever the degree of their exposure; with or without injuries; alone or lost in a crowd; on the domestic, national, or international scale, in their accounts these survivors sketch out a field of research that their symptoms are exploring. All agree on the following points:

Whether others realize it or not, in a certain sense they are no longer part of the world of the living. Hypersensitive or unable to feel, they are beset by untimely images that are too vivid or, on the contrary, ghostly though not always frightening. T. S. Eliot (1929), author of "The Waste Land" (1922), praises the visionary ability of people in the time of Dante; nowadays, he says, this cognitive technique is granted as a sad privilege only to nerds or illiterates. Whether their life is normal or eccentric, people who went through hell oscillate between distrust and excessive trust. In short, they feel that they are in exile in our world. They no longer believe in anything. They are outside of time.

Their psychotherapies or psychoanalyses, recommended by their relatives or doctors, are usually soon broken off, do not take hold. Take hold of what? Of whom? Of another, but not just any other. Instead, they complain that, at best, they have found only fine words, at worst, procrustean terminology,[27] be it psychiatric, psychoanalytic, or even anthropological if they come from a traditional country. They are fitted into abstractions that they see clearly but that do not "say" anything to them. Finally, whatever the medications they have tried, whatever the succession of diagnoses, their dread persists, especially when they say they know it but do not even feel it.[28]

---

27. Jeffrey Jay (1991) describes one such case:

Joseph's memories and nightmares, he was told, were "flashbacks" and "intrusive thoughts," his anger and despair were "persistent symptoms of increased arousal," and his sense that nobody understood him or wanted to were "feelings of detachment or estrangement from others." He was suffering from PTSD, he was told, and was advised to attend regular group counseling sessions with others who shared some of his problems. Joseph joined a support group for PTSD sufferers, . . . and, as he said, "I learned to behave better and hide better." [p. 21]

28. Cf. the films of Bertrand Tavernier (1992) about veterans of the "nameless" war in Algeria and Peter Kosminsky (1999) about the United Nations peacekeeping forces in the former Yugoslavia.

"I could write a book," they all say, and then fall silent. Now, almost a century later, and, for us, fifty years after the Second World War, the Salmon principles draw from the same experience as Faulkner did when he began writing fifty years after the Civil War. What a strange affinity between literature and the treatment of traumas and madness!—although, of course, inscription is at stake for both, and this common stake has always placed them on the same level. Fiction, here, is neither an ornament nor a cultural product: it is a necessary instrument of historicization. The same necessity holds true for the stories we are telling here. Beyond directives for action, the Salmon principles thus constitute a theory developed in the face of the need to speak of the real disasters of space and time.

4.3.3. The Salmon Principles

Proximity opens up a new space of trustworthiness amid chaos.
Immediacy creates a living temporality in contact with urgency.
Expectancy constructs a welcome to the return from hell.
Simplicity emphasizes the obligation to speak without jargon.

These four pillars define the space-time of a new language game for an experience that is not so much unspeakable as inaudible, for the experience of the real consists in there not being any Other to respond to it. Today, their precision may seem simplistic in the context of the different forms of violence that keep on exploding all over the planet. For, along with this violence, the guarantees of speech, trust, continuity, safety, and the law explode as well.

But it is just this same context of the breakdown of all value that authorizes us to posit more than one homology, a common ground uniting trauma and madness where survival is at stake for body and mind indissolubly linked. Thus we shall be referring to these principles as a rigorous foundation for the dynamics of a transference aimed at the creation of a new social bond on the ruins of loyalty and hence of speech. This kind of minimal society emerging from absolute aloneness is the only way out of a situation in which men have become things and in which all otherness that is not murderous has been banished from this death zone, sometimes for several generations.

In this way, the Salmon principles for forward psychiatry are closely associated with the beginnings of the psychoanalysis of the psychoses in the United States. The wars of the twentieth century have seen them successively annulled and then revived. Nowadays they tend to be dissolved in the ideological reductions of managed care, the imposition of cursory managerial instructions that claim to govern mental health on a worldwide scale. In peacetime, not much importance is granted to psychic casualties insofar as they are not counted in unemployment statistics.

It is only in so-called enlightened times that so many babies are thrown out with so little bathwater, observes the hellenist E. R. Dodds (1959), noting that rationalism enables people to justify their bestial conduct in their own eyes. Like Dodds, Schrödinger (1954) deplores the intellectual destitution in which we find "the grotesque phenomenon of scientifically trained, highly competent minds with an unbelievably childlike—undeveloped or atrophied—philosophical outlook" (p. 12).

Thus, until we are once again confronted with the real cost in the loss of men, the Salmon principles are debased into cheap recipes. *Proximity* quickly becomes a slogan for discharge from the hospital and return to the community, with a reduction in the cost per day (and a proportional increase in the drugged-up population). *Immediacy* apparently serves to encourage brief therapies based on cognitivist problem solving with no reference to history. *Expectancy* surreptitiously preaches adaptation to group ideals on the pretext of returning to the collective whose pressure was exactly what made the patient crazy. *Simplicity* is reduced to the simplistic reduction to stupidity of the high level of research attained by madness.

4.3.4. Koan: "Let Me Die, or I'll Perish"

This cry, screamed out in the clinic by one of the analyst's patients, gives a remarkably concrete form to what Chinese T'chan calls the koan. In the face of this enigma, "an act of speech must be produced, . . . seized at the spring from which words well up . . . from the relation between unarticulated reality and its articulated forms" (Izutsu 1978, p. 26). Patients who frequent the borders of the unarticulated—we would say, of the Real—are familiar with such enigmas. All the analyst has to do is accept the challenge, pick up the glove, and a sparring match begins that may enable the patient to pass from the asphyxia of a lethal impasse to the respiration of words exchanged to name the unnamable.

In looking into this comparison with the philosophical and psychotherapeutic practices of the Orient, we were guided by extraordinary scholars like Paul Demiéville (1972). In his translation and comments on Lin Tse (in Japanese, Rinzai), Demiéville calls this ninth-century master—one of the great figures of the school of Buddhism known as T'chan (in Japanese, Zen), in the very particular form this school took at the end of the Tang Dynasty (618–907)—a practitioner of psychotherapy. Might we say: Of psychoanalysis?

Lin Tse is basically asking the same question posed by these patients, who are specialists in the outer edges of language and time. Demiéville presents Lin Tse in just such an apocalyptic context. In the wars that were tearing China apart in that period, he says, the Zen master might just as well have been a warlord. For the T'chan monasteries were refuges that turned into bedlams and led to a movement of return to praxis instead of theory, of anti-intellectualism pushed to the limits of the rational. Madness was always part of the tradition of Chinese wisdom, even sometimes in the art of calligraphy.[29]

When a patient says, "When I'm well, I'm not well, and when I'm not well, I'm well," this is another form of the same riddle. It would obviously be inane to do an abstract, scholastic analysis of the aporias that patients hurl at us from the shores of life and death, and to draw a brilliant conclusion about their paradoxical nature, incapable of logical solution.

---

29. "In the ancient history of the Tang written by Liu Xu between 941 and 945, the calligrapher Zhang Xu is mentioned in the biography of his friend, He Zhuzhang (659–744). The latter was connected with Zhang Xu, who excelled in cursive calligraphy and liked to drink. When drunk, he shouted, tossed about, and called for his brush; his writing then unfurled in infinitely varying forms, so that he might have been said to be helped by the gods. He was nicknamed Xhang the Madman" (Hsiung 1984, p. 3). Prints of this turbulent calligraphy can be seen in the museum at Xian, in China.

The war psychiatrists were dealing with a variant of precisely this same aporia: "If you cure my symptoms, you'll be sending me back to death on the battlefield; if you don't cure me, I'll be a mental invalid for the rest of my life." The First World War was the training ground for this type of paradox, and a veritable psychoanalysis of madness emerged from this challenge (Barker 1992).[30]

---

30. Barker's *Regeneration* trilogy (*Regeneration, The Eye in the Door, The Ghost Road*) begins with a similar, apparently insoluble, riddle posed to William Rivers by the poet Siegfried Sassoon. Sassoon, escorted by his friend Robert Graves, was referred to Rivers after writing an open letter to the House of Commons, in which he criticized the pursuit of the war. He had thrown his decorations into the river. The therapist either had to diagnose Madness, thereby destroying the meaning of his act, or to declare him mentally fit, sending him to a court-martial and the firing squad. On the work of Rivers, see Sassoon 1937.

5

Proximity: Constructing Space in a Boundless Space

5.1. GETTING IN TOUCH

5.1.1. The Challenging First Interview: Close to the Uncanny

One may ask what closeness to the battlefield involves when the war is over and no one wants to hear about it anymore. On the other hand, the present wars are enough of a preoccupation for people day to day, in minute-by-minute live broadcasts; everyone can be stirred by human misfortune, reassured in the knowledge that the victims are in the hands of specialists. Everyone nowadays knows that one has to talk, be debriefed: "Go see a shrink; that's his job." All too often confused with the microphone held toward the suffering of the planet, this job in fact generates a remote proximity, virtually steeped in indignation and good intentions.[1]

But in reality, even when it's right under our noses, we do not see war. As the Chinese proverb says, the stupid person, when a finger shows him something, looks at the finger. To begin with, this is because, beyond discourses of convenience, the proximity of disaster is marked by an effect of repulsion. For their part, these patients are resis-

---

1. "Television companies were quick to see the potential of 'trauma.' . . . 'Trauma' became one of the staples of daytime talk shows, the cheapest form of entertainment" (Shephard 2000, p. 386). "Debriefing programs seemed to do more to meet society's collective need to be seen to help victims than to address the clinical needs of the individual patients themselves. Why, it was asked, was debriefing so successful as a social movement and so believed in as an ideology when there had been no adequate demonstration that it did victims any good or prevented post-traumatic illness?" (p. 390).

tant to analysis from the outset. They come in order to please a relative or friend who had a good experience with therapy, or they come once or twice at a doctor's recommendation. They may possibly return on their own later on. Physician or not, the person who refers them must surely already be situated in a certain proximity.

The announcement of what isn't going well is made suspiciously and hesitantly: what's the use of talking about it further; it can all be said in a few sentences. Horrendous suffering, paralyzing apathy, indifference, months and years of missed work, crying and shouting when one is home alone, the shame of evoking and reliving the intensity of the burn or wound: all this is hardly worth talking about. The analyst is the nth in a long list of abortive attempts. Besides, if the emergency staff couldn't do anything, this proves that it's an illness, as everyone says: PTSD, depression, even the ultimate verdict of endogenous depression. And the medications pile up at home, at least with a view to putting an end to things.

As for the analyst, he hovers among benevolent listening, some questions—more or less well received—about the history, and the wish to stop there, for the sake of peace and quiet, and send this ambivalent demand back to the miracle doctor and his prescriptions. Here we see that a touch of violence has slipped into this generous re-referral, one that the patient, of course, immediately registers. Let us make no mistake: we are at war; the battlefield is right there. This is not the usual riot among specialists arguing about how to explain symptoms and their treatment. The front line in fact involves prior, and much more striking, ruptures that have already been actualized in the proximity of the transference.

The analyst—but first his "visitor"[2]—may be aware of the underlying violence that has just manifested itself, more or less hidden by a surface tolerance. This confrontation destabilizes the therapist's neutrality and brings him close to affects he would prefer not to experi-

---

2. "When host and visitor see one another, the visitor says a few words to test the host in front of him. . . . [The host] is offered some insidious words shot from the side of the visitor's mouth" (Demiéville 1972, p. 112). In his learned note (p. 113), Demiéville readily compares this joust, in Chinese T'chan, to the situation of the analysand facing the analyst.

ence. At least not right away, when the work hasn't begun and he is not yet able to get his bearings in relation to history—the patient's history, he thinks cautiously.

Is it only that he resents this unwelcome visitor who scorns his work and puts him in a senseless competition with medicine? Or has he fallen head over heels in a conflict he knows nothing about? The analyst then tries to know, to guess, to form hypotheses by extracting bits of anamnesis. On the other side of an invisible line, he tries to orient himself in a geography alien to him, but just as alien to the person who is revealing himself. Why trace the geography of a distant past, while the patient, for his part, is trying in the present of the interview to interrupt evocations he knows all too well—or not at all? In any event, only the present matters to him.

In fact, this entire protocol is aimed at marking the boundaries of an arena for one-on-one combat, a combat on the level of a logical paradox, a koan: "Either you acknowledge that this is an illness, and why not entrust myself to the progress of chemistry and electricity, or you deny this and thereby deny the reality of the suffering. What's your answer to that? Anyway, I'm leaving."

This aporia is the initial form of a challenge, in the best chivalric tradition. The analyst does not have much time to locate himself in the arena—between throwing down the gauntlet, which the patient has just done, and throwing in the towel, which the analyst is sorely tempted to do. Yet the situation is absolutely not the same as a game of professional roles.

For, when looked at more closely, throwing in the towel refers to the boxer's trainer, who thereby stops the fight for good. Throwing down the gauntlet, on the contrary, calls for an object of the action: someone throws down the gauntlet to someone else. This challenging gesture abruptly calls for a response in the same language: the other person must take up the gauntlet. The violent admission of the most extreme heterogeneity is, at this moment, equivalent to defining a place of intense proximity: the proximity of the unknown, the uncanny, which has no chance of getting out of its entrenched positions unless an other comes to look for him. "Looking for someone," in quarrelsome French, has the meaning of provoking him.

5.1.2. After the Battle

"You're not being paid enough for this work. You're going to wear your-self out. Even babies, they do too much for their age. . . . At 5, I was a little old lady of 80. I understood all about life; all about life I under-stood. . . . I'm going to tell you about the incomprehensible, the terror of the world. . . . With a wave of the historical wand, they turned into lime-stone. . . . Does it think it's alive, a baby? They'd have to tape a little baby to know if it thinks it's alive or dead. It all depends on its tone of voice. . . . If the baby doesn't smile, it's because there are things it doesn't dare to do to its mom. Because then *she's* sick, and the baby isn't glad to have been born. They work, babies; I inherit babies. . . . It's the war that made me crazy." [Davoine 1998, p. 8][3]

Most of our patients arrive like this, long after the battle, more than a generation after the cease-fire. Often a random event, important or microscopic, opens a breach in the continuity of their daily life, one in which incongruous geographies break through. This event should always be considered a traumatic revival, that is, an autonomous pro-cess without memory, since there was never a subject to carry a trace of it, even a repressed trace.

This warping of space-time defines particular criteria of proxim-ity in which the analyst will find himself forced to invent his place within the very movement of the transference. He cannot embody the assumed knowledge[4] of what is happening or what has happened. He is driven to be the spectator of an act that could not possibly be in-scribed by and for a subject, a Real that signals its presence only in the urgency of the onset of new hostilities.

These spaces, turned into limestone by a wave of the wand of his-tory, are revealed with very sharp contours: everything is set forth there from the beginning, often in the course of the first interview. But the

---

3. These words were spoken to the analyst, in the depths of the psychiatric hospital where she was working, by a patient who called herself Sissi, Empress of Austria-Hungary. When she left the hospital where she had been committed for over fifteen years, she never said anything more about this war unless the analyst, un-aware of this issue at the time, asked her the right questions. See Davoine 1998.

4. "As soon as the subject who is assumed to know exists somewhere—I have abbreviated it for you today at the top of the blackboard as S. s. S. [*Sujet supposé savoir*]—there is transference" (Lacan 1964, p. 232, translation modified).

idea of asking for associations to such material proves sterile and may even provoke the patient to end the meeting: "That's all I have to say." In fact, the incomprehensible is imported into the analyst's office as a "strange attractor." The therapist will find himself propelled into it without knowing when or how or why, right from the beginning of the work. The proximity actualized in this way becomes the very locus of the transference.

5.1.3. The "Unsung Battle"[5]: In Touch with Facts Stricken with Nonexistence

"Taking up the gauntlet" consists, first, in showing that there is no question of letting oneself be annihilated by this kind of force of negativity that specializes in the destruction of all otherness. This force not only emanates from the patient's disorganization; it corresponds to long practice in the active atomization of the other, resulting from contact with zones of destruction.

A seed of otherness, however, may then take refuge in things: the found objects and other "readymades" dear to the Surrealists. Such were Ernest's objects (3.3), which he mentioned right in the first interviews: "As an analyst, you should be interested in three objects, the only ones I took with me into the streets." At that time, the analyst had no idea what to do with them, nor could she relate them to the fateful baby deaths of which they were the geological outliers. At the intersection of story and history, as Auguste said, they also marked the violent period of the contemporary wars of decolonization in which his family was caught. These objects would soon make their presence felt "in person" in the strange and threatening session we described above. Although they looked worn, ready to be thrown out, for this young man they were more stable, trustworthy, and faithful than the human beings who were busy justifying themselves.

---

5. "As the officer in charge of this organization, [Bion] deliberately assessed the situation in military terms, identifying a foe and determining the strategy and tactics with which to fight it. This unsung battle of the Second World War was against neurosis. It then became necessary to assist the men in identifying this enemy and hold the retreat in which, as he saw it, all patients and staff up to that point had been engaged" (Harrison 2000, p. 186).

Because we are positing the real existence of such a danger zone that threatens all continuity, it becomes possible to state at the outset—and state to the patient as well—some definite points:

—There is no reason to invoke an internal personality disorder, cognitive or affective deficits, or mental handicaps. Moreover, there are no boundaries, here, between internal and external.

—These symptoms establish a boundary and are produced in contact with danger, in the proximity of terrifying situations. They may afflict anyone in situations like these.

—They constitute normal reactions to abnormal situations. At the moment when he discovers the reality of trauma, Freud himself (Freud and Breuer 1893–1895) emphasizes that one would have to be crazy not to react to it with madness or to let oneself be persuaded that it is nothing.[6]

—Apathy is the guardian of knowledge concerning this catastrophic space that, in normal times, no one wants to or is able to approach with impunity.

—This knowledge is indispensable to survival, even if the extreme aloneness in which it is employed makes it unfit for communication.

—Given these premises, it hardly makes sense to speak of the past, since a catastrophe like this, which eludes transmission, could not be inscribed in time.

Even the patient who seems most regressed, withdrawn as far as possible from the analyst's words, is not unable to hear them. On the basis of bits and pieces of statements barely mentioning an alcoholic grandfather, a mute or violent father, or a depressed or cruel mother, dates and places speak for themselves about the various wars the gen-

---

6. "If we go into the mechanism of 'idées fixes,' we find that they are based upon and supported by so many experiences operating with such intensity that we cannot be surprised to find that these ideas are able to put up a successful resistance against the opposing idea brought forward by suggestion, which is clothed with only limited powers. *It would have to be a truly pathological brain from which it was possible to blow away by mere suggestion such well-founded products of intense psychical events*" (p. 99, emphasis added).

erations of the patient's family passed through, if only the analyst can recognize them:

"In my family, we never wished for any holiday."

"Would you by any chance be from the north or the east," asks the analyst, "where no one sang anymore after three waves of disaster?"

"I'm from Dunkirk, Boulogne, the Somme, the Ardennes, Verdun, Wounded Knee, Bataan, Angola, Rwanda . . . ."

"And these names no longer mean anything to you?"[7]

Sometimes the "castrating father" and "omnipotent mother" have already been brought in as a couple in stereotyped oedipal interpretations that are obviously inadequate. They have blurred the lines of the landscape, including the names and songs that accompanied the memories of the patient's immediate ancestors. It can really be said that, in France, songs fell silent after the Second World War—at least those that were sung in the evening among family or friends. Didn't Marshall Pétain definitively mark with infamy the words "work, family, fatherland" by making this the motto of his government of collaboration with the enemy? Along with the old people, "the dear voices have fallen silent" (Verlaine 1866, p. 48), the voices that sang the old songs to us.

But songs cannot be annihilated so easily, as we see from the reissue of a book by the musicologist Davenson (1946), presenting a collection of songs gathered "between 1941 and 1943, in the darkest days of the Second World War, when France, torn by defeat and occupied by the enemy, was threatened by discouragement, despair—and betrayal" (p. 1). The book originally appeared clandestinely, as an act of resistance, during the war and, in order to be published, had to be entrusted to a member of the maquis from Savoy, who carried it across the Swiss border. Among the "dear voices" from a time when the country seemed to have lost its voice, the author, in a learned note written during the war, offers the following comment, which echoes alongside the tragedy of Adam, the novelist we mention at the beginning of this book. Referring to the concentration camp at Holzminden during World

---

7. The reader to whom these names do not mean anything may substitute the names of other, more recent or more familiar, battles, for example those of the Normandy invasion. If even those have been erased for him, let him look in today's headlines for names that, despite their foreign sound, are on everyone's lips for awhile before being erased in what is called public opinion.

War I, it resounds for us today, too late, with Adam's family's living ghosts and unsung deportation:

> In fact, each time a happy researcher thought he could grasp the origin of one of these songs, his discovery was immediately contested. Thus P. Olivier thought he could attribute the lament of "The Living Ghost," the song of a mother who did not want to recognize her boy, to a certain Guinoiseau, a peasant from the north of Mayenne, who was said to have composed it *in the spring of 1917, in the prison camp of Holzminden* in Germany. . . . This Guinoiseau was the son and grandson of village fiddlers: an admirable example of the persistence of the poetic gift in a family! Alas! These village fiddlers were above all gifted with a good memory: P. Coirault has shown that this lament, which, by the way, was known and published well before 1917, goes back at least to the wars of the First Empire, since it was read in a manuscript songbook of 1814. [Davenson 1946, p. 56]

5.1.4. Only Psychoanalysis Can Find the Trace of the Breaking Point[8]

We do not hesitate, then, to tell the descendants of such living ghosts about the presence, on these erased battlefields, of a forward psychiatry and about its close connection with the work we are doing together. In this way we create a field of recurrent analytic experience, constantly destroyed and rediscovered, that serves as an ancestor for both analyst and patient.

The establishment of this judgment of existence puts objectivity back in its place, not as a diagnostic label but in the reality of an event. An interpretation referring to fantasy or to prior psychic weaknesses is not relevant.

What we see here, in all its vanity, is a causalist preconception of madness. It leads directly to "therapies" aimed at bringing the force of the event back into awareness, to the point of administering pentothal or amphetamines and conducting narcoanalysis (Crocq 1999, Sargant and Slater 1944), even to forcing somebody to watch a videotape of the traumatic scene if by chance it has been filmed, in the chimerical at-

---

8. See the quotation from Claude Barrois on pp. 129–130.

tempt to integrate a dissociated scene forcefully (Legendre 1989). On the contrary, what is important is that the judgment of existence be brought into the transference, where the analyst is, willy nilly, engaged. Those who have been threatened with vitrification by the impact of the Real do not need to be turned into objects yet again.

On the basis of his experience fighting on the Austro-Russian front in World War I, Wittgenstein firmly maintained this position. During World War II, he initially asked to work as a dispensary porter in a London hospital during the Blitz. There he handed out medication but advised the patients not to take it (Monk 1990).

He was later summoned to take part in studies of wounded airmen in the military hospital in Newcastle, where he recommended that not even the word *shock* be used. He felt that this word, equivalent to a stigma, could only sink patients further into their depressive slump, creating an entirely disastrous psychic inwardness, stricken by the absence of any other. In the official report he worked on, he even suggests that the word *shock* be written upside down as a sign of its uselessness and harmfulness. He was very firmly of the opinion that the patient be allowed to describe his experience in his own way. Wittgenstein was still reading Freud at this time and wondering about the difference between dreams of fear and wishful dreams (Monk 1990).

Even the notion of stress, universally disseminated today by the diagnosis of PTSD, is inadequate, as Claude Barrois (in Briole et al. 1994) emphasizes:

> What we are trying to name here is not a mechanical, purely physiological, post-accident reaction but the existence of a response to a tragic misfortune, to the meaninglessness that has befallen the world, to an existential threat that reifies the subject. It is as though each psychic victim embodied the gap in the social fabric. If there is no other to whom to speak, the trauma reduces the individual to an interiority invaded by annihilation anxiety and terror. An object among objects, he is doomed to aloneness, to an absolute abandonment, to a break with all communal and cultural bonds. Nothing in contemporary culture is available to help reintegrate the victim into the world of the living. Psychoanalysis has the merit of being the only discipline that can really do something: find the trace of the

breaking point and of a prior time in which fantasy and dreams had their place. For death, one's own, that one has looked in the face, has no representation. [p. 73]

It has none, that is, except, occasionally, through a horrified other.

5.2. THE MIRROR OF HISTORY[9]

5.2.1. Madness, Trauma: The Same Combat

Rejecting diagnoses, then, is not a bias on the part of a particular school of thought or a global disparagement of medicine. Let us look more closely at this question. A distinction is generally made between the two entities: on the one hand, *normal* traumatic symptoms understood as a survival mechanism and an adaptation to extreme conditions, and, on the other hand, the same symptoms, described in the same semiological terms but, this time, presented as an illness described in large tomes of psychiatry. In the second case, we see that the link has been severed to one of the primary modalities of the knowledge of history, the modality that, as Sophocles says, seeks to bring bits of history without any images, words, or voice into existence for an other. Now there is no reason to make this into an illness, especially when these symptoms confront the suppression of truth.

The details of the real traumatic situation will inevitably appear in the transference. But, outside this dynamic, the upsurge of this past without a past is always socially disastrous. It is precisely the nothing, the nothing to be learned from history (Braceland 1946), impossible to inscribe and hence to learn. It is that no-thing, that negativized thing[10] that constantly returns to the same place in madness, so as to try to find its way back into history, when the trace of the traumas has been lost.

The proof of this is that, each time theory tries to dissociate madness and trauma, the social cost increases. Let us recall the consider-

---

9. In the Middle Ages, the word *mirror* was used in the titles of works reflecting the image of an aspect of the world (*Mirror of the World, Mirror of Good Women*, etc.).
10. In this case, the no-thing or negativized thing is the Freudian *das Ding*.

able error of Harry Stack Sullivan when the United States entered the war at the end of 1941. Called in as an expert, he advised that certain recruits be discharged on the basis of a prophylactic diagnosis of mental fragility. This recommendation had the quantifiable result of a percentage of psychic casualties twice as great as that of 1917, despite the discharge of over one and a half million men who received this diagnosis. All that was discovered is that a good half of young American men were fragile.

Without being aware of what he was doing, Sullivan had renounced his own definition of madness, though he had been defending it for years. He had always stated that madness is neither endogenous nor structural but eminently reversible in a context in which the value of speech could once again be taken into account: that is to say, in an interpersonal relationship. He had forgotten his one-genus postulate that "we are all much more human than otherwise" (1974, p. 271),[11] which, in times of war, is expressed as "each man has his breaking point" (Grinker 1945, p. 731),[12] whatever the antecedents.[13]

Close to the frontlines and the reality of combat, or, long afterward, in the hospital, clinic, or analyst's office, proximity is thus a crucial element of the transference: patient and analyst are put to the test of

---

11. In her commentary on this passage, Helen Swick Perry (1982) writes:

One phrase in the article is especially worthy of note: "The difference is wholly one of degree, and not one of kind." In this instance, Sullivan is referring to the difference between the schizoid and the schizophrenic, but this also includes any differences between the well and the disordered. This is, again, an early formulation of the one-genus postulate which underlies so much in this book. The expression itself was later made memorable by Frieda Fromm-Reichmann, M.D., in her work with schizophrenics at Chestnut Lodge. [p. 271]

12. "We found that no matter how strong or normal or stable a man might be, if he had to endure stress sufficient to reach his personal threshold, he would succumb to a war neurosis. A man's threshold is variable, and stereotyped performance from each human, as from an airplane engine, could not be expected" (Grinker 1945 p. 731).

13. "After 100 days of continuous combat, it appears that almost everyone becomes a casualty. . . . It has been recognized that there is a finite quantity of courage and bravery" (Kentsmith 1986, p. 93).

danger, terror, and confusion. The comparison with the battlefield situation is not specious: mortal danger is very much present. Analysts who confront it with their patients share with war veterans the tendency to tell those close to them about the adventure and its fortunate outcome. They have the opportunity to experience the polite silence, slightly scornful, that greets "stories" where a good, solid diagnosis would have done the job and confirmed everyone in the certainty of public opinion.

And yet the danger of psychic murder committed by diagnoses has long been known. Diagnoses may be made innocently by physicians, shrinks, or anyone who professes to keep at a distance the "ghosts" returning from hell. This is undoubtedly why the physicians of the first aviators initially rejected the term *neurosis* as "unpalatable" (Grinker 1945, p. 729). They replaced it with *combat fatigue*.

This "psychosomatic compote"[14] that offers protection from the tyranny of diagnostic labels is surely a litotes, not a denial. For the return to civilian life, or even the cessation of hostilities, does not stop the war. Therapists had observed, for example, that certain veterans, struck by the injustice of having been hastily diagnosed, could turn to "demagogues, psychopathic characters, and destructive personalities" who offered them the same unquestionable certainties.[15]

---

14. "The Greeks probably had a name for this fatigue. They did not call it 'combat fatigue,' but we did, and we withstood a great deal of criticism for so doing. . . . [L]et us admit at once that combat fatigue is a psychosomatic compote if you will, a semantic expedient and an emotionally neutral way out of a difficult diagnostic dilemma. . . . To be a purist about these diagnoses is all right, providing that one is far enough removed not to have to cope with the tyranny of diagnostic labels" (Braceland 1946, p. 591).

15. In his discussion of postdischarge problems, Grinker (1945) writes as follows:

We are also concerned with attempting to send men back to civilian life as independent as possible and as free from regressed trends as can be accomplished. Giving a man a medical discharge invites him to descend the toboggan of dependency, since perpetual veterans' medical care and pensions are his for the asking. The prognosis for good recovery should be as high in civilian life as in the Army, provided that rational and adequate methods of therapy are utilized. There are not enough psychiatrists to carry the load successfully and probably never will be. . . . The task is tremendous, but it must not fail, because the consequences would be a profound disturbance

For, stigmatized in this way, upon returning one is rejected or ignored by the people back home. Better to go in search of the disaster zones that are familiar to them, offered, in this case, by the fictitious constructions of those who, fearing neither God nor man, preach in a spirit of hate and the politics of love the apocalypse and destruction of all those who do not join them.

5.2.2. The Memory of Freedom

The enigma of this influence was especially well analyzed by a young man in the sixteenth century, Etienne de la Boétie. The celebrated friend of Montaigne (1580), who described their *philia* (the ancient Greek word for friendship) in the famous words: "He is myself" (*parce que c'était lui, parce que c'était moi*, literally "because it was him, because it was me") (p. 142), was only 18 when he wrote his *Discourse on Voluntary Servitude or The Anti-Dictator* in 1548, which was, incidentally, the occasion for the meeting of the two men. Attempting to understand why so many men are bewitched by the name of a single man, La Boétie writes as follows:

> I should like merely to understand how it happens that so many men, so many villages, so many cities, so many nations, sometimes suffer under a single tyrant who has no other power than the power they give him; who is able to harm them only to the extent to which they have the willingness to bear with him; who could do them absolutely no injury unless they preferred to put up with him rather than contradict him. Surely a striking situation! Yet it is so common [to see them] delighted and charmed by the name of one man alone. [Montaigne 1580, p. 4]

Now this leader is not so strong as he claims to be. He is in fact "a single little man, . . . the most cowardly and effeminate in the nation" (p. 6), one of those tyrants who, "if not one thing is yielded to them, if, without any violence, they are simply not obeyed, they become naked

---

of our social structure, since regressed personalities are followers, equally susceptible to leadership by demagogues, psychopathic characters, and destructive personalities. [pp. 738–739]

and undone and as nothing" (p. 10). Where does he get his power, then? From the fact that the body of the people has become the very body of the tyrant:

> He who thus domineers over you has only two eyes, only two hands, only one body, no more than is possessed by the least man among the infinite numbers dwelling in your cities; he has indeed nothing more than the power that you confer upon him to destroy you. Where has he acquired enough eyes to spy upon you, if you do not provide them yourselves? How can he have so many arms to beat you with, if he does not borrow them from you? The feet that trample down your cities, where does he get them if they are not your own? How does he have any power over you except through you? What could he do to you if you yourselves did not connive with the thief who plunders you, if you were not the accomplice of the murderer who kills you, if you were not traitors to yourselves? [pp. 11–12]

This complicity weaves an iron bond in which, paradoxically, loyalty has no place. Everyone, welded together by compromise, comes to the rescue of a being who is hardly alive, who is animated and excited only by destruction. Thus, gradually, "the fire from a little spark will increase and blaze even higher as long as it finds wood to burn" (p. 10), the transference of all the energies and goods to the aid of this single individual who does not love but instead seduces and makes himself into an idol in order to survive.

Thus La Boétie entreats the people reduced to servitude by the name of a sole man not so much to fight him as to neglect him: "I do not ask that you place hands upon the tyrant to topple him over, but simply that you support him no longer; then you will behold him, like a great Colossus whose pedestal has been pulled away, fall of his own weight and break in pieces" (pp. 12–13).

What has to be done is to step aside and be guided by the mirror of history: "There are always a few, better endowed than the others, who feel the weight of the yoke and cannot restrain themselves from attempting to shake it off" (p. 26). Such people never become accustomed to servitude:

> They cannot prevent themselves from . . . remembering their ancestors and their former ways. These are in fact the men who, possessed of clear minds and far-sighted spirit, are not satisfied . . . to see only what is at their feet but rather look about them, behind and before,

and even recall the things of the past in order to judge those of the future, and compare both with their present condition. These are the ones who, having good minds of their own, have further trained them by study and learning. Even if liberty had entirely perished from the earth, such men would invent it. For them slavery has no satisfactions, no matter how well disguised. [Montaigne 1580, pp. 26–27]

This is the case with our patients, who indeed come to look around and "cannot prevent themselves from . . . remembering their ancestors and their former ways"—though without knowing it, for they remember in the present tense, as it were. Instead, they ask us to recognize the forbidden link with their ancestors. They are the ones for whom "slavery has no satisfactions, no matter how well disguised."

Recent wars have shown the extent to which these passages, over four hundred years old, are still relevant. For how can we forget that the bond of therapeutic proximity that can assure a way out of traumas is ultimately rooted in an essential memory: the memory not just of the ordeals but also of the name of freedom: "the memory of their ancient liberty" (Machiavelli 1513, p. 21).[16]

5.2.3. The Political and Transferential Outcomes of Trauma

Although one of the possible results of traumatism is adherence to ideologies whose watchword is the eradication of memory, it is important to note that traumatic symptoms are themselves the sign of a memory that is too close, that is inscribed at the level of the body and represents a constant torment. The potential subject fights to get out of the

---

16. La Boétie had read Machiavelli (1513):

And whoever becomes patron of a city accustomed to living free and does not destroy it, should expect to be destroyed by it; for it always has as a refuge in rebellion the name of liberty and its own ancient orders which are never forgotten either through length of time or because of benefits received. Whatever one does or provides for, unless the inhabitants are broken up or dispersed, they will not forget that name and those orders and will immediately recur to them upon any accident. . . . [T]he memory of their ancient liberty does not and cannot let them rest, so that the most secure path is to eliminate them or to live in them. [pp. 20–21]

space governed by the whim of that flawless other whom we have called the Real other.

Analytic discourse is not immune to this risk. Quite the contrary: at certain times, the analyst becomes the incarnation of the tyrant. It is up to him to disengage himself and, using his own landmarks, to gain the proximity not only of the ordeals but of the memory that does not leave them in peace. In cases of madness and trauma, analysis thus starts out from that fact so well expressed by Machiavelli: the prohibition against, and impossibility of, recalling the very name of freedom.

Analytic experience with traumas and madness takes us, transferentially, through the different social and political situations described by La Boétie, including the worst of these. What does this experience teach us? Like it or not, analytic discourse can be established when speech emanates from a locus without a subject or from someone who experiences himself as a reject. In the proximity of combat and risk, this speech can be addressed only to a therapist who is familiar with the same field.

Thus a particular mirror is constituted, a mirror of history in which the intersection of two trajectories allows for a triangulation. Only in this way can essential facts, expelled from transmission, sometimes be located. Their existence becomes possible once again, after having been annulled, because an other attests to them, from an independent source, on the basis of his own experience.

When this transference, common to psychosis and trauma, is not theorized, everyone is tempted to hide cautiously behind the couch of the classical analysis of the neuroses and offer fine words and nice interpretations. Benevolent and condescending neutrality reinstates the rule of detachment and psychic distance. Fear of a crisis can lead to the killing of speech,[17] by always postponing it or reducing it to insignificance. The rigor of the search proposed by the patients is challenged, and the hermetic seal between patient and analyst is reinforced. Experience un-

---

17. Barker (1992) describes a session of electroconvulsive therapy, conducted in the presence of W. Rivers, by the neurologist Yealland, on a mute patient who had been sent home from the Somme: "'I am going to lock the door,' Yealland said. He returned to stand before the patient, ostentatiously dropping the key into his top pocket. 'You must talk before you leave me'" (p. 229). "Then he added, with great emphasis, 'You must speak, but I shall not listen to anything you have to say'" (p. 231).

dergone at the cost of so many ordeals is emptied of its validity, of its very contents.[18] Such a ready-made psychoanalysis discredits proximity, as though proximity were to lead to fusion or confusion. A totalitarian situation then slips into the banality of the sessions, perverting the analytic relationship into a scenario of submission (Milgram 1974).

A natural—or, rather, social—inclination thus distances everyone from the impressive knowledge of the Real these patients bring with them. In any event, from our world to the world of catastrophe the distortion of perceptions is considerable, as Gilda said (1.1.5). What was most important was to break the windowpane behind which she said she had been entrenched, in a monochrome and flat world, to create the relief she needed.

5.2.4. Interferences. The Birth of a "Transitional Subject"[19]

Though withdrawn into this background, as though she were behind a two-way mirror, Gilda was nevertheless able to observe and analyze the degree of fear—indeed, of terror, scorn, or cruelty—with which everyone approached her. When their delusions left them some respite, she and her fellow inmates compared notes on the caregiving abilities of the medical staff. They assessed the degree of fear of each doctor, psychologist, or nurse by means of tests consisting of the fits of madness of one or the other of them. The therapists were constantly evaluated, even, and especially, when they tried to escape this dangerous proximity.

---

18. "A question arises about how trauma develops: can the Real perceived here be absorbed into the Symbolic? In other words, is the trauma erased? The answer is no. The event may be genuinely erased, but the trauma has an incurable aspect" (Briole et al. 1994, p. 165). Our patients have taught us the opposite.

19. The term is Gaetano Benedetti's (1996). Benedetti practices in Basel, but we met him for the first time at the Austen Riggs Center in 1982, on the occasion of the jubilee of Otto Will. Trained at Burghölzli in Zurich and at Chestnut Lodge, where he met Will, Martin Cooperman, and many other analysts of schizophrenia, Benedetti developed an original theory of transference in cases said to be inaccessible to transference. It involves a profound understanding of psychotic symptoms as seen from the patient's perspective. Benedetti founded a triennial symposium devoted to the psychotherapy of schizophrenia, but psychoanalysis has eventually come to play an increasingly smaller role, even in the programs of these meetings.

The practice of proximity is not an attitude of easy conviviality displaying a demagogic intimacy with the patient. Everyone has his style, familiar or reserved. If it happens to be familiarity, this is none other than the uncanniness described by Freud (1919).

Geographic in origin, therapeutic proximity first of all entails the constitution of a safe space near the battlefront, where it is possible to recover physically and psychically while experiencing the possibility of speech in the proximity of the Real. This proximity then becomes the condition of the transference in the case of madness and trauma. It has taken the form of the "potential space" that Winnicott (1971) established with the children of the Second World War.[20] For Gaetano Benedetti, in his work with schizophrenia, it is the place not only of the transitional object but also of the transitional subject arising from an unconscious proximity shared by patient and analyst that Benedetti calls the therapeutic unconscious.

This is the proximity in which the analyst finds himself projected when the meaninglessness is such that he is reluctant to approach it, a proximity that he has been explicitly taught to mistrust. This spatial and transferential concept denotes a space-time between person and person that the Japanese call *ma* or *aïda* (Isozaki 1978, Kimura 1972).[21]

---

20. "The place where cultural experience is located is in the potential space between the individual and the environment. . . . From the beginning, the baby has maximally intense experiences in the potential space between the subjective object and the object objectively perceived, between the me-extensions and the not-me" (Winnicott 1971, p. 118).

21. The character *ma*, which can also be read as *aïda*, is written to represent the light visible between the two sides of a double door:

In Japan, both time and space were conceptualized with the word *ma*, meaning the space or vacancy between things. . . . Space was basically void, and even objects were supposed to have a vacuum within. *Kami* (minute spiritual elements) were considered to descend there and to fill the space instantly with spiritual force. It became immensely decisive for all artistic endeavor to perceive that very instant. . . . Space is perceived only in relation to time flow. The western concept of space is three-dimensional, but spatial depth is perceived within the structure of several time scales. *Ma* was used to describe both time and space, and this fact correlates with the mode of cognition in which space was perceived within the structure of a facet with time scales. [Isozaki 1978, p. 8]

We, for our part, have given the name *cut-out unconscious* to the place, beyond the looking-glass (cf. Carroll 1865), in which appear the double, ghosts, the *horla* (Maupassant 1887).[22]

Analysts who, in their individual styles, have been able to state and demonstrate in practice a proposition that is still scandalous for many today—no, psychosis is not unanalyzable—have thus established that it calls for rigorous and transmissible tools. Such instruments are correlated with the rifts in each analyst, which have made him sensitive, like a vibrating string, to imperceptible resonances. These potential harmonics are detectable to each clinician's reading or listening, though he is not always able to explain the flaws at the origin of the movement and form of his interventions, as Bion did from the beginning to the end of his work.

Such resonances, perfectly discoverable in the course of a session, reveal the fundamental dimension of the psychotic transference that leads patient and analyst, at first unknowingly, to find themselves on the same battlefront, not on one and the other side of a line of demarcation, of discrimination. In this framework the patient can no longer be defined by something radically different in the structure of his psyche, endogenous or primary, and deficient.

On the contrary: in a state of alertness he registers with an implacable precision all the elements necessary to his survival, with the aid of sense images that totally isolate him. Thus he is able to detect the slightest unusual modification of the human and nonhuman environment (Searles 1960).

The analyst has no choice but to let the impressions speak in him, impressions that will inevitably emerge in contact with someone on the alert, for whom everyone else is part of the world's hostility. One's spontaneous tendency is to trivialize these strange interferences, to normalize them, silence them, set them aside. The effort required to

---

This presentation was able to materialize the concept of *ma*, giving access to it at the boundary of the concrete and the abstract. In the theater, for example, there is the process of going from one place to another, in which space is considered as time flow perceived through the characters' experience. A bridge connects our world to the spiritual world, the entrance onstage signifying the appearance of a spirit from the underworld. Cf. also Lacan 1959–1960, Ch. 21, and Davoine 1989.

22. Maupassant's *horla* is cited by Freud in "The 'Uncanny'" (1919).

make oneself formulate them, or, more exactly, to relocate them in the place from which they come, is the materialization of this concrete proximity. The impressions are always uncanny, since they proceed from what has not yet become part of a language game. These points of interference are the site on which "everyone else" can turn into a single "someone else," as we see in the following story.

5.3. THE CHILDREN OF WAR

5.3.1. The Mother of Vinegar: Making Use of Coincidences

A woman who was a few months pregnant entered into a state of apathy and withdrawal from the world. She knew what was happening: the father of her children had left her once again, this time for good. That had also been the case with the preceding child. At this very time, her grandfather died in a distant province, where he had taken refuge in the period between the two world wars, fleeing the poverty and, no doubt, the dictatorship in his country of origin. Her pregnancy did not allow her to go to the funeral. Seeing her in such desolation, the analyst asked about this grandfather.

The patient replied that her despair was deepest when she thought of the vinegar that her grandfather made, several bottles of which he would give her every year. "The mother of vinegar[23] will dry up and die," she said, as though she were in a trance. The analyst, who did not want to let her slip further into that distant state, all alone, had a crazy idea:

"I make vinegar, too. Would you like me to give you a piece of my mother, as people used to do in the country, although we're in the middle of Paris?"

The analyst was aware of how egregious her suggestion was and apologized, laughing. But the woman was present once again, and she

---

23. This is the gelatinous mass that forms in alcoholic liquids during acetic fermentation (a cluster of cells of *Mycoderma aceti*). Without stating its Latin identity, this fungus used to be found, in every home, in the vinegar jar into which leftover wine was poured. It was considered a neighborly gesture to give a bit of one's mother of vinegar to someone whose own had turned bad.

agreed. The analyst went into her kitchen, cut off a bit of the gelatinous fungus in her vinegar jar, and put it in a plastic container. The patient took it with her, as though it were something precious.

The delivery went well. The child was a sturdy little girl, the delight of her parents (for her father had come back). Several weeks after the birth, the analyst got to meet the infant. But, three months later, in a state of panic, the mother brought to the session a moaning baby who, though she was being breast-fed, had not had a bowel movement for four days. She had already seen the pediatrician. The analyst would have preferred to send her to the emergency room of the nearby children's hospital, but the mother insisted on staying, as though this office were the only field of operations: proximity.

"What happened four days ago?"

The two *parents terribles* had had a huge fight, which must have frightened the child. The cause? The father's projected purchase of an old house in the mountains that he wanted to remodel; the wife wanted nothing to do with it. But the name of the village was immediately familiar to the analyst. This region of mountain pastures, resounding with cowbells in the summertime, was near the place where she was born. Everything professional in her protested against this coincidence. At the same time, she was looking at the child and imagining her physical suffering, since she herself had been subject, since childhood, to a similar symptom: intestinal blockage in response to the violence of meaninglessness. An intestinal occlusion had resulted in the past, one year after the "Chinese" operation (2.3.2).

Even as she told herself that, as an analyst, she most certainly did not know how to work with babies, or what to say to them or do with them, the name of this place evoked a gesture, and she took the little girl firmly in her arms, leaning the bloated little belly against her. For she knew, from experience, that these light massages help. In an authoritative voice, she told the child, while also speaking to the mom, "Well, they're really bright, your parents! They fight like cats and dogs, and here you go, thinking it's your fault! It's no use trying to block with your belly all that stupid rage, like a shield against nonsense!"

The baby did not take her eyes off the analyst. Suddenly, she let out the most marvelous fart, as long and sonorous as one could wish, delighting the two co-mothers and making them burst out laughing. The baby reacted with a half-smile.

The analyst had to be away the following week. When she returned, she learned that the poop that had been held in for four days had poured forth, that very evening, like fireworks.

"What was the magic?" asked the mother, perplexed.

"There's nothing magical about it," replied the analyst, after a moment's hesitation. Should she tell this mother about the irruption of the coincidence that had led her to take the baby in her arms in spite of her own resistance?

"This village that set off the war between you and your husband is the very one where I was evacuated, during the Second World War, when I was barely two years old. Battle was raging in this Alpine Valley, especially on the border, in the Petit Saint-Bernard Pass,[24] from which the city where I was born was bombed relentlessly. After the Liberation, battles continued between the Germans and the united forces of the Resistance of the Alpine Army. This episode in French history is not well known."

"You were 'evacuated,'"[25] the mother interpreted cleverly.

The analyst was surprised; she had not made the connection. A metaphor had just been born, amid poop and geopolitics. Against the explosion of hatred in the home of the little girl, as in that of the analyst as a baby, a safe space had been constructed, a sort of refugee camp, in an odd contemporaneity. The play on words had transformed the negative forces of the Real into liberating laugher. Thanks to this proximity, baby and analyst were ready for the next round. For this holiday was to be a brief one.

A month later, the mom once again brought her little one in a state of emergency, this time on the way to the nearby children's hospital.

---

24. Twenty-one hostages, among whom the analyst's father was to have been included, were killed here. This pass has been in use since prehistoric times. It recurs several times in this book, like the hobbyhorse of Uncle Toby in *Tristram Shandy* (Sterne 1759–1767). Uncle Toby constantly brings the Siege of Namurs into the conversation, and, like Don Quixote, enters the lists on this subject of fortifications on every possible occasion, boring everyone. But what would an analyst be, after all, without his hobbyhorse?

25. This word was epoch-making for French people familiar with the period of World War II. It refers to the measures taken by civilian and military authorities to relocate in advance all the inhabitants of towns and cities due to be attacked or occupied by the enemy.

Completely apathetic, the baby no longer reacted to sound, light, or anything else and no longer cried or laughed; the pediatrician had diagnosed autism and sent her for tests. Lying in the baby carrier between the mother and the analyst, the little girl was indeed far from the human world, a bit like her mother during her pregnancy. War had broken out again between the parents, with screaming and shouting. This time, as was the case every time, the father said he was leaving for good. The only thing they could agree on was observing their child and improvising tests, seeking objective evidence of abnormality in her. But, when fingers were snapped in her ears and candles passed before her eyes, the baby presented a stony face to her parent's inquisitive gaze.

The analyst, encouraged by their earlier proximity, leaned toward the child, telling her, in the same firm and angry voice, "So you've become a resister. You certainly have reason to. But just leave them to their Punch and Judy show,[26] and let's you and I talk a bit together."

The baby turned her head to the familiar voice and made a faint sound.

"Listen! She's talking," the analyst exclaimed. "All that has to happen is that her father sit in my place and that the three of you talk about what's going on, instead of hunting for your own circus freaks in her. That wouldn't be any harder."

The rest of the session was spent talking with this mother, whom her daughter now accompanied with babbling that became more and more audible, as in a crescendo. The three of them were really talking.

Mother and daughter came together for a few more sessions, during one of which the analyst happened to be holding the baby on her lap. The child continued to babble and smile while the two women spoke. One day the telephone rang, and the analyst, turning her head to answer it, abruptly broke the harmony of this three-way conversation. The baby screamed inconsolably, and it took the rest of the session for her to agree to forgive this gross impoliteness, which reminded her of the harshness of other situations. Since that time, the child has grown: she talks, she plays, she goes to school, and her mother has learned how to reassure her children with words of truth.

---

26. *Grand Guignol*: this was not only the puppet battle but also a kind of street theater that had its heyday during the nineteenth century and the Belle Epoque, in which the spectators were regaled with bloody crimes, dripping red with ketchup.

It was she herself who, one day, revealed the truth about the mother of vinegar. Her own mother, the daughter of the deceased grandfather, had just received a letter from a cousin, containing information about the family's past history. The mother immediately called to report what she had found out.

Seventy years earlier, the patient's mother had been a baby herself, the daughter of the young couple who had taken refuge in France after crossing the border. Her own grandmother had come from her village on the other side of the mountain to pay them a visit. She found the baby apathetic and without reaction and immediately diagnosed that the child was dying of hunger: her mother's milk was not nutritious enough. Her refugee parents were no doubt too preoccupied to notice this and look for a solution. The good advice of this third party led them to take the baby to a doctor immediately, which saved her life. So it was thanks to this great-great grandmother that the present baby could have the benefit of a grandmother and thus exist.

"The mother of vinegar," the patient interpreted, "was just an acidic mother who had lost her sweetness in the context of exile."

The analyst, who herself grew a mother of vinegar at home, had similar thoughts: she had nearly been born in prison, where her pregnant mother had been incarcerated by the Germans at the end of 1942, right in the middle of the war. She now said to the patient, "We owe our lives to mothers who were far from ideal, far from 'good enough.'"

"As long as other motherly women took over, who themselves had been through worse," concluded the patient.

5.3.2. Children on the Firing Line

After the wars of the period of decolonization, military psychiatrists were struck by the proximity of symptoms affecting soldiers, civilians, and even children, who had had no direct contact with the fighting. Today we have come full circle, with child soldiers being sent to the front lines in a real and organized proximity with gunfire.[27]

---

27. Cf. Arendt 1959. No matter what ideologies seek to legitimate such engagements, Arendt warns us to recognize the signs of totalitarianism.

In 1986, an investigation into the dramatic collision, eleven years earlier, between two American ships ascertained that not only the sailors but also their families had been affected in a major way. The wife of one of the crewmen consulted a pediatrician: her baby was not gaining weight. The doctor saw that the child was not being fed enough. Its mother, distressed about her husband, who had begun to drink after the collision, had her mind elsewhere. Six people had been killed and forty-six wounded on his boat (McCaughey 1986).

In 1977, it was finally admitted officially that such symptoms were similar to those found in soldiers, and it was decided to reactivate the Salmon principles[28] for traumatized patients and their relatives. For a long time, the magical belief in pharmacology as a panacea had rendered them obsolete.

For, even in children, the widespread use of psychotropic drugs leads to increased dosages in the face of resistance to treatment, to the point where a veritable chemical straitjacket is created and called upon to provide protection. The relevance of the allegedly serious studies that have multiplied since the 1980s, based on the illusion of objective observation and statistical curves, has finally been challenged, "for, in this regard, they in fact seem tautological, biased, at a time when neutrality is being questioned even in the basic sciences" (Bailly 1996, p. 13).

Children are the first to be pushed into proximity with strangeness, even if it is silent. From this interface, they bring back eloquent symptoms. As the child psychiatrist Lionel Bailly puts it, when "children hear the voices of the dead" these are most often the voices of those who died without burial, without a rite. This brief hallucination will cease as soon as it is heard by a therapist in whom the voices of the dead can resonate instead of remaining a dead letter. If the voice finds no echo, he says, "we have the seed of psychosis. . . . In the face of this call for symbolization, the causalist biologistic explanation in terms of the release of neurotransmitters deals with the vector and loses sight

---

28. "In January 1977, staff at the Portsmouth Naval Hospital Psychiatry Department observed that the kinds of psychological problems generated by military disasters were similar to those encountered by the battlefield soldier. It was hypothesized that the same early and aggressive intervention techniques developed during World Wars I and II could also be used to treat disaster victims" (McCaughey 1987, p. 133).

of the message being transmitted. There is no discontinuity between trauma and psychosis" (Bailly 1996, p. 32).

Frieda Fromm-Reichmann (1946) stated that emotionally traumatic experiences underlie all psychoses. The therapist's proximity consists of the exercise of tact to a superlative degree. For, in trauma, huge quantities of rage and resentment are expressed in response to this experience, and expressed toward the therapist as well. Fromm-Reichmann goes on to explain that the meeting must take place on an egalitarian footing, not that of preordained authority, even if the psychiatrist is an officer. What is this equality like?

In the case of children, who sometimes demonstrate excitation—including sexual excitation—that they are unable to articulate in words, so as to feel alive, the only possible reply, Bailly writes, varies with the interference of the transference. Far from pushing the child to abreaction and arousing affects that quickly get out of control, the analyst must not give in to a fascination, intrusive or passive, that consists in wanting to know everything or wanting to know nothing by simply observing. There is only one way to do this: he must begin by saying what he knows about the history, the situation, his impressions, and the therapeutic unconscious activated in him by the power of the images that have not yet entered a language game.

This renunciation of neutrality can be reassuring, in that it makes it possible not to deny death or the truth, however painful: yes, it is normal to have nightmares in such a situation, and this can happen to anyone. But, at the same time, we are well aware that the analyst's words also give rise to a negative transference and attract the destructive force of the traumatic event. In both cases, haven or tinder, it is important "to exchange one's own knowledge of catastrophes for the child's terrible knowledge, so that the child is not longer the only one holding it" (Bailly 1996, p. 102).

5.3.3. They Have Good Reason to Be Crazy[29]

We have been describing traumas that are identifiable in time and space. Even when the symptoms affect a descendant, the connection with the

---

29. Cf. *tô orthôs manenti* (Plato, *Phaedrus*, 244a).

traumatic catastrophe is often clear. But sometimes it is impossible to rewind the film. At those times, if the elements of the Real that have been cut off from the world of the living are to be made visible, recognized, and inscribed, we need history to act as our compass. Investigating history in the making means getting one's bearings when the compass needle is spinning in the zones of the spasms of time. The search is for names lost, people betrayed, facts covered up on the border with the wild space in which the Erinyes of vengeance fill the air with their formless howling (Loraux 1990). John Ford's film, *The Man Who Shot Liberty Valence* (1962), is a perfect representation of such a moment when time stops and official history is rewritten on the basis of betrayal, silence, and lies; the tone is on the level of classical tragedy, and the name of the sacrificed hero, Tom Doniphon, is a phonetic sign to those who understand Greek, since it means "the monster slayer."

There is no relativity when it comes to betrayal: whether the scale is that of a nation, a village, or a family, the lethal zone opened up by this catastrophe in the domain of giving one's word results in the same confusion. Where there is no trust, inscription—that is, transmission followed by forgetting—becomes impossible.

In Sophocles's *Antigone*,[30] Polynices, who betrayed the city, is killed in a fratricidal war. His body is rotting, given to the dogs on the order of King Creon. In his commentary on the play, Lacan (1959–1960)[31] defines the space into which the heroine enters in order to bury her brother as the space between two deaths.

Between real death, which belongs to the cycle of decomposition and life, and death inscribed in the register of the Symbolic, between the rotting of the body and the ritual inscription of the name, a spacetime is inserted, that of the tragedy, which shows how the Real never stops not being able to be inscribed. In this permanent skidding with-

---

30. Aeschylus, Sophocles, Socrates, and Thucydides were war veterans.

31. Poe's story, "The Facts in the Case of M. Waldemar" (1845), also illustrates the suspension of time characteristic of this intermediate space, as well as decomposition as one of the attributed of the Thing: "[H]is whole frame at once—within the space of a single minute, or even less, shrunk—crumbled, absolutely rotted away beneath my hands. Upon the bed, before the whole company, there lay a nearly liquid mass of loathsome—of detestable putridity" (p. 663).

out traction, monsters, figures of the unspeakable and unrepresentable, make their appearance. All reference points are lost, all otherness, and hence the dimension of the subject, is banished. At the same time, the death instinct and the repetition compulsion are in fact reaching toward a tentative inscription. Antigone keeps on provoking the king so as to assert the unwritten laws, the sacred laws of duty toward the dead, even at the cost of her own death. And this is, of course, why she is crazy, as the increasingly exasperated Creon complains.

This is the madness of children who have seen too much. Whatever their age, to accompany them into the field of their rigorous action means leaving aside the fascination that always brings about the presence of the formless Real. Taking up this very question, Plato emphasized the connection between the Real, "that entity without color, form, or name, whose being is being" (*Phaedrus*, 247c), and madness, ultimately conceived as an implement of cure (244d). We offer here our own translation of this luminous passage, often obscured by inexact interpretations:

> But diseases, immense sufferings come from ancient [divine] angers and exist in certain members of a lineage. By occurring and doing the work of interpretation in those who need it, madness has found the way to remove them. By recourse to prayers and services to the gods, by carrying out purifications and ceremonies, madness frees [from illness] those whom it possesses, for the present and afterward. Thus it finds a way to release whoever is caught in a just madness [who has reason to be crazy] from his present evils. [244a]

Thus babies have direct access not only to domestic violence but to the rage of the Erinyes, which, charging down the course of several generations, can slip into a simple household quarrel. Suddenly the validity of the child's perceptions is denied, and the official doctrine offers him deceptive gestures, words, and silences. As a result, the baby knows too much for his age.[32] "I have legacies from babies. They work, babies, they work too hard for their age," the patient who called herself Sissi, Empress of Austria-Hungary, told the analyst from the depths of the mental hospital (5.1.2).

---

32. Cf. the expression *parentified child.*

5.3.4. They Know Too Much for Their Age

Let us call this knowing too much the knowledge of the Real, not able to be remembered as past but occurring as an arousal without chronological perspective. It is a knowledge that has no subject to bear it. At certain moments—birth, imminent death, becoming a father, childbirth—where the radical novelty calls for the giving of a name to inscribe what is happening here and now into the process of exchange, there is always a great risk that the tool of names will break. Then the continuity of transmission is interrupted on this point, and into this weak link in the signifying chain, in the "string of words" (Sullivan 1945, p. 214), there irrupts something that cannot be spoken in words, the Real, the uncanny, constantly seeking the doorway of language.

Hannah Arendt (1971) contrasts this signifying welcome of the new arrival with the anonymous mechanism, still current nowadays, in which people are reduced to numbers: "The sheer naming of things, the creation of words, is the human way of appropriating and, as it were, disalienating the world into which, after all, each of us is born as a newcomer and a stranger" (p. 100). It is in the name of this radical newness and its potential that Arendt always opposed the deliberate use of children for the purposes of war or to serve their parents' claims, however justified.

Now in the cut-out unconscious of a family line this knowledge of the Real may sometimes rush, with an incredible concentration, into a mind and a body too small to contain it. It is always the baby in the adult who knows too much for its age. The Real is the impossible, according to Lacan. Its irruption is a catastrophe that cannot be metaphorized, a break of continuity in the world and in discourse. But, since its nature is to burst the boundaries of the self, it activates similar zones in the analyst. When that happens, interferences and coincidences become the sole referents of what has disappeared from the exchange between people. How do we spot this moment?

The irruption of the Real into a session is made apparent by the fact that everything becomes "as if" and begins to obey a pseudo-rule of free association or even the rules of etiquette. The analyst is suddenly relieved of his role as other. Like Henry (2.2.5) or Ernest (3.3), the patient wants to stop right there: trust has been broken; words do not hold good anymore. This rupture may be repeated several times.

In the inaugural moments when the analyst must speak as an equal, all he can trust are impressions that, likewise, come from an excess of knowledge acquired on the shores of the catastrophes in his own family line. The analyst's own analysis introduces an asymmetry, but this is not the same as inequality: it has enabled him to approach these zones before such patients teach him to use it as a tool. Analysts approach these phenomena, in their variety, in terms like *countertransference, counteridentification,* and *projective identification.* Each has its validity, but we shall not go into detail here.

What can *project* mean, though, when the inside and outside of an oriented space are not constituted in this particular regard? In any event, the analyst's impressions are registered from the outset by these perceptive patients. Their formulation by the analyst simply relieves the patients of having more to do in taking care of him. "You can't imagine," Henry said one day, "how much we patients take care of you, even when we don't seem to."

In order to constitute an Other where one never existed, the analyst must thus name what is happening, aware of the makeshift structure being put together with the bits and pieces of these interferences, which are the only evidence of the registering of the inaudible and the annulled. He is never very proud of communicating these details but offers them as tentative trial runs, corresponding to precise moments, that he would, however, never dare to boast of publicly before his colleagues.

Supervision sessions teem with such anti-exploits, which some analysts relate shamefacedly even though they have been endowed, in fact since childhood, with the ability to work with patients like these. This knowledge, explicitly cut off from official conferences, is comparable to the knowledge of trauma. Unofficially acknowledged in the context of limited transmission to one's peers, it is exposed to the condemnation of official institutions considered guardians of the *doxa.*

5.4. THERAPÔN

5.4.1. Betrayed by One's Own

"Homer has seen things that we in psychiatry and psychology have more or less missed" concerning warriors, writes Jonathan Shay (1995,

p. xiii).[33] It hardly needs to be added that the same holds true for their descendants. There is no great distance between the elite babies summoned to fight on the battlefronts down through the generations and soldiers completely dependent, in battle, on the most basic needs: food, clothing, hygiene. They suffer from cold, heat, lack of sleep, and diarrhea, with constant fear in their bellies, always on the alert in a treacherous environment, in a state of perpetual change, alongside the wounded and dying who are shouting and groaning, "Mom."

But, like Barrois (1988),[34] Shay describes the second phase of traumatization, which is too often disregarded. It has to do less with the

---

33. "In particular," Shay states, "Homer emphasizes two common events of heavy, continuous combat: betrayal of what's right by a commander and the onset of a berserk state. . . . To my astonishment, I was told that knowledge could also flow in the opposite direction, that scholars of the *Iliad* would be better able to interpret the great epic if they listened to combat soldiers" (p. xiii). Shephard (2000) missed the relevance of Homer, when a therapist works with traumatized patients, as a transcultural and transhistorical invariant. Despite his keen historical analysis, he seems to confuse such a theoretical position with new-age revivals. There is no need for Shay to simulate cathartic rituals copied from Epidaurus or Sioux ceremonies.

In his comments on "ceremonial man," Wittgenstein (1930–1933) states that "Frazer is much more savage than most of his savages, for these savages will not be so far from any understanding of spiritual matters as the Englishman of the twentieth century. His explanations of the primitive observances are much cruder than the sense of the observers themselves" (p. 8e). Wittgenstein goes on to say:

> The most noticeable thing seems to me not merely the similarities but also the differences throughout all these rites. It is a wide variety of faces with common features that keep showing in one place and in another. And one would like to draw lines joining the parts that various faces have in common. But then a part of our contemplation would still be lacking, namely what connects this picture with our own feelings and thoughts. This part gives the contemplation its depth. In all these practices we see something that is similar, at any rate, to the association of ideas and related to it. We could speak of an *association of practices*. [p. 13e, emphasis added]

A convincing example of this method is Nagy's (1996) comparison of Homeric poetry with the songs of the medieval troubadours and ritual Apache chants.

34. On the second phase of traumatization, Barrois writes as follows:

> The last question is: What to do when all possibility of action has been annihilated and the man is reduced to passivity and impotence? In any case, uncertain charges of responsibility, scientific ideologies, and the frequent

absence or destruction of the imaginary orientation points in space and time than with the collapse of the symbolic bond, the betrayal by one's own: one's commanding officers or those who stayed home and spit on the veterans returning on the ghost road. This betrayal changes them radically. Whatever their previous problems, the dimension of otherness has been shattered. The social contract collapses. In this place of maximal insecurity monsters arise, chimeras that are part beast and part god. This was the way the pitiless, berserk Achilles appeared in Book 22 of the *Iliad*.[35] Defiling Hector's body, he no longer respects any law, even the laws of war that call for the honor due to the dead.

Is the Other who is the guarantor of the symbolic forever compromised, then? How to enter into contact with these inhuman sufferings, as well as with the capacities for resistance that likewise go beyond the human? When the analyst gives the patient his word along with his words, from his own fund, he is actually returning to him what belongs to him. It is in some way what is owed him of the language he has been robbed of in and by the silences in which he finds himself.

Jonathan Shay refers to Gregory Nagy's (1979) study of the *Iliad* in discussing the crucial importance of the buddy. According to Nagy, the wrath of Achilles exemplifies the problematics of trauma, inflicted

---

mediocrity of interventions by the media will never be able to answer the true questions that arise from the being who, often for the first time in his life, is placed before the absolute truth of death. Psychic traumatization is this journey among oneself, others, and the Powers. After the abandonment of the rupture, the second abandonment comes from men and society, who, after an initial attentiveness, assuage their consciences with a few months of various interventions and are of the unilateral opinion that everything is in order: the victim "is doing fine" and is not complaining, and there are always good souls who tell him that he has to forget all that, that with a little willpower . . . . As a result, a very great number of traumatic neuroses are aggravated by this second, purely social, rupture. Psychoanalysis has the merit of being the only discipline to really do something. . . . [It allows for] the necessary time, . . . in a pact that is in many respects extraordinary and often misunderstood by our culture. [pp. 172–173]

35. "Entreat me not, dog, by knees or parents. Would that thy heart's desire could so bid me myself to carve and eat raw thy flesh, for the evil thou hast wrought me, as surely is there none that shall keep the dogs from thee, . . . but dogs and birds shall devour thee utterly" (p. 410).

less by the horrors of battle than by the betrayal by one's own commanding officers, in this case the commander-in-chief Agamemnon. When the spoils were divided, the king of kings took for himself the captive Briseis, who was supposed to go to Achilles, the best of the Achaeans. As in *Antigone,* the betrayal of justice opens a zone of catastrophe, of the collapse of the Symbolic, in which our laws are no longer obeyed.

5.4.2. Proximity to Combat

In the space of proximity that is thus beginning to take shape, we find ourselves coming back to the etymology of the word *therapôn,* a word found several times in the Homeric epic. It designates a relationship the paradigm of which is that of Achilles and Patroclus. Linguists teach us that the word is very old. We can define its usage nowadays by examining its occurrences in Homer.

The *therapôn* is obviously in place in the context of war: he is the second in combat and the ritual double. He is the one who takes care of the other's body and soul, during life and after death. He inherits his weapons and is in charge of the burial rites; he is the one who will sometimes be visited in dreams by the soul of the dead man.

Jonathan Shay (1995) has inferred a transferential place for him: "the keeper of the mind" (p. 44) for the other soldier. The affects animating this vital relationship, in Greek *philia,* transcend those of sexual or filial love. The usual interpretative stereotypes completely bypass the needs and obligations of this mutual role. In the cases presented here, the therapist's words, the therapeutic space, and the therapeutic unconscious have their roots in this usage as old as war and words.

We cannot understand this notion, Shay explains, "if we do not know the human attachment which battle nourishes and then amputates" (p. 39).[36] As Bion (1997) testifies, the death of a comrade is a tragic

---

36. Shay continues: "Combat calls forth a passion of care among men who fight beside each other that is comparable to the earliest and most deeply felt family relationships. . . . We often hear that the death of a special friend in arms broke the survivor's life into unhealable halves, with everything before his death radically severed from everything after" (p. 39).

leitmotiv for all veterans. "You didn't live through it, you can't understand it." When we were children, our respective fathers drummed this into our heads. Both of them were taken prisoner during World War II and escaped several times.[37] They returned to be part of the resistance to the occupying forces; certainly not out of heroism they said, since they always had fear in their bellies, but because they could not possibly do otherwise. "You didn't live through it . . .": Was this refrain an attempt to erase from their memories the fact that we, too, as children, had been exposed to bullets, bombs, and imprisonment in the zones of combat and occupation? Or did they need to reassure themselves that a baby born in 1943 was too little to understand?

Combat evokes in those who are fighting side by side a passion for taking care of the other physically and psychically, equivalent to the earliest and deepest family relationships. Patroclus (like Sancho Panza in the comic register of another epic) is the buddy, the comrade, the squire, who can only be an equal in these moments of extreme danger. His death leaves the survivor feeling like an incurable half, as long as the dead man has not received a burial, the necessary but insufficient condition for the restoration of the social link.

No one has any idea of the proximity of those two. Each man is his buddy's other self. The Greek word *philia* thus refers to an unconditional bond, one that is sometimes stronger than the bond to one's relatives, unless, like Penelope and Telemachus, the latter rise, on the home front, to the level of that war. In such a context, the proximity of this bond is the condition of speech itself: only the *philoi* and *philai* can understand what the others, who did not live through it, cannot understand. It is to them that the chants and epics of the veterans are addressed.

Back to the war of 1914. A soldier learns via telegram that he has just become a daddy. In the trench, he shouts to one and all, "Who wants to be my daughter's godfather?" His buddy volunteers. Deprivation and the terror of combat transforms the men into one another's mothers: "The grief and rage that they experience when the special comrade is killed appear virtually identical to that of a child suddenly orphaned, and they feel that the mother within them has died with the

---

37. Thus both also have their place in Shephard's (2000) discussion of prisoners of war, pp. 313–323.

friend" (Shay 1995, p. 49). From that time, they live at times like walking ghosts.[38]

For the bond of combat erases the distinction between oneself and the other. When a soldier speaks of his buddy's death, we always hear, "It should have been me." Or, in the words of Chronis Missios (1985), who was a political prisoner for thirty years in Greece and learned to read and write in prison at the age of 16, at least you, the buddy, "got to die first." Some of the men who survived the Napoleonic wars, like Captain Coignet or Balzac's Colonel Chabert, as well as the wars of the Second Empire or the world wars, also learned how to transmit their epic by writing, in spite of their destitution as veterans (Balzac 1832, Coignet 1850, Déguignet 1999). These accounts all describe the dead comrade to whom one owes one's life.

The veterans of modern wars have the same feeling as those of antiquity, even if they do not have a theology that can explain it.[39] Some find a solution in suicide, in which self-inflicted death seems less meaningless than a living death. Suicide is also a way to get a name inscribed on a tombstone. Freud (1919) could see traces of primitive thought in this ghostly double that can call you to the hereafter, animist beliefs that have not been surmounted.[40] But should they be surmounted, and, if so, how?

---

38. Our grandfathers, who had been gassed and wounded, returned from the war of 1914 taciturn and touchy. All they wanted to do is get together and talk about the war, singing and weeping at banquets. This is what we heard from our parents, who registered these scenes in the period between the two world wars. It seems that, after the defeat of 1940, the songs fell silent. We became psychoanalysts.

39. As Shay (1995) observes,

In the words of one veteran, these stories were "sacred stuff". . . . No single English word takes in the whole sweep of a culture's definition of right and wrong. . . . The ancient Greek word that Homer used, "themis," encompasses all these meanings. . . . What has not changed in three millennia are the violent rage and social withdrawal (Achilles' *"menis"*) when deep assumptions of what's right are violated. . . . When a leader destroys the legitimacy of the army's [fate] by betraying what's right, he inflicts manifold injuries on his men. The army's order is determined by *moira*: the lot, the right way to share, the spirit of sharing itself. [pp. 5–6]

40. "Most likely our fear still implies the old belief that the dead man becomes the enemy of his survivor and seeks to carry him off to share his new life with him.

This relationship—so intense that the Greek word *philia* that names it is hard to translate, since it is more and other than friendship and love—is a feeling woven in the domain of the Real, which it is difficult to approach in normal life.

In a novel entitled *Le non de Klara* (*Klara's No*) (Aaron 2002), the sister-in-law of a woman who had been deported to Auschwitz and Birkenau publishes her own diary, written in 1945, fifty years later, describing Klara's return. Klara kept on talking about three dead women, her inseparable friends—the Krakow friend, the Prague friend, and the Linz friend—none of whom she would mention by name. Several months later, Klara leaves for the United States, changes her name, and never again sees her little daughter, born one week before her arrest in 1943.

The most important point is that the sister-in-law, the narrator of the book, who takes in the baby, is also located in the dimension of *philia*, outside of which Klara would not even be able to speak. And yet Klara seems to have no feelings, and the exchanges are not without a certain harshness. Even after the war, however, *philia*, which made it possible to survive, is what makes survival possible in the written account after the same fifty-year delay that we have mentioned before. Outside this dimension, no *epos* (meaning "a saying" in Greek) is possible.

Gregory Nagy (1979) describes the basic framework of the epic as the account that veterans address to other *philoi,* who are themselves veterans, actors in the same battles, or their descendants. Only they know what it's all about, since they take part in this terrible knowledge of the Real. But such knowledge does not consist solely of information. It is a powerful expectation, an unconditional assent that mobilizes the survivor, or the poet, animating the desire to sing the epic.

This "mover," as Nagy (1996) calls it, also mobilizes the transference in this situation, a transference so special that, without it, nothing can be said about trauma or madness. Nagy sought the origins of this concept in the language of southwestern France in the twelfth-century cradle

---

Considering our unchanged attitude toward death, we might rather enquire what has become of the repression, which is the necessary condition of a primitive feeling recurring in the shape of something uncanny" (Freud 1919, p. 242). "Nowadays we . . . have *surmounted* these modes of thought; but we do not feel quite sure of our new beliefs, and the old ones will exist within us, ready to seize upon any confirmation" (p. 247).

of the poetry of courtly love sung by the troubadours, some of whom, incidentally, were rough warriors like Bertrand de Born (Nelli 1974).

As we have seen, a baby may be assigned the role of *therapôn*, keeper of the mind, for its parents, the boundary of their irrationality, remaining welded to them by a bond that may prevent any other attachment. This therapeutic relationship in the story of the mother of vinegar that we have related, a story in which the baby is the real hero, had its origin a very long time ago, well before her parents' quarrels into which the Erinyes rushed, pursuing with their cries for vengeance both family lines after emigration. In her aloneness as unacknowledged *therapôn*, the child found in the analyst a buddy, and also a body, exposed at the same age to the hazards of war, and on the same battlefields.

5.4.3. Psychoanalysis Upside Down

Such encounters are quite common; they establish therapeutic proximity. What happens here? In disaster zones, defined by the occurrence of the unspeakable, the signifying chain is interrupted, broken. What remains are disconnected things, events, images, and words: thoughts without a thinker, as Bion (1977) would say. On this point there is no subject of speech.

Once again we find the spatial metaphor of foreclosure.[41] Repression is not possible, since it depends on the signifiers of an inscription,

---

41. In 1954, Lacan developed his concept of foreclosure in connection with Freud's (1918) case of the Wolf Man. "We are not dealing with repression (*Verdrängung*)," Lacan (1966) explains, "since repression cannot be distinguished from the return of the repressed, in which the subject shouts through all the pores of his being that which he cannot speak about. This subject of castration, Freud tells us, did not want to know anything in the sense of repression. And to designate this process, he uses the term *Verwerfung*, for which, all things considered, we shall suggest the term *retranchement* [cutting off]" (pp. 385–386]; Lacan goes on to say that "foreclosure" might be the best translation. In his seminar of 1959–1960, he observed: "The frightening unknown on the other side of the line is that which in man we call the unconscious, that is to say the memory of those things he forgets. And the things he forgets . . . are those things in connection with which everything is arranged so that he doesn't think about them, i.e., stench and corruption that always yawn like an abyss. For life after all is rottenness" (pp. 231–232).

which is impossible in this case. Whereas the repressed unconscious can be defined, with Lacan, as the memory of what we forget, what we are dealing with here is a memory of what we cannot forget. Any effort, quasi-muscular, to repair this hole in the continuity of the linguistic fabric reveals these creases, despite any attempt at mending; they will quickly be discerned as social abnormalities. At the same time, they are the bearers of truth: *a-letheia*, the truth in Greek, is that which is not forgotten.

The first consequence of the break in the chain of signifiers is that, on this point, time stops, sometimes for several generations, with bizarre and maladaptive effects. For human time is made solely of signifying matter. If one of the vital signifiers in a chain is missing, as we have seen in the case reports, the clocks stop.

The second consequence is that, on the edge of the impossible where he has disappeared, the subject tries desperately to invent an otherness in the place where he experiences its inextinguishable absence. If mouths cannot speak, stones, animals, and the heavens begin to howl. *Griten las piedras*, as a famous Mariachi love song from Mexico has it. Reducing these phenomena to an auditory hallucination is obviously an inadequate approach to the stakes in question, which are always of a historical, political, and social order.

What, then, can get started on its way in the transferential establishment of proximity? We have seen that proximity is formed by making mutual use of the reliving of contact with the Real. "Might we say that, from the encounter of two unlinkings, a new link can arise?" asks David Foster.[42]

At those times, it seems as though the psychoanalysis of madness were a psychoanalysis upside down. Far from lifting a repression, it becomes the tool that makes repression possible and puts an end to the catastrophic effects of the Real, which, to be sure, never stops not being written, as Lacan says, but—let us add, following the veteran Wittgenstein—also never stops being shown, or appearing, to those who do not profess blindness.[43]

---

42. Oral communication at the Fondation du Nant, Corsier sous Vevey, Switzerland, October 1992. Foster is a psychoanalyst in nearby Montreux.

43. "Could there be human beings lacking in the capacity of seeing something as something, and what would it be like? We will call it 'aspect blindness'"(Wittgenstein 1945–1949, p. 213).

In this case, analysis initiates a sharing of speech on the basis of minutely recounted details, in a process that is, ultimately, close to epic. Those who encounter an other who is capable of this sharing, a *philos* equal to the task because he or his relatives endured similar ordeals, cannot prevent themselves from speaking, can no longer stop speaking.

5.4.4. The Man without Qualities

It is up to the analyst to analyze himself and, in contact with his patient, to investigate what has made him familiar with this field, working out the knowledge that enables him to respond to the transference and to vouch for the transference in the case of the Real. If he moves toward contact, he cannot do so under conventional professional armor. Let us recall that this field we are calling the catastrophic zone has been robbed of all customary imaginary consistency, all reliability. Thus the analyst can venture into it only if he keeps a low profile. What is more, the patient, who is used to being in this field, awaits him by knocking him off his pedestal, demonstrating his lack of qualification. The only quality that holds good there is that of being a man without qualities (cf. Musil 1930–1942), who is not unrelated to the "true man without a situation" and the "man with no rank" of Lin Tse.[44]

The analyst, too, overcome by details, risks, and coincidences, short on interpretations, carried along with the patient, can only state "what speaks in support of" these strange effects.[45] This is the only response

---

44. "Demiéville (1972) compares the man without qualities to "the true man without a situation": "A monk asks what this is like. Lin Tse gets down from his chair, grabs hold of the monk, orders him to answer himself. The monk hesitates, the master lets go of him and says, 'The true man without a situation is a shit-wiping stick' (formerly used in China as toilet paper). And he returned to his cell" (p. 31). Cf. Izutsu 1978.

45. Wittgenstein (1930–1933) makes this point as follows:

[W]hy does Frazer use the word "ghost"? He evidently understands this superstition well enough, since he uses a familiar superstition word to describe it. Or rather, he might have seen from this that there is *something in us that speaks in support of these observances by the savages*—If I, who do not believe that somewhere or other there are human-superhuman beings which we might call gods—If I say "I fear the wrath of the gods," then this shows

commensurate with the challenge. Thus our patients appear to us as potential warriors, not by tradition or by choice, but by experience, thrown into the fray early on as they have been. If the analyst is willing to join in the combat and not hide behind his mask, he will be able to tame the impossible by uttering an initial link in the signifying chain, one that arises from the therapeutic unconscious in the intermediate space of the session.

At such times, the analyst is moving toward a zone whose borders have been abolished. A battle gets underway, at first, in an attempt to reestablish them. In this way, madness becomes reason, "follisophy." In these clashes, the analyst finds himself doing what he must not do as a rule, such as speaking of the reverie he brings about and that comes over him.[46] This reverie unfolds as the auxiliary space of the fold, the tiny space into which a subject under pressure has taken refuge in resistance to destruction.[47]

Thus the analyst oscillates between, on the one hand, rendering the inquisitorial verdict of a psychoanalysis reduced to psychiatric labeling that confuses different categories of the unconscious (repressed and unrepressed) and, on the other, playing the resistant role of the double, who knows what is owed to the dead and knows that, if it is not given, the decay will continue to stink. He oscillates between the revisionist denial of the impressions that assail him and the utterance of an unconscious to which he has to reply. At the outer edges of the human, what must be done is meet up with the Thing with the Medusa gaze, not so much in order to humanize it but to bring it back into the pact of language and put it into circulation among men.

---

that with these words I can mean something or express a feeling that need not be connected with that belief. [p. 8e, emphasis added]

"Don't believe a word of what I say": Stanley Red Bird, the Lakota leader on the Rosebud Reservation in South Dakota, said these words from time to time as he was translating for us the ceremonial words of his friend, the medicine man Joe Eagle Elk, whose ritual double he was in some sense. Cf. Mohatt and Eagle Elk 2000.

46. Bion (1962) emphasizes the importance of maternal reverie in the positive outcome of projective identification.

47. What is a fold? "When a space is under pressure, that is, when it is projected into someone smaller, he accepts the pressure, except at a certain number of points at which he concentrates, as it were, all his original individuality. *And it is in the presence of these singularities that resistance occurs*" (Thom 1991, p. 23, emphasis added).

René Thom (1991) describes the properties of the catastrophic zones as the very ones encountered by fighters: a field of uncertainty and indecision, of coincidences and "the undeniable 'compliance of chance'" (Freud and Jung 1974, p. 220), in which signs are upside down, the arrow of time may turn back, and animals may begin to speak. Even analysts.

When Thom, a mathematician, cracked up after receiving the Fields Medal in 1958,[48] the year in which John Nash (Nasar 1998), his chief competitor for the award, cracked up when he was denied it, he emerged from the abyss with his catastrophe theory. Should his research be condemned on the pretext that he used theory and delusion at the same time in order to fight with the Real?

The hobbyhorses[49] ridden by analysts when they try to leave, with their patients, the same zones of breakdown, are sometimes also scorned

---

48. Thom (1991) gives the following account of this episode:

I think I was productive from 1951–1952 and 1958–1959. . . . It was at this time that I set up a discipline (the English would say, a gadget): cobordism. . . . This is what got me the Fields Medal in 1958. I think I stopped being productive in the years following this award. At that time, I constructed a sort of half-philosophy. This is how I characterized catastrophe theory. Some people said this was bad science coupled with bad philosophy. They may be right. But it seems to me that it is something quite original and, ultimately, quite valuable. [pp. 20–21]

Thom continues:

I experienced a sort of phase of depression. . . . I had to "let go of the pedals." But one has to do something nonetheless! . . . It was then that I turned my attention to catastrophe theory. . . . No longer able to follow, I returned, in a certain fashion, to more concrete situations. . . . Catastrophe theory met with considerable media success in 1974–5; thereafter, a rather more virulent critique descended upon this theory. It came essentially from the other side of the Atlantic, from the established science that basically never accepted this kind of theory. [p. 25]

49. The term is Laurence Sterne's (1759–1767):

A man and his HOBBY-HORSE, tho' I cannot say that they act and re-act after exactly the same manner in which the soul and the body do upon each other. Yet doubtless there is a communication between them of some kind,

as old warhorses. It is surely that that makes them suspect. But they also have something of Rosinante about them. Like a tiny trotting mouse, not much of a swashbuckler, the mount takes its time, stumbles, gets back up, and finally leads the entire retinue as the driving force of the transference.

We might as well name our hobbyhorses, since the patient guesses that they are there. "You're working on your own stuff," he says to the analyst, who is surprised to be seen through. Is this hobbyhorse a stuffed horse? "But it isn't yours any more than mine," the patient continues, seizing hold of this object that thus becomes an agreement between them. And what might "your own" mean in this case? "Neither you nor I exists, in this regard, as owners of well-delimited egos or of well-trained chargers, when you and I are struggling on a path strewn with pitfalls—what's more, a path on which we are always in the same place. Right?"

---

and my opinion rather is that there is something in it more of the manner of electrified bodies,—and that by means of the heated parts of the rider, which come immediately into contact with the back of his HOBBY-HORSE, by long journeys and much friction, it so happens that the body of the rider is at length fill'd as full of HOBBY-HORSICAL matter as it can hold. [p. 61]

6
Immediacy: The Coordinates of Time When Time Stands Still

6.1. BEYOND THE CAUSALITY PRINCIPLE

6.1.1. The Mad Tea Party: Speaking to Time

Pastor Rivers, the father of William H. Rivers, had a sideline that enabled his son to meet some interesting people. He treated stammering with a method he had invented, and he counted Charles Lutwidge Dodgson, better known as Lewis Carroll, among his patients; Katharine Rivers, William's sister, was one of the models for Alice (Rivers 1976). It is with guides like these that we approach the loops, twists, and dead-ends of time to which our patients lead us. The guests at the Mad Tea Party (Carroll 1865) have begun our work for us: "'If you knew Time as well as I do,' said the Hatter, 'you wouldn't talk about wasting *it*. It's *him*. . . . I dare say you never even spoke to Time! . . . Well, I'd hardly finished the first verse, . . . when the Queen bawled out, "He's murdering the time! Off with his head!" . . . And ever since that,' the Hatter went on in a mournful tone, 'he won't do a thing I ask! It's always six o'clock now'" (pp. 69–70).

Alice and the Hatter teach us that a time that does not pass is disruptive even when it comes to the normal functioning of metaphors. When the urgency of an attack of madness makes us feel that we don't have time, this is actually because "we don't have time," because we have just entered, with someone, into a world that is unacquainted with our everyday chronological dimension, so everyday that we forget it by assuming it to be a time of things. In any case, time no longer functions there in its customary direction, which goes without saying. As the Mad Hatter says, when Time speaks, it is best that everybody be prepared to answer him.

163

At a moment when his suicidal crises left him some respite, a survivor of one of those totalitarian worlds politically constructed as a
perpetual movement without ancestors[1] said to the analyst, "Little by
little, we're building a house of time. Take your time."

 And, indeed, one has to "take time," take it by the feelings, take it
around the waist. For the symptoms brought to the analyst have nothing to do with neurotic repetition. They are the stammerings of history.

The dynamics of the transference are complex at these times: on
the one hand, we must act on the emergency basis of a crisis or of acting out. But, on the other hand, these very symptoms reveal a time that
is not passing. The danger arises precisely from that oxymoron. How
can we stop motionless haste? Danger also arises from the collision
between the everyday time that manages human affairs and the time
of madness that could not care less about this management. Not to
mention the collision with the analyst's time.

The stories we have told have shown that getting time going again
depends on interferences that take the analyst back to problematical
points in the temporality he inhabits. He may recognize them and sometimes make use of them; he can never anticipate them. The production
of the future, as a grammatical tense, becomes possible at these bizarre
intersections, in the transference, of time loops or untimely moments.

The clinical vignettes that we shall be presenting try to sort out
these various stages of the production of time, which is the principle
issue at stake in the work of madness with regard to the history of family
lines.

6.1.2. Urgency

In the face of an imminent danger, the first therapeutic reaction must
take place as quickly as possible: this is the immediacy posited as the
second of the Salmon principles. In its application by war psychiatry,
immediacy calls for intervention in the twenty-four to seventy-two

---

1. "In the interpretation of totalitarianism, all laws have become laws of movement" (Arendt 1951, p. 463). "Terror is the realization of the law of movement; its
chief aim is to make it possible for the force of nature or of history to race freely through
mankind, unhindered by any spontaneous human action" (p. 465).

hours following the traumatic event (Holloway and Ursano 1984; cf. Marshall 1944).[2]

Speaking of civilian victims of air raids, Frieda Fromm-Reichmann (1946) adds that the psychiatrist should see them immediately after the trauma and provide physical and moral comfort. But that is not all. In the proximity of the transferential relation, the gaps in the story of the catastrophe and the emotional reactions are gradually explored, no matter how distressing this may be. This is done in an attempt to prevent the splitting off of the traumatic impact, which quickly makes its

---

2. "Memory and social context: S. L. A. Marshall noted that the experience of battle is confusing and its recall is rapidly modified—only immediate debriefing of an entire surviving combat group can provide a reasonably detailed, accurate representation of what actually happened" (Holloway and Ursano 1984, p. 104). The dimension of transference is essential. "The recall of events is likely to vary with the occurrence of different life circumstances, group memberships, and aging" (p. 107). In the islands that, coincidentally, bear his name, Marshall, as historical officer, devises the psychoanalysis of a battle that took place just after the fighting on the atoll of Kwajalein in January–February 1944:

> For four days, we went over and over that one night of battle, reconstituting it minute by minute from the memory of every officer and enlisted man who had taken an active part. By the end of those four days, . . . we discovered to our amazement that every fact of the fight was procurable, that the facts lay dormant in the minds of men and officers, waiting to be developed. . . . We found that the memory of the average soldier is unusually vivid as to what he has personally heard, seen, felt, and done in the battle. We found that he recognizes the dignity of an official inquiry where the one purpose is to find the truth of a battle, that he is not likely to exaggerate or to be unduly modest, and that he will respond best when his fellows are present. [Marshall 1944, p. 18]

Marshall continues:

> All soldiers, including officers, are equal in the informal court. They are simply looking for the truth. . . . The success of the inquiry comes of their good judgment and good faith. . . . Almost invariably the clearest statements came from the privates. We asked them not only what they did in the fight, but what they actually said and how they felt. They were usually quite sure of their recollections of their emotional reactions. But they rarely remembered just what they said in the midst of action. It was the man who heard another man say something who was most likely to remember the words, and not the man who had said them. [pp. 23–24]

way out of awareness, and begins its doubly silent work, if one waits too long.

It was in this emergency situation that the psychiatrists learned their profession in the combat zone. They learned above all to observe in themselves the effects of these times out of joint, and they learned how to analyze those effects. It is said that those who had formerly been child psychiatrists found it easier to depart from their stock of traditional training, which had surely already been undermined by their young patients.[3] These psychiatrists found no correlation between a brutal collapse and any given personality structure. They learned the hard lesson of the here and now of the transference, without systematic recourse to the cautious reconstructions of anamnesis.

But the dimension of immediacy is not so easy to handle, and not so readily tamed. After the initial successes come repeated crises, with symptoms that may sometimes be delayed for several years. Public opinion reasserts its rights: "Talking did no good; we told you so; you were deluding yourself."

This is to misunderstand the nature of the dimension of time on the edge of the Real. The forms of communication, verbal or nonverbal, take on considerable importance here, as long as we take into account the transferential relations that make them possible. For acute disturbances get worse or better essentially as a function of the Other. If the latter panics, or scorns, or accuses, or gets discouraged, he amplifies the symptoms and fixes them in place.[4] But the therapist's composure and sensitivity do not guarantee a lasting improvement either. On the contrary, after a period of immediate relief, the worst can come to the fore and be expressed precisely toward the therapist who was at first, like the others, being tested.

---

3. Braceland (1946), who makes this observation, states that it is "purely empirical," and that one can "simply intimate that the advance of psychiatry and the increased responsibilities of psychiatrists in many new fields call for a thorough revision of our educational methods" (p. 588).

4. "A treatment environment which communicates tension, helplessness, or disability continues symptoms and noneffective behavior. . . . Prior experience with complicated treatment techniques which rely upon drugs, prolonged bed care, subshock insulin, or frequent psychiatric interviews have indicated that only mediocre results were obtained despite the large outlay of personnel and supplies" (Glass 1956, p. 340).

Thus what is commonly called debriefing is not a routine procedure. If it excludes the transferential dimension, this communication may perhaps come up with inaccessible details, but it will only leave the subject more confirmed in his aloneness. Then everything must begin all over again, and with still more difficulty.

That having been said, the frozen time we encounter in immediacy always makes it necessary to begin all over again. Some people will feel the need, after the event, to repeat, to keep on telling what happened, in order to overcome their excitation; others will remain silent. Some sons of heroes, traitors, or victims will enter a crisis state with a fear that their parents did not experience. In those cases, we tend to think that their illness is internal, ongoing, whereas what is ongoing is this temporality out of time that abruptly opened out for their ancestors and endures, for them, in the very suspension of time.

Hence we find the paradoxical aftereffects that these events bring about in family lines and that call for the same immediacy in critical moments, sometimes fifty years later. For intervention *in situ*, in the midst of the crisis, is not sufficient. In these cases, urgency is the major parameter of time that does not pass. Urgency persists.

6.1.3. The First Crisis, the Nth Crisis

Such a temporality without future or past eliminates all pertinence from a causal chain. This is because causality implies the orientation of the arrow of time from the past toward the future. The principle of immediacy, then, does not make it possible to anticipate the crisis in the hope of preventing it. Nor do the times and spaces explored by madness correspond to the saying that where we have an effect, there must be a cause. Here we cannot refer to this reassuring program that to avoid the effect, all we have to do is act on the cause.[5]

---

5. On the inadequacy of a philosophy that interprets atrocities with the idée fixe of the "best of all possible worlds" and inflicts the principle of causality in a catastrophic field where it is manifestly irrelevant, see Voltaire (1759): "Master Pangloss taught the metaphysico-theologico-cosmologico-logic. He could prove to admiration that there is no effect without a cause, and that, in this best of all possible worlds, the Baron's castle was the most magnificent of all castles and My Lady the best of

In fact, it is only fear of the psychotic crisis that leads specialists to seek refuge in causalist reasoning of all kinds and to entertain the illusion of a possible mastery of a problem only if one intervenes in time.

It is clear that a patient who is given the opportunity to speak from the beginning of his first hospitalization will certainly be less prone to the disillusioned dejection that sets in with repeated stays in the asylum (Goffman 1961), less likely to become one of those despairing figures of formerly gifted young people who have adapted to a drowsy routine after years of treatment with mood stabilizers, like the brother of the Norwegian author of *Angels of the Universe* (Gudmundsson 1993).

We always wish we could have been there the first time around. But what does "the first time" really mean when time does not pass? In what time should we begin dating when it is as irrational as the demand of a patient who insulted the analyst for not having intervened ten years before his, the patient's, birth? The analyst would have been two years old then!

It is better to conceive of all crises of madness as beginnings: "The Thirteenth returns. She's still the first" (Nerval 1854, 1.1).[6] This kind of temporal paradox is exactly what enables us to receive a "chronic"[7] patient in a time of "first time," the first time of a possible encounter.

---

possible baronesses" (p. 16). In a general context of wars, shipwrecks, slavery, and fanaticism, the background of Chapter 5 of *Candide* is the Lisbon earthquake of 1755, which claimed over twenty thousand victims.

6. The French poet Gérard de Nerval (1808–1854) underwent attacks of madness more than ten times from the age of 33 until he committed suicide: he hung himself from one of the brand-new street lights in the middle of Paris after several hospitalizations. The sonnet "Artemis" continues: "She is still the only one, or the only moment" and ends: "The saint of the abyss is holier in my eyes." Nerval had lost his mother when he was 2. She died somewhere in Poland, having left the child in France to follow her husband, an army surgeon, in the Napoleonic campaigns. Nerval went back over the itinerary of this catastrophic topology in one of those uncanny journeys familiar to children of the wars. A powerful contemporary analysis of such a journey toward a haunting childhood in the context of World War II is W. G. Sebald's *Austerlitz* (2001).

7. This word paradoxically identifies the patient with time itself, according to its Greek etymology, *chronos*. In mythology, moreover, *chronos* is identified with the monstrous figure of Cronos devouring his own children out of fear of being dethroned by them.

Here youth is not the youth of one's arteries but that of a potential beginning, with its effects of surprise, awakening, astonishment, and amazement.

On the other hand, we remain baffled in the face of programmatic formulations that tend to resolve the crisis with the instruments of problem solving: what must be done, what must be avoided, what must be said or not be said. For, right from the first meetings, the analyst always has the feeling that he is saying what must not be said, not saying what must be said, doing what must be avoided, and not thinking of what must be done. The shock of this encounter forces him to wonder what is happening to him, the analyst, as much as to the other.

Gilda had something to say on this issue. When she came to the hospital, she had, she said, met doctors who wanted to tranquilize her, shrinks who listened to her in neutrality, nurses who spoke to her as though she were a baby, and occupational therapists who had her make clay pots. All this time, she was looking for someone who could sustain the shock of her experience.

Is this type of encounter the "solution" kind? In fact, the apparently logical sequence—first the problem, then the solution—is not relevant here. For, from the outset, an initial crisis is a solution, even a symptomatic one, that dissolves the customary reference points of understanding and abruptly offers others in a tone that expects no response. Transferentially, the response comes first, then the formulation of the problem of which the analyst will come to be part once he has become confused. It is up to him, once he becomes part of the problem, to formulate the intersection and coordinates of histories that go beyond both of them. Without denying the urgency and the need for clarity, it seems that the requested rigor ought to be brought somewhere else than to the causalist model: toward the deployment of interference, instead, and the keen noting of gaps, the analysis of which is suggested by the crisis.

6.1.4. A Minor Character

At this first contact, the analyst is thus not the repository of a piece of knowledge, even a supposed one. On the contrary, he is, as he begins, actually connected to the crisis, and as such he, too, has become the object of inquiry. Whether he wants to or not, he is part of the critical moment in which all expertise has its limits. Very quickly disqualified, he finds himself reduced to a minor character, scanned by someone who is apparently spaced out, confused, disconnected, indifferent to the impressive appearance of social roles but focused on what the analyst does not know about himself. A piece of knowledge without a subject is trying to get back into contact with the flaws in the other, beyond the professional mask.[8]

From this conjunction a potential subject may be born, indispensable to research but hardly more triumphant. Antonin Artaud and Erwin Schrödinger, contemporaries, theorize this crisis as a theatrical one whose center of gravity is an unpretentious minor character, the "double" of Balinese theater for Artaud, who looks on in alarm at the apparitions of the beyond. Schrödinger (1956) describes him, almost in the same terms, as the figure of the subject of knowledge.[9]

> Only a small fraction of species have embarked on "getting themselves a brain." And before that happened, should it all have been a performance to empty stalls? Nay, may we call a world that nobody contemplates even that? . . . But a world existing for many millions of years without any mind being aware of it, contemplating it, is it anything at all? Has it existed? . . . Sometimes a painter introduces into his larger picture, or a poet into his long poem, an unpretending subordinate character who is himself. Thus the poet of the *Odyssey* has, I suppose, meant himself by the blind bard who, in the hall of the Phaeacians, sings about the battles of Troy and moves the battered hero to tears. . . . To me, this seems to be the best simile of the bewildering double role of the mind. On the one hand, mind is the artist who has produced the whole; in the accomplished work, however, it is but an insignificant accessory that might be absent without detracting from the total effect. [pp. 146–148]

---

8. Cf. Bion's (1975) "thoughts without a thinker" (p. 176) and Wittgenstein's (1945–1949) observation: "Any interpretation still hangs in the air with what it interprets and cannot give it any support. Interpretations by themselves do not determine meaning" (§ 198).

9. Artaud (1931–1936) mentions "warriors in a state of trance and of perpetual war. . . . There is still the eminently realistic performance of the double, who is terrified by these apparitions from the beyond" (p. 216).

There can be no better way to compare the discrete emergence both of the subject of the trauma and the subject of scientific discovery. Schrödinger finds it in the echo linking an anonymous wanderer washed up on a beach to the song of a bard representing Homer, who enables Ulysses to weep and to name himself. Gregory Nagy,[10] too, emphasizes the moment in which the tears of things in the universe, and the certainty that the soul of the other is touched by them (cf. Virgil's *Aeneid*, I.462), can, through this echo, finally lend depth, relief, to flat, filmy representations.

The transference of the crisis responds at this very moment, in which it is urgent to recognize the subject producing a picture of the world that no one is contemplating. At the same time, this subject knows perfectly well that his role is an auxiliary and unpretentious one. It may be that, for some people, this acute knowledge gives rise to the belittling crises that follow the reception of a Fields Medal or a Nobel Prize. "I'm older than the earth," Sissi would say, to formulate the knowledge of which she was the repository.

This untimely knowledge is not immediately receivable. It rests, instead, on intuitions that the analyst absolutely must either disconfirm or confirm, even if they are sometimes embarrassing. This takes time, for the patient derives this expertise in beginnings from the larval phases he has passed through, in which there germinates a language in quest of an other to initiate a language game, an other who will respond to him and vouch for the relevance of his suggestions.

There is no reason to read a deficit into the fragility of beginnings; what there is, instead, is an immediate competence in the techniques of survival. There is a knowledge of the crisis that, shamelessly and with a complete loss of face, enables this man or woman with no rank whatsoever to locate in the analyst the points at which language is inchoate, not very well anchored.

Catastrophic zones call for the survivors and their descendants to have a baby's skill in an adult's body. These are beings who are on the alert, dependent on the unknown that is imminent, hardly sleeping, inured to a wide-ranging vigilance, extremely attentive to the subtle

---

10. Personal communication in our seminar on Madness and the Social Link at EHESS in Paris, May 2002.

variations in faces and atmospheres that already constitute an incipient language game with a cosmos in perpetual change. Thus they are quick to detect, in the analyst, the slightest connections to these tiny moments when the universe may tip over into chaos—whether the analyst knows this or not.

In the same way, analysts talk among themselves of their beginnings, of the first patient to make them tip over into a story of madmen in the uniqueness of a single, mind-blowing moment that will later be repeated on the occasion of other meetings. The crises of the patient, which are always the first crises, are answered by the analyst's critical moments, which are, each time, initial moments.

6.2. A TIME THAT DOES NOT PASS

6.2.1. Joseph: Presence of the Thing[11]

A man of 28, overwhelmed by threatening and ongoing suicidal ideation, was sent to the analyst by a psychiatrist. Joseph's father was employed in the civil service. His mother stayed home; she had been born in a very small village in provincial France, and Joseph was ashamed of her.

Stigmatizing her as an uprooted native, he described her as a savage, out of place in the capital: "My mother's stupid." This was his word. His father, more of a city man, found nothing wrong with this or, for that matter, with anything else, since, according to Joseph, he never showed any reactions. The marriage had transplanted his mother to Paris, far from a countryside and a culture neither she nor her ancestors had ever left. She lived in exile, in the middle of nowhere, as sometimes happens when populations are displaced.

---

11. "Let me add *das Ding* [the Thing], insofar as it is the very correlative of the law of speech in its most primitive point of origin, and in the sense that this *Ding* was there from the beginning, that it was the first thing that separated itself from everything that the subject began to name and articulate" (Lacan 1959–1960, p. 83). According to Lacan, the process of sublimation through which beauty tames the horror of the Thing is also connected to the boredom that signals its proximity, its presence, in a suspended time without a desiring life.

In fact, time had stopped, in the suspension of all modernity, around the period of the Debacle of the 1940s.[12] But, in the analysis, this time of war and occupation was never mentioned, although it corresponded to their move to Paris. The uprooting seemed to have left no trace. Perhaps only Joseph's eyes were able to detect a dullness, as well as an omnipresent boredom. On this point, in France today the 1940s still have a kind of negative existence. Like Auguste, who entered into secession, Joseph in his entrenchment rejoined the shame of this secluded epoch in history.

The analyst had the opportunity to meet Joseph's mother on one occasion, during a perilous phase in her son's therapy. Sometimes patients who take part in a symbiotic economy of survival bring to their sessions those to whom they are vitally linked. What the analyst saw coming into the office was a lively, elegant woman, precise in her account of the situation, very different from the disoriented being her son had described. Yet at the same time she really seemed, like Elliot or even Phineas Gage, to be living outside a world of which she could nevertheless speak pertinently and intelligently. During the analysis she would say important words to her son; these words would always be spoken in the context of the house in which she was born, in the village to which the family returned each year on vacation.

Joseph had never been hospitalized before. He had even had a nearly normal period of schooling, although he described this as a constant exercise in maintaining a wobbly balance, always linked to best friends to whom he had a vital attachment. Not one of these friends would fail him during the ordeals he was to experience, including during the analysis.

The first crisis came after a sentimental breakup with a girl whose life and medical studies he had shared for several years. When they separated, it was the end of the world for him. He returned to live with his parents, and, in the eight years that followed, he lived completely cloistered in his room. No career, no studies. He violently forbade anyone to enter, even to straighten up or change the sheets. Before this, he

---

12. In France, the Debacle is the dreadful period of World War II when civilian populations poured into the roads, by car or bicycle or on foot, fleeing in panic the advance of the German invader.

had accumulated in this room a diverse collection of objects picked up at random from streets and garbage cans. It was impossible for him to throw anything out, and the floor of the room had not been visible for a long time. Nor did he differentiate between his days and his nights, which were filled with unspeakable nightmares.

The analyst asked him, at the beginning, to bring in a piece of this sedimentation of time. He was quite reluctant but finally brought in a brass ingot weighing about forty-four pounds, stolen from a construction site just before he shut himself in. He dropped it on the floor. This weight, the analyst told him, could be an anchor, in the office, for the work they had to do together. Immediately after this, he found a little job to pay for his sessions.

At the same time, he became dependent in the transference: he would phone, often right after his session, then at all hours, even at night, saying only, "It's me." In this proximity, it even happened that, when his parents were away, the analyst fed him bread and cheese, since he would easily forget to eat for the several days between sessions. He was often forgetful, as well, when he spoke, no longer able to recall the beginning of the sentence he was uttering. When he tried to read, the memory of the beginnings of the printed sentences would get erased even before he got to the next line: "I have no memory," he would say, in the grip of a terror that made it impossible to confuse this observation with an ordinary deficit.

During these eight years, his primary occupation had been turning the pages of the same four albums of family photos. At the analyst's request, and very reluctantly, he finally brought them in. A baby, always the same one, was depicted twenty times on each page, as though he had been photographed every five minutes. In the albums there were also curls of blond hair, dried flowers, and small boxwood branches.

"Who is this?"

"My older brother, who was born and died nine years before my birth. I have nothing to do with this old story."

The analyst decided to keep these albums, against the patient's will.

Joseph continued: "One day, a kid in my class asked me the name of this baby whose photo had always been displayed on the dining-room wall. All I could answer was, "'It's me.'"

Then, in a sudden fury: "Why didn't you take care of me when I was a baby?"

The analyst was taken aback at this question; he calculated that he would have been 9 years old at the time. Thus he was about as old as Joseph's brother, whose short life had been spent at the end of the war. This period remained blank, like Joseph's blank, sleepless nights.

The reply to this displaced question arose the following night, in the form of a surrealistic dream of the analyst's in which there occurred the image of an "exquisite corpse"[13] at the very point where words and images no longer come into ordinary exchange. The analyst was in a hospital looking for his grandmother, who had died twenty years earlier. A nurse took him to a room where she, the grandmother, appeared to him, in a kind of crate, as a plucked, headless fowl that attempted to touch him with the stumps of its wings. This nightmare reactivated the immediacy of an uncanny state "between two deaths" in which, for Joseph as for the analyst, one of the living dead was trying to touch them: when his grandmother, to whom he had been very close, died, the analyst had not had the opportunity to be with the body. At the burial, for a few seconds he had had a sharp, hallucinatory vision of an empty coffin.

As bizarre as this might seem, he had had this dream in the place of Joseph, whose nightmares were always inaccessible. He decided to tell him about it, as a speakable piece of evidence from that zone between two deaths (Davoine 1989) at the intersection of their two histories. The immediacy of arrested time had found representation, whether by coincidence or, as the Surrealists would have said, by objective chance (Breton 1928).

Joseph listened to him attentively and, as was his habit, replied, "I don't understand anything at all; that has nothing to do with me." And yet this embryonic contact with the Thing, a naked and cold "little

---

13. The Surrealists were very fond of this society game, which consisted in taking turns writing a word or expression, or even a sentence, without knowing the content of what had been written by the previous players. The result is always surprising, sometimes comical, sometimes poetic. They used a strip of paper that was rolled up as they went along. The name "exquisite corpse" had always seemed odd to us, until we encountered the *cadaveras* of Mexico on the Feast of the Dead. On similar strips of paper are written poems and aphorisms aimed at and addressed to the person whose disappearance one so generously wishes in this way. Along with the skeletons of all kinds that are displayed or eaten and that walk about on those days, we find here the "exquisite corpse" of the analyst's dream.

chickadee" (as one would say affectionately to a child), haunting his aloneness, feeding on its younger brother's life, received in the analyst's dream the welcome of a grandmother from the land of ancestors, and not without terror. The inscription—if not in the imaginary realm of immediate understanding, then at least in the signifying chain linking an experience of the Real to "the words of the tribe" (Mallarmé 1876)— had an immediate effect.

Several weeks later, Joseph suddenly emerged from the grave of his room and found a paid internship in the computer field, which he then made his career. Shortly thereafter, he met his future wife, married, and had children, just before his father died of cancer.

His mother, who had moved back to her province, then made a strange request: she asked him to throw a large black stone into a well belonging to the family house in the village. The stone had always been in the yard, and she could not bear it anymore. He pointed out to the analyst that his brother's name, Pierre,[14] could be inscribed in this way, now that it no longer needed to be permanently represented by the object of the same name. He made the trip, performed this ritual gesture, and brought the analyst another stone, a white one, in order to "throw it into" the session, performing in this humorous way the same quasi-ritual gesture in the framework of the analysis.

After Joseph had illustrated for him, in this way, the theorem of the murder of the Thing at the origin of the signifier in the symbolic order as a process that got time moving again, the analyst returned his family albums to him, images that, from now on, would be those of the past and no longer of the present.

In this way, traumatism, science, madness, and poetry open a field of research in which we are not surprised to find that rituals have a place, rituals that we may just as well invent if they are not already available.[15] Lacan (1959–1960) describes this field as follows:

---

14. In French, the name Pierre also means "stone." The name of the village itself sounds like "Tournepierre" or "Turnstone."

15. In *Remarks on Frazer's Golden Bough*, Wittgenstein (1930–1933) writes:

Just how misleading Frazer's explanations are, we see, I think, from the fact that one could well imagine primitive practices oneself and it would only be by chance if they were not actually to be found somewhere. That is, the

What, then, is this famous field that we must not cross into? We are told: it is there that the unwritten laws rule, the will, or, better yet, the Δίκη [Diké, justice] of the gods. But, look, we no longer have any idea what the gods are. Let us not forget that we have lived for a long time under Christian law, and, in order to rediscover what the gods are, we have to do ethnography. . . . In other words, this field is hardly accessible to us anymore except from the external point of view of science, of objectivation, but, for us Christians, it is not a part of the text on which the question is actually based. *This field of the gods*, we Christians, we have actually swept it away, and *it is precisely what we have put in its place that is in question here, in the light of psychoanalysis.* In this field, what remains as a limit? A limit that has no doubt been there forever but that, alone, no doubt remains and marks its ridges in this field that, for us Christians, has been deserted, *that is the question I venture to ask.* [pp. 259–260, translation modified, emphasis added]

6.2.2. *Inferno:*[16] Appearance of the Real Other

But before these intersections that are the children of the transference,[17] we find ourselves being brought back violently to the starting point, where time stopped. Nothing changes, nothing has changed, nothing can change. It's always the same thing, no progress. The refrain is:

I'm at exactly the point where I was when I came to see you. Or worse. I'm going back on my meds. By the way, I've already gone back to a doctor who prescribed them for me and told me that, in my case, our

---

principle according to which these practices are ordered is much more general than Frazer shows it to be, and we find it in ourselves: we could think out for ourselves the different possibilities. . . . Think how after Schubert's death his brother cut certain of Schubert's scores into small pieces and gave to his favorite pupils these pieces of a few bars each. As a sign of piety this action is just as comprehensible to us as the other one of keeping the scores undisturbed and accessible to no one. And if Schubert's brother had burned the scores we would still see this as a sign of piety. [p. 5e]

16. Strindberg's autobiographical work *Inferno* was written in French in 1897. Published in Sweden in that year and the following year in France, it described Strindberg's experience of madness in Paris, between the Jardin du Luxembourg and the rue d'Assas, adjacent to EHESS and the Maison des Sciences de l'Homme.

17. And not "children of my silence" (Valéry 1921–1922), even psychoanalytic!

meetings are useless. Or they may be making things even worse! I read it myself in the paper. It's definitely medical. Is it or isn't it a disease? Positively genetic. It runs in the family, and my children are already showing signs. What do you have to say to that?

This is the most visible mark of arrested time and entry into the hell of despair. Like Dante on the threshold of Hell,[18] the analyst leaves behind all his illusions and, more or less secretly, wishes that this kind of talk and these meetings would stop for good—if only this patient could follow through and stop! Maybe his case isn't a matter for analysis after all. Surely psychiatrists are sometimes right.

From the biological argument to the psychoanalytic argument, the analyst runs very far away from the proximity we have described. But sometimes the therapist ends up "fleeing up to the need for flight, [arriving] at the foot of the wall of time" (Guimarães Rosa 1956, p. 100). The paradox is enough to make him change his mind abruptly. He suddenly sees that, where he is now with this patient, time is no longer functioning as it did before. The clocks have stopped. At that point, the hands may very well turn backward. "Where were you before you were born?" Zen asks in this regard.[19] Where are we when time stops? What point have we gotten to?

The temptation, as always, is to take recourse in the purely causalist explanation: "It's a relapse. It was inevitable; his illness is taking hold again. The upturn didn't last long. The problem is essential, endogenous, and has to do with structure."

But then he changes his mind again. A little more causality is helpful at these times. As a psychoanalyst, he rummages around in the past and, first of all, finds a way to account for present disasters in terms of past traumatizations. So as to be better able to analyze them later on, he tells himself with a bit of hope. Wasted effort. Like a donkey, the patient refuses to budge.

Here again, the fable shows that, of the two of them, the donkey isn't the one we might think. Wearing his dunce cap, the analyst has done all he can do. He is stuck in the pillory, exposed to public derision. It is as though the analysis had become a torture chamber to

18. "ABANDON EVERY HOPE, WHO ENTER HERE" (Dante 1309, III.9).

19. "What face was yours even before your parents were born?" (Izutsu 1978, p. 135).

annihilate one or the other member of the therapeutic couple—indeed, one *and* the other. We hear that psychoanalysis causes patients to decompensate, that the shrink is crazier than the madman, and so forth.

In this confusion, at one moment the analyst shrivels under the insults and the inquisitorial gaze of his patient, who is taking the place of other doctors and public opinion; at the next moment he is transformed, despite himself, into a monster capable of killing, since suicide is thrown in his face as the result of his irresponsibility. For suspended time may well degenerate into a time of suicide, and it is not rare for the abyss to open up, without warning, after an initial time of proximity in which the mere fact of speaking had produced an improvement and reason for hope.

Born from the collision with the Real, immediacy makes a break in the slow death of chronicity and also in the continuity of the initial progress. There is a fierce rebellion against any analytic interpretation that would posit the past as a cause. There is no "once upon a time." The analyst comes up against "that's how it is" (Beckett 1953, 1961). "Once upon a time" becomes "once upon no time."[20]

"So what is it?"

"The Nothing Thing.[21] 'That which in life might prefer death.'[22] Something. Any-thing. No-thing."

---

20. In French, we would say, "there was a time" or "there was no time" and might pun on *fois*, "time," and its exact homonyms *foi* ("faith"/"there was no faith"). To these homonyms, a nursery rhyme adds the place name *Foix* and the liver (*foie*):

> Once upon a time (*fois*),
> In the town of Foix,
> There was a liver merchant (*foie*)
> Who said, "Upon my faith (*ma foi*),
> This is the first time (*fois*)
> And the last time (*fois*)
> I shall sell liver (*foie*)
> In the town of Foix.

21. The French word for "nothing," *rien*, comes from Latin *rem* (from *res*, "thing").

22. "It is an ethical paradox that the field of *das Ding* is rediscovered at the end [of Freud's "Project for a Scientific Psychology"], and that Freud designates there as that which in life might prefer death" (Lacan 1959–1960, p. 104, in the chapter on the Object and the Thing).

In Gounod's opera *Faust* of 1859, the title character sings:

Nothing!
In vain I question in my ardent vigil
Nature and the Creator;
Not a voice slips to my ear
A word of consolation!
I languished, sad and solitary,
Without being able to break the tie
Which attaches me to the earth!
I see nothing, I know nothing! Nothing! . . .
O death, when will you come
To shelter me under your wing?
Well then! Since death flees from me,
Why don't I go toward her? . . .
And I am, with this beverage,
The sole master of my destiny!
Damned be happiness!
Damned, science, prayer, and faith!
May you be damned, patience!
Come to me, Satan! Come to me.

To which Mephisto replies, "Here I am!"[23] A bit kitschy, this aria of Faust's, sung at the depths of depression just before he takes hold of the flask of poison. Nowadays he would take his meds, perhaps overdosing. Fortunately, Mephistopheles is on guard: "Here I am!"

Faustian aloneness is being present to the Thing, to the exhaustion of time. The Thing is exactly that which never finishes not dying. But the devil, who invites himself there to an odd feast and breaks this dangerous face-to-face, is not at all like an empathic guardian angel. All he can do is promise the seductive other face of the Thing: beauty mummified in eternal youth (Lacan 1959–1960).

In our experience, the appearance, in the sessions, of the Real Other, of an other without otherness, for whom nobody is someone else but is reified into his Thing, has thus taken forms we would have much preferred to do without. For hardly have we recognized it but it is already seated in our chair, as Martin Cooperman said to us at Riggs. Facing the Real Other is an obligatory point of transition practically and theo-

---

23. Translation by Lea Frey, *www.area-database.com/translation/faust.txt.*

retically: it is the *pons asinorum*, the donkey bridge, of the psychoanalysis of madness.

At such moments of immediacy, we have been taken to task under the name of Mengele by the patient whose mother had been deported; we have been called Stalin in person by a son of apparatchiks. We have been assailed as Incompetent Medicine, responsible for the death of Joseph's brother, as Genetic Misfortune by Ernest, as the incarnation of Italy's Shame by Gilda and France's by Auguste and by survivors (or their descendants) of the colonial wars and the collaboration.[24] In the same way, William Rivers (Barker 1995) saw his twitching and jerking patient in the grip of the "Guilt of England" (p. 226). How could he have separated himself from that?

6.2.3. A Summons from beyond the Grave[25]

The only way to stop the repetition of such violence is for the analyst to acknowledge, reluctantly, that the monster has assumed his place and to take the time to name it, detach himself from it, and exorcise it. The experience is, again, that of time falling into immediacy, but in this case it is falling onto the analyst. This is an occasion on which he must not fail to undertake the battle, in his place, with the ghosts from the beyond. Interpreting as the patient's projection something that really concerns the analyst, as though nothing had happened on his side, or taking refuge in silence, procrastination, neutrality, and avoidance amounts to evading this encounter and its therapeutic potential.

---

24. The upper-case letters here emphasize that it is never a question of abstractions derived from causalist reasoning. "They have personality," says Bion (1963, p. 22). They are real characters, like Time for Alice's Mad Hatter and like the characters named and incarnated in the medieval Theater of Fools of the fifteenth and sixteenth centuries (Davoine 1998). According to Henry Rey-Flaud (1980), "the study of psychology has little reason to be in this world of marionettes. The interest lies elsewhere: in decoding the characters as bearers of meaning, insofar as each of them, as it were, represents a living part of speech, and in knowing that each of them alongside the others, and then all of them together, form a coherent discourse" (p. 102).

25. Cf. Faulkner (1936): "The quaint, stiffly formal request which was actually a summons, out of another world almost" (p. 5).

Now the identification of the monster haunting the analyst is a precondition for any remobilization of time. Whatever the culture, this dynamic takes ceremonial forms. Thus the killing of Bonhomme Carnaval is a prelude to the return of the sap. Masks, incarnating the return of the dead, suddenly invade everyday life in order to restart the flow of time, desire, and renewal (D. Fabre 1992, Zumthor 1978). More often than he would like, and when he least expects it, the analyst in his office puts on the mask of a wandering soul. Similarly, identifying the Real other who is returning in this way ensures that immobilized, frozen time will once again resume its course.

For, at these critical moments of the analysis, the living dead burst onto the stage with the force of the explosion that made even their name disappear. Such an erasure is not the privilege of the totalitarian regimes of the twentieth century. It can just as well occur on the scale of a family or community in the ordinariness of everyday life. Totalitarian regimes, for their part, exploit the wearing down of time in order to maintain the lie of a fictitious world based on arbitrariness and betrayal. In this case, in which the sole aim of betrayal is to perpetuate itself, another character, Violence, *la Violencia*, as they say in Colombia (Pécaut 1987), breaks loose, blind and berserk,[26] sometimes turning children into instruments of killing who use their own families as their first targets. This is the "banality of evil" (Arendt 1963) that establishes itself in place of all guarantees.

Now it is not easy to fool the devil: to dine with him, you need a long spoon. First, as we have said, right there in the session the analyst must recognize the Real Other who has taken his place, the very other whom the patient would like to defeat by suppressing his Thing. It is in the reflexive pronoun *himself* that the monster in fact lies hidden, difficult to dislodge from the alleged interiority. It pretends to act in the secrecy of harm that is self-inflicted, not only at the worst moment,

---

26. The word *berserk* comes from the Old Norse for "bare skin" or "bare shirt," referring to a physical effect that overcomes someone who goes before the enemy with no protection, animated by a deadly frenzy like that of Achilles when he threw himself on Hector, profaning his corpse, after the death of his *therapôn*, Patroclus, and the betrayal by his commander, Agamemnon. According to Jonathan Shay (1995), the *berserker* has broken the pact of language with humans. He commits atrocities because he is already dead and is no longer part of the land of the living.

often even when things are going better. In fact, the Thing that is to be killed is always alien to the self, as pure hatred, an attack on the link to otherness. Let us not forget that, in Greek, *diabolé*, the act of disuniting, is the exact opposite movement of *symbolé*, the act of reuniting before being able to name.

This is why the fight with the analyst involves real risks for both parties: the risk of putting to the test of the transference the violence that has cast bits of history into the limbo of nonexistence, where the consensus prefers to leave them. And yet not all blows are permitted, for while, in this complex arena, the analyst finds himself really incarnating a fiend, he must at the same time guarantee the safety of the maneuver. This is a paradoxical ordeal in which time, otherwise confiscated, can experience birth.

6.2.4. Rough Music[27] in the Face of the Confiscation of Time

The increasing rate of suicide among the young and the constant rise in deadly violence may be responses to such a confiscation of time. Charivari was the noisy, indeed, violent, but ritualized demonstration of young people in gangs. On certain occasions, for example the marriage of a graybeard[28] to a young girl, they would make a great hue and cry, banging on pots in front of the old man's door and demanding compensation for the girl who had been taken from their generation in this way. This was a way of reaffirming the laws of alliance in a situation in which the confusion of generations was a threat.

In this way, a social place was given to young people's rage. During the time of the ritual and the masquerades, they in fact embodied

---

27. On rough music (charivari) and the role of juvenile associations in the return of the dead, the Mesnie Hellequin, the wild hunt, the raging army, and the army of the dead, see Le Goff and Schmitt 1981 and Rey-Flaud 1985. Henry Rey-Flaud is a medievalist and psychoanalyst.

28. On the figure of the graybeard, which, incidentally, Molière himself was with regard to the daughter of his wife, Armande Béjart, see Molière 1662. On the battle between the deadly time of eternal youth and the regeneration of time, in which graybeards and bearded duennas play a role, see Cervantes 1605, 1614, Ch. 38 (let us not forget that Cervantes's father was a barber, a farcical way of inscribing the name of the father again).

the irruption of the army of young men killed in combat who were crying out for vengeance and demanding reparations. If he refused to pay, the old man at whose door the charivari was being held with all kinds of pots and pans and dissonant instruments was placed facing backward on a donkey and led through the villages as an object of derision. This custom was still in force in the Alps before the war. But it can also get out of control and become a manhunt, as in the film *Hunting Scenes from Bavaria* (Fleischmann 1968), in which the young people, in turn, are confiscated in the service of a totalitarian ideology.

For tyrannies have no scruples about extending the domain of youth to a youthfulness mummified in the imposture of suspended death. Nowadays they condition children and teenagers by means of images of virtual or real murders that desensitize them, glued as they are to their screens. As we know, professional training in the act of killing uses exactly the same techniques as certain video games (Grossman 1995). Thus the return in the Real of criminal acting out questions the denial of our societies in the face of death and killing.

As for psychoanalysis, which has worked for a hundred years to lift the repressions of Eros, desire, today it finds itself in direct confrontation with the effects of the trivialization of Thanatos. Here we see live massacres invading drama films and television news reports placed on the same level. The patients we are quoting here are quite insistent that this crucial question be asked, and asked precisely of psychoanalysis. Their symptoms hold a veritable charivari until they find an analyst able, first and foremost, to distinguish between fantasies and the Real.

6.3. FIGHTING THE GHOSTS

6.3.1. *Satori*[29]: An Omnipresent Danger

Jacques, a truck driver, was referred to the analyst by one of his pals at his karate club. His violence was getting out of control: he was beating up his girlfriend and fighting at work; he had just gotten fired yet

---

29. In Japanese, the title of this legend connotes illumination and awakening.

again and was talking about killing. At karate he seemed completely berserk.

Coming into the office rather tipsy, unshaven, charming, and provocative, he was visibly wondering what this woman, the analyst, wanted from him. He refused to sit down and inspected every nook and cranny of the room. Quickly, the analyst told him a brief story about martial arts, ordering him to sit down in order to hear it: a story of immediacy.

"Do you know the story of the *satori*? It's an invisible monster that suddenly appears from every direction and can guess the thoughts of the person it's chasing. One day it attacks a woodcutter who is busy felling a tree with his ax. 'Your final hour has come,' says the *satori*. The woodcutter immediately thinks up various strategies, which the monster anticipates right then and there, instantly announcing what had secretly crossed the man's mind.

"Tired of resisting, the man prepares to die, asking only that he be allowed to finish his task. He raises his ax. As chance would have it, the blade comes off the handle and kills the *satori* without any premeditation being involved."

On the spot, the analyst invents a moral for the story: it's OK to kill monsters in here, but not living people on the outside.

Jacques had listened with a distracted air, his gaze wandering around the room. Then he looked straight at the analyst. He knew that, he said. His father had died when he was 7. He had never been able to bear his alcoholic stepfather, who had aimed his rifle at him several times. He alone, of all his siblings, had been sent early on to boarding schools and reformatories, where he grew up as the living image of his father and a living remorse for his mother each time he returned home. This year he was going to reach the age that his father was when he died. So there could be no possible life for him after this. Something had to happen, or else . . . .

He got up, very agitated once again. And, once again, he had to have a very quick response. The analyst mentioned the hospital, the clinic. He replied that he'd had his fill of Social Services. He had always been in the hands of social workers and youth workers. So, the analyst said, she would see him here, in her office, once a week, on condition that he stop drinking.

"Forget it! You're not going to give me a lecture."

The analyst, however, ordered him to bring her his bottles and to find a job in order to pay her.

"These hands I see," she added, "seem to me to be strong enough for you to put them back to work." To calm him down, she continued speaking to him with an authority that surprised her. Her voice took a turn toward a language she thought had been lost to her. More precisely, it was the tone her grandmother in the country had taken when she spoke to young people, like this man, to whom she always gave work to do in the same way that she collected abandoned cats: she used to say that this reminded her of the time of the war.

Today, the analyst realizes that her grandfather, back from the trenches in 1918 after having been at the Chemin des Dames,[30] where he was a stretcher-bearer, along with the American or Canadian soldiers in both world wars who had been stationed near her home in the eastern part of France, must have acquainted her grandmother with these young men who had been turned into ghosts (Ducharme 1976; Ducharme's title, the neologism *Les Enfantômes*, puns on *enfants / fantômes*, "ghost-children"). This grandfather was a member of the regimental band, and, it was said, this is why he became a stretcher-bearer in the First World War.

This connection remained a mystery for a long time, until the analyst read an article by an Irish psychiatrist who had taken part in the war in the Falklands in 1982. As usual, specifically psychiatric resources were scarce, but he discovered that this psychotherapeutic role, essential for the morale of the troops, was traditionally that of the regimental band, in this case the Royal Navy Band. They therefore performed other medical tasks, in particular stretcher-bearing while under fire, and this was their traditional role in wartime (O'Connell 1985). This is how one learns to be a psychoanalyst, under the aegis of an ancestor who was a "music therapist" on the scale of microhistory.

For it is to the perspective of microhistory that we must return, like Sabina Loriga in *Soldiers* (1991), so as to overturn the purely repressive and negative view of power put forth by Foucault. "By orienting our perspective from bottom to top, we can reconsider the preconceived ideas

---

30. This was a failed offensive of the French Army on May 16, 1917. The failure and the losses that were sustained marked the beginning of a crisis of confidence and a state of unrest in public opinion and in the army.

that have gradually clouded our gaze. Only then can we break through the bureaucratic silence and let some furtive voices be heard, emerging from anonymity" (Loriga 1991, p. 225).[31]

The analyst continued talking to Jacques like this, in a tone that, at that time, she would have been ashamed to use in Paris: too loud, too many gestures, too many concrete images, the twisted syntax of a local dialect, crude words, proverbs, a mixture of mockery and respect, a kind of challenge to welcome the stranger after a silent period of observation.

The following week, he was not there at the time of his appointment. A little later, the analyst got an enraged phone call. He had come and had found the door locked. Had she, too, shut the door in his face? She began to have inner doubts: embodying arbitrary power once again, had she forgotten the appointment? Upon checking, she found that he had been mistaken about the day. He protested. Something did not correspond in their respective measures of time. She therefore told him to come in right away. He arrived in a worse state than the first time. He was going crazy and was thinking of killing himself; maybe he should be hospitalized?

She asked him at what time he had found the door shut. He had indeed come at the right time, but on the day before the appointment. At this very moment, the analyst had been working at the psychiatric hospital. Making use of this coincidence, she immediately gave their missed meeting the form of a story, as though it had taken place on another level of reality. We shall see how.

---

31. This book analyzes "the reasons why men need institutions and the constraints brought to bear on hierarchy" (Loriga 1991, p. 23). From this perspective, institutions are thought of, not as an impersonal system but as a formation of mutually dependent individuals. "The soldiers were easily subject to 'attacks of distress.' The sadness some called nostalgia was one of the deepest wounds of military life. It took hold of entire battalions. . . . Several superior officers hoped to overcome it through music and its ability to shake up the nerves by the effects of mechanical vibrations and rhythm, according to the physician Jean-Pierre Buret (1665–1747). Jean-Jacques Rousseau opposed this idea, arguing that music acted as a 'commemorative sign' that reactivated 'a bitter sorrow at having lost one's native land, one's former pleasures, one's youth.' In addition, the horizontal ties between the soldiers were strong. It did not take much for the barracks and cafés to turn into veritable echo chambers for the complaints of each of the soldiers" (p. 165).

6.3.2. Potential Simultaneity According to Schrödinger

To understand the mechanism of transformation into a potential simultaneity of two different juxtaposed temporalities, let us listen carefully, even with our modest means, to the physicist Erwin Schrödinger (1956) when he, too, comes down to our level and explains how he speaks to Time. After showing how to construct a "region of 'potential simultaneity'" between events that are in a "relationship of mutual non-interference without a link of cause and effect" (p. 161), he tells how it is always possible to adopt a spatiotemporal orientation that makes these events simultaneous.[32] He goes on to say that such things

> have become very concrete reality to us physicists; we use them in everyday work just as we use the multiplication table or Pythagoras' theorem on right-angle triangles. I have sometimes wondered why they made such a great stir among the general public and among philosophers. I suppose it is this, that it meant the disthronement of time as a rigid tyrant imposed on us from outside, a liberation from the unbreakable rule of "before and after." For indeed time is our most severe master, by ostensibly restricting the existence of each of us to narrow limits—seventy or eighty years, as the Pentateuch has it. To

---

32. Schrödinger (1956) writes as follows:

Given an event A, contemplate at any later time an event B outside the sphere of radius CT around A. Then B cannot exhibit any "vestige" of A, nor of course can A of B. Thus our criterion breaks down. By the language we use we have, of course, dubbed B to be the later. But are we right in this, since the criterion breaks down either way? Contemplate at a time earlier (by t) an event B' outside that same sphere. In this case, just as before, no vestige of B' can have reached A (and none from A can be exhibited on B'). Thus in both cases there is exactly the same relationship of mutual non-interference. There is no conceptual difference between the classes B and B' with regard to their cause–effect relation to A. So if we want to make this relation, and not a linguistic prejudice, the basis of the "before and after," then B and B' form one class of events that are neither earlier nor later than A. The region of space-time occupied by this class is called the region of "potential simultaneity" (with respect to event A). This expression is used because a space-time frame can always be adopted that makes A simultaneous with a selected particular B or a particular B'. This was Einstein's discovery (which goes under the name of the Theory of Special Relativity, 1905). [p. 160]

be allowed to play about with such a master's program believed un-assailable until then, to play about with it albeit in a small way, seems to be a great relief; it seems to encourage the thought that the whole "timetable" is probably not quite as serious as it appears at first sight. And this thought is a religious thought, nay, I should call it *the* religious thought. [p. 161]

The analyst, then, was constructing this kind of region of potential simultaneity to connect two events that presented no mutual relationship of cause and effect, but instead a "relationship of mutual non-interference":

"You came at the exact time to bring me the thing that is haunting you, so that I could enclose it in the boundaries of the asylum where I was then. This thing, which is beyond good and evil, must be enclosed in a safe place. If it's a matter of your father's troubled soul, as they say, we'll work toward his being able to find rest."

Jacques then burst out in hatred of his stepfather, who could not stand the sight of him: he looked too much like his father. He also mentioned an enigmatic act that came over him when he was a teenager in boarding school. He had charged like a beast of prey onto a 12-year-old girl who was crossing the yard. His pals had had to restrain him so that he would not kill her. She was not pretty; when he attacked her, she seemed sad, despairing, like a little old woman with her head lowered. He remembered her first name: Valentine.

"Of course," he concluded, "you can always talk to me about repressed sexuality. But, no thanks, things have always been fine in that department. I'll tell you: she actually looked like the misery of the world, and that's what I wanted to kill."

He had always found a job, as a matter of fact, even though he was fired periodically because of his fits of temper. The analyst would be surprised, he said, to learn that he was a safe driver who had never had an accident.

The analyst asked him to talk about his grandparents. "A bunch of drunks," he replied, admitting that he did not know anything about the preceding generations. She asked him to make inquiries. It turned out that they were no more drunk than any others; he was descended from skilled workers, blacksmiths, whose trade had disappeared around the time of the war. Their families had not held together either. Yet his father had tried to pick up the torch, and he was in the process of rising in society when brain cancer killed him. The family then sank back into difficulties again.

Several years after this session, his motorbike took him, as though of its own accord, to the village in which his stepfather had been living after the separation from his mother. He found him dying of cirrhosis in the hospital. They had not seen one another for nearly fifteen years and, shaking hands, were able to say good-bye: the farewell that Jacques' father had not been able to receive from his son. At present, Jacques has a family of his own and is self-employed.

In the meantime, this initial crisis was often repeated, until words and images could be supplied for traditions that had disappeared and lost voices that had fallen silent in the analyst's history as well. A rebel against any cause, this truck driver was in fact fighting to enter time. Time cannot be entered without a crisis.

6.3.3. Here and Now: An Interpretation in Search of a Subject to Interpret

The reader will have understood that the imminent acting out in the form of "killing the misery of the world" is an objective utterance that knows no time and whose subject is still to be born. Under these conditions, such a pending proposition can only be shown. To give the ostensive definition (Wittgenstein 1945–1949), things or acts speak in place of people. Wittgenstein would say that we do not choose the mouth that says, "An end must be put to the misery of the world." He believes such occurrences to be interpretations without a subject: "Any interpretation still hangs in the air along with what it interprets and cannot give it any support. Interpretations by themselves do not determine meaning" (§ 198; cf. Bion's [1982] "thoughts without a thinker").

Here we are entering the realm of excess (Gaudillière 1995), which even the rules of a martial art can no longer manage to contain. The betrayal of his own people, who barred him from the household, drove Jacques to this utterance, as it were shown rather than spoken, that began its violent course in search of a subject to interpret. For us, this quest covers exactly the same area as the transference.

When violence sets in at the beginning of the analytic work and during it, analyst and patient find themselves immediately objectified by it, becoming its Thing in a total loss of orientation points. Fascination can even set in when confronted by the sheer shapeless energy given off by the misfit, this desperado who has the face of an angel and knows no limits whatsoever. At such times it is important to speak quickly, in the here and now. But what *here*, what *now*?

The here and now of the Cause of the Immemorial Misfortune that triggered the catastrophe and that, in the course of the work, the analyst will not fail to embody—to the point where he is tempted to give up and hand the patient over to the pharmacologist. But where there is a danger of death, there is an urgency to survive. And if madness is going through so much trouble to lead its analyst into a mess, this is because the subject's survival entails passing through a world that has collapsed and resembles nothing but a formless and sticky paste. The sessions themselves do not resemble anything much.

For, if the analyst somehow manages to maintain the framework of the experience, he feels himself drawn in by uncanniness. Into this timelessness of arrested time, in this space without boundaries, there rush coincidences. They are usually the favorite object of delusional interpretations, to which an analyst must nevertheless not yield; at least this is what the clinician cautiously believes at first. But it must be admitted that the field of the analysis then becomes the ground for the "compliance of chance" (Freud and Jung 1974, p. 139).

Should the analyst let himself be carried along into this bizarre space, using "readymades,"[33] whatever lies within reach, he can link up with it "surrealistically," as Salvador Dali would say. Then the birth of a form begins to be woven, a morphogenesis, at the edge of the unnamable, that will later make it possible to inaugurate a language game where one had been impossible. In the case of Jacques, the readymade consisted of an old way of speaking in proverbs and concrete images that is not really used in Paris anymore and can be considered prime words, initiating a new language game with him.

---

33. Duchamp planned to investigate prime words, which, like prime numbers, are divisible only by themselves and one: "Planning for a future moment (such and such a day, date, minute) 'to inscribe a readymade'—the readymade can then be sought (with all time limits). Therefore, what is important then is this clockism, this quality of being of-the-moment, like a speech given on any topic whatsoever but at a given hour. It's a sort of appointment" (Duchamp 1934, p. 49; cf. Duchamp 1967).

Jacques' outbursts of violence, for example, detected the destruction of the symbolic functions of alliance and of promises by inciting catastrophes. Only the unexpected use, in the transference, of these ancient ways of expressing oneself, no longer customary now that everyone speaks through TV, demonstrates their symbolic efficacy. Stigmatized as obsolete and slightly ridiculous relics, or mummified in folk festivals, they were able to bring old accents of silenced voices back to life, forming a link between two country people, lost in the big city, who would never have met. For, in truth, this truck driver was not programmed for a psychoanalysis.

Waiting for symptoms to appear, all seems to be going well in families—except for one person, who is thought to be addlebrained. On the brink of acting out, he has, as he says, no self anymore, no personality, and may become "a danger to himself and to others."[34] Though fragile, he is nevertheless affected by a solid hatred, to the point where he fends off the best intentions and brings the severest acts of brutality down on himself. The analyst may possibly be able to take up the challenge if he first acknowledges that he was hit like a target.

Here madness appears as the investigation of a temporality snatched from history, an investigation through the modalities of the transference that sometimes looks like a tragic *agôn* where what is really at stake is a battle against ghosts. The cultures of warrior societies have given it various forms, including, for example, the Nô theater in Japan.

6.3.4. Ghosts of All Nations: Unite!

Nô, writes René Sieffert (1979), who translated these Japanese theater pieces into French, goes back to the High Middle Ages but continues to thrill our contemporaries.[35] It was theorized in the fifteenth century by Zeami (1420), an actor and producer who wrote Nô treatises and

---

34. Cf. the wording of the rules and regulations governing emergency psychiatric intervention, including, in France, the old law of 1838 that has been applied in the same terms for 150 years.

35. The more than three thousand Nô librettos are divided into "Nô of apparitions" and "Nô of the real world." It is the former that concern us here.

librettos. In the so-called Nô of apparitions, gods, demons, or phantoms of human beings appear, usually showing themselves to a pilgrim, of whom it is often specified that he sees the hero or heroine from the past in a dream. "In a process that is literally psychoanalytic, these ghosts render concrete the multitude of passions, like that of the fit of rage of warriors killed in battle" (Sieffert 1979, p. 21). The berserk state, in which the dead besiege the living, was thus familiar in the world of the samurai as well, as in the worlds at war today.

And so, when the eternity of time without a subject rushes into the very place where the analyst is, and the battle against the demons is joined, the field of the analysis encounters an invariant of all cultures and all times. A space of the sacred is marked out there. As an approach to these places and practices that are obligatory in times of catastrophe, Wittgenstein (1930–1933) invented the term *ceremonial man*.[36]

Thus it often happens that we tell our patients about the customs of other cultures in which man is not left alone to face monsters the way our children are in front of their screens. For example, in the case of Tristan, the master craftsman who was astounded at the awakening, in his analysis, of a fact that had lain dormant for forty years (the scene of the accident in which his sister had died before his eyes), the analyst related a Nô story. This form of theater was contemporary with the masters who, from the seventeenth century on, had imparted their skill to him. The evocation of this art of the intermediate space between two worlds, this practice of *ma* (see 5.2.4), enabled him to build and then to cross the bridge leading to his sleeping beauty. Unbeknownst to him, she had been omnipresent, haunting his creations and his existence.

Certain plays from the Japanese Nô tradition, famous for the beauty of its wooden masks, constituted a ceremonial theater aimed at awakening these facts that had lain dormant for centuries, for example in the form of lies, so as to affirm their truth before a public inhabited by these same lies of official history. This form of theater is very similar to a psychoanalysis of trauma. The setup is always the same (Sieffert

---

36. Using the notes and correspondence of William Rivers, Pat Barker (1995) explains the way his anthropological knowledge, acquired among the Melanesians, was interwoven with his therapeutic practice when confronted with the madness of war. His informant on the Solomon Islands appears to him, coming to his rescue, when he, the doctor, must deal with so many young men dead in battle.

1979): on a small stage, hardly larger than the analyst's office, a pilgrim, the *waki*,[37] arrives, on the way toward some destination. As he comes onto the stage, he meets another individual, a humble character busy at some menial chore, perhaps a gardener or servant. He asks this person where he is.

This is not just any old place. It is marked by a famous event, a battle, shipwreck, or massacre, whose memory the gardener or servant is honoring. The stage is set up as the "crossroads of dreams" (*yume no shimata*), where the pilgrim meets the humble character, who in reality is the one who performs the action (*shite*). In speaking to Tristan, the analyst explained the most important point: on the stage is a narrow bridge, the materialization of the intermediate space connecting to an elsewhere on the other shore, indicating in the East as in the West the beyond of our world: the world of the dead.

Tired from his journey, the pilgrim falls asleep in a corner of the stage. Then, from this elsewhere, a character from another era walks slowly across the bridge. His face now covered by the famous white mask, and dressed in the sumptuous kimono of the time of his former splendor, he chants the epic of his lineage and his disaster. On the stage, to the rhythm of percussion instruments and in a strangely violent voice, he shows and dances, in the temporality of the dream of the other, the perfidious murder that caused his death or the ignored offense that dishonored his name.

Without hesitating, the analyst added that, in her opinion, the analyst is like the pilgrim on a motionless journey through meetings with his or her patients. On the bridge linking the different temporalities, they show her, here and now, ghosts who are offended and furious at having had to come to a disowned death. They engage the analyst to approach this dangerous footbridge.

Under what conditions is the analyst capable of this encounter "at the crossroads of dreams"? Sometimes he actually does happen to dream; sometimes he is brought back to a bygone era when he, too, was a child who witnesses acts of violence that were covered over afterward as though by the ash from the eruption at Pompeii that engulfed Gradiva (Freud 1907). The child in the analyst comes to the rescue of the child

---

37. The use of the *waki* may overlap with that of the double as described by Artaud (1936).

in distress, frozen in a crease of time. Tristan remained petrified at the crossroads where his sister exploded before his eyes. Ernest, in a stupor, kept waiting to be summoned by the children who had disappeared before him. Others, like Gilda, stand still in the place where young men killed in battle lie unburied, Jacques goes berserk where populations, cultures, languages, and professions were destroyed. Like the *therapôn* in the epic, the analyst is set in motion (Nagy 1996) by this boundless energy found at the brink of the Real.

In this immediacy, which corresponds to very precise moments of the analytic work, there occurs a switching of places—rapid, instantaneous, unprepared for, involuntary—that contrasts sharply with the usual interpretative work. In supervision, analysts complain about this, apologize for it, and come to unburden themselves of a moment that, according to the official *doxa*, certainly is not psychoanalysis. This kind of alarm marks the precipitated (in the chemical sense of the term) encounter with an event out of time. In this case, supervision serves less to oversee analysts, who do not need this control, than to lend credence to a discovery: the discovery of an inscription that has been validated in this way, both in sitting with the patient and in the dialogue with a colleague. This double occasion is in fact a single thing: transmission.

To stay in Japan a bit longer, Zen has formalized this temporal paradox in which the boundaries of before and after, other and self, are blurred in the combined dialogue and challenge called the *mondô*, in which the visitor poses a riddle to his host. As we have seen with regard to the *koan*, if the latter does not immediately reply, he is pulled off his chair and the visitor replaces him at once. In this technique of suddenness, what is at stake in changing places is the production of words on the basis of the impossible. One of these riddles, which has spilled much ink in commentaries, is expressed simply as: "The child with white hair." It abruptly reveals the moment in which an archaic[38] youthfulness appears, the imperious youthfulness of the beginning of time of which we are the old contemporaries.

The vitality of these practices is still accessible to us through other ritual theaters handed down since the dawn of time. A Korean scholar, Kim Jeon-ok, tells us that, in his country, there is no theater, at least not as it exists in the West. Theatrical performance is intimately con-

---

38. In Greek, *arché* means both beginning and commandment.

nected with shamanistic rituals (*kut*), in which the actors, acrobats, and mummers, like the jongleurs of the past in Europe, are ferrymen who enable various different time periods, heterogeneous to our modern or postmodern primitivism, to irrupt onstage.[39]

6.4. THE CHILD WITH WHITE HAIR[40]

6.4.1. Mayday! The Measure of Time

"It's May, it's May, the merry month of May"[41]: at the beginning of the twentieth century, this song was still being sung in Paris by Yvette Guilbert, the famous singer and fin-de-siècle diseuse painted by Toulouse-Lautrec, who was Freud's acquaintance.[42] This old French song resonates with the celebration of May Day in the Elizabethan period of Merry England, before the disenchantment following the condemnation of holidays of pagan origin in the following centuries (Laroque 1988).

---

39. The program notes for *Flower, Water, Tree*, staged in Paris by the Korean Jayu theater troupe in March 2002, describe the play as follows:

> An imaginary country is undergoing a period of historic upheavals. The dominant classes are dead or have committed suicide. A princess who is still alive performs a *kut*, along with a company of women shamans (*mudang*) and street acrobats, to appease the anger of the dead. The past comes back and merges with the present. . . . The *mudang*, of common birth, have often experienced physiological or psychic harm in the course of their youth. These illnesses, considered to be omens, then take on the meaning of trials. Having overcome them, the shaman knows that, through ecstatic practices, he can serve as an intermediary between worlds. In Korea today, the *kut* are very active.

40. "The child's hair hangs down, white as silk threads" (Demiéville 1972, p. 51).

41. "The Song of the Birds," by Clément Janequin (1485–1558), begins: "In this merry month of May, let us all be of good cheer, let us arise, sleep no longer; let us dance, skip, and everyone have a try at the game of hugging and kissing."

42. On Guilbert, see Brécourt-Villars 1988. Freud, who knew her when he was staying with Charcot in Paris, came to hear all of her annual concerts in Vienna after World War I. Each time, he would send her flowers and his card. She soon came to confide in him, as to no one else, and asked him to help her understand the essence of his art. Yvette Guilbert's photo was in Freud's library in his apartment on Berggasse.

As we know, this day corresponds to one of the chief festivals among the Celts: May first was the holiday of madmen, fairies, and witches: it is Walpurgis Night. The feast of Beltane, it was thus the counterpart of Samain, the first of November, dividing the year in two. At the beginning of the summer and winter periods, these two dates permitted and restricted the irruption of supernatural and irrational forces so as to bring an exhausted time back to life. On May first, the maypole was carried ceremoniously from the forest to the village.

On Mayday, the Lord of Misrule would authorize the overturning of laws and would summon for the ritual May Games sacred figures including the Fool, the Clown, and the Hobbyhorse, who gave themselves over to war dances like the Sword Dance. Sometimes the Fool would fight with the Hobbyhorse, who was formed by a wicker mannequin around a man's waist, covered with a cloth down to the ground.

Isn't this figure, taken up by Laurence Sterne (1759–1767) in *Tristram Shandy*[43] to denote the slight craziness of all of us, a wonderful presentation of the clash between our patients' madness and the hobbyhorses of their analysts?

We may recall, for whatever purpose it may serve, that "Mayday," a phonetic transcription of the French *m'aidez* (help me), is also the final call of distress in cases of disaster. Here, it is surely the analyst who is about to shout it out.

In the month of May, Gilda's analysis had just reached a phase of progress. She had had no delusions for a long time. And yet, on that day, she came to her session stating, in a tone that brooked no reply, "I am the Goddess sent down to earth by extraterrestrials, with whom I am in communication, to announce that time is finished. The end of the world is at hand. In one month, I must return there. They are calling me back to them. My mission on earth is over. What do you think about this? I'm sure it isn't a delusion; they told me so."

---

43. "When a man gives himself up to the government of a ruling passion—or, in other words, when his HOBBY-HORSE grows headstrong—farewell cool reason and fair discretion!" (Sterne 1759–1767, p. 76). We want to emphasize the importance, in this book, of the figure of Uncle Toby, a veteran severely wounded in the groin (like the king in the Percival legend). In his garden, along with his *therapôn*, Corporal Trim, he constantly reconstructs the siege of Namur, where he was wounded, as well as all the sieges of contemporary wars.

She looked not anxious but terribly affirmative. The analyst immediately sensed the emergency of an announced death and thought that the extraterrestrials were the companions of her father, the young soldiers who died at El Alamein. She said not a word about this, since she, too, knew that the time was not in the past. Using the grammatical past tense was therefore of no use here. It was urgent to speak to Time itself, and hence in the present:

"Yes, you're right. But this time span of a one-month deadline by the extraterrestrials, from their world, may correspond to an entirely other length of time in our world: years, maybe even centuries. Light takes a crazy amount of time to reach us from the stars. So I doubt that the due-date thirty days from now is exact."

The analyst had said these words not so much in her haste to find an expedient as with an uncanny sense of a break in the continuity of time. It was precisely what would happen at moments when, in her own home, the gaze of some family member would go light years away and no longer be reaching her in the present.

Gilda let out a sigh of relief and agreed to the relativization of the deadline. After this abrupt incursion of a time of imminence, the analyst pursued a more reassuring course, and the two women parted calmly for their respective vacations.

Nevertheless, toward the end of this period, the analyst received a postcard depicting a Canadian rock group called *Sépulture* (Burial). This name, which seemed like a funereal omen, startled her.[44] When she returned, Gilda said that she had attempted suicide by overdose but had called the fire department herself before it was too late. Though she never took these pills, she admitted that she was continuing to get them prescribed so that she would have a supply of ammunition.

She had been hospitalized during this time in a military hospital, for she had been spending her vacation near a naval base. There, a psychiatrist had added a new diagnosis to her record of achievements, which was already quite full. But she told the analyst straightaway that her father's companions had now received a burial, a *sépulture*, as a

---

44. In connection with the funereal impression given by certain games or rituals, Wittgenstein notes (1930–1933) that "this deep and sinister aspect is not obvious just from learning the history of the external action, but *we* impute it from an experience in ourselves" (p. 16e).

result of her gesture. For they had always been present in her current life. For example, her father never stopped looking at the young people on the beach. This would make her uneasy. Was he looking at dead people or living ones?

Her own madness had lasted twenty years. Mussolini's dictatorship was of the same duration. She was now reading histories of the Mussolini period (1922–1943). For all of this time, she said, her parents, born in the 1920s, had "drunk the milk of the fascist Great Mother." Books had been written on the atrocities, but little mention was made of what might have been their childhood, their youth, their enthusiasm, their hopes. Never had her parents or their friends spoken among themselves about their childhood memories. After the war, only the present counted: one had to go forward. But, for Gilda, a silent negationism, erasing the past, had prevented the future from existing.

Twenty years: this was the time when her madness had explored the hell of our civilized societies. Like the Angel Lucifer, whom she might have been incarnating in her delusion, she had actually met men who were monsters in the public display of high political virtue and wondrous therapeutic intentions. She had exercised the art of unfolding the creases of time, in which the horrors of men try to escape the gaze of children, generation after generation.

6.4.2. The Transmission of a Catastrophic Immediacy: An American Gilda

How to hope when hope is impossible? How to think of the future when the future is impossible? How to think, at one and the same time, the suddenness of immediacy and the endless time needed for transmission? In going her "bloody rough way,"[45] Gilda had found that her parents had something to transmit to her. Before her analysis, since she could not express this in words, she had embodied, given her body to, this task in such cases; the transmission of what is essential is so much likelier to occur in convoluted and violent ways than in submission to the conformity of a given society.

---

45. Wittgenstein, in a letter to Rush Rhees in the autumn of 1949, wrote: "Please go the bloody rough way! Complain, swear, but go on" (cited in Monk 1990, p. 476).

A case marked by a more recent war (Jay 1991) teaches us what Gilda may actually have gotten from her parents. A black Vietnam veteran becomes unglued, over twenty years later, while watching pictures of the Gulf War on television. When his daughter returns late from a party, he rushes at her and beats her up: she "violated curfew." She is 17 years old, the age he had been when he left for Vietnam.

As he speaks to the therapist, his voice and his use of the present tense express urgency and self-disparagement, conveying a vital situation:

> "I know what those guys are thinking out there in the desert; I know exactly what it's like at this moment for them, because they don't know what's going to happen to them. They don't know that what they're going to do will last them day and night for the next twenty years. . . . When they come back, everyone who was never there is going to tell them what happened. And if they're stupid enough to really talk about it, . . . everyone will give them *that* look. You know. 'You got a problem?' It's hard to keep taking this shit." [Jay 1991, pp. 20–21]

Meanwhile, his daughter is the one who gets the shit. Perhaps one day she, in turn, will find a way to make this kind of knowledge known.

Her father, who had been drafted at 17, swore that he would never fire against the enemy. Then his buddy, standing next to him, was shot in the chest:

> In a frenzy of rage and fear, he aimed his gun directly at the enemy soldiers, trying to wipe out everyone he saw. From that moment, he became like two people living in two different worlds, sharing one body. . . . The self he had discovered in combat had become part of himself. . . . When he tried brokenly to describe his war experience, his parents, friends, even his wife did not want to hear, lost patience, withdrew, grew stone-eyed. He needed, they said, not to dwell in the past. . . . Since the Gulf War began, the ugly, vivid memories had erupted once more. . . . He found he could not suppress his anguish, could no longer keep the silence that was his ticket to normality. . . . The counselors, and even the others in the group, told him that the problem was within himself. [p. 20]

There is absolutely no question of repression or, as the counselors suggest, of externalizing what is inside. The past is present; the world is dangerous.

The American therapist admits that he has twenty years of experience and failures with this type of patient. The various specialized approaches have at best served to make the limits of these attempts understood, but they have been unable to relieve the veterans' permanent despair. Hypnosis makes them recall things they know only too well but does not help them explain to their wives why they close all the shutters at night and hide a gun under their pillow. Gestalt practitioners say "be honest with your feelings" but are at no time concerned with history. Only when the therapist admits that he is lost do they speak of the lessons learned in hell. We know these lessons, but we have to rediscover them each time.

The delimitation of a space-time between two deaths:

> The traumatized victim is not inclined to make a quiet request for understanding but feels driven to a howling, self-centered outrage that exactly corresponds in ferocity to the pain and terror of trauma itself. . . . The ultimate trump card is shame. . . . The shamed person feels both exposed and condemned, uncovered and seen through, in a sense flayed by the community's disgust and contempt. The trauma survivor already wishes on some level to disappear, to withdraw, to die.

The challenge of *satori*:

> [The trauma survivor] is challenging society's vision of itself, bearing witness to uncomfortable moral truths and demanding from everyone, including the therapist, a kind of moral accounting: "And where do you stand?" the victim asks, not on abstract issues of truth and justice, but on *this* war, *this* violence, *this* brutality, and *this* terrible thing that happens every day in our world, yours as well as mine. [p. 26]

No one chooses this, and most people refuse to see it, receiving this terrible knowledge with condescending pity, then with boredom, then with rage, finally with disgust.

The recognition of the knowledge of the Real: "The society that requires survivors to sacrifice their knowledge as the price of belonging is thereby itself morally and spiritually depleted" (p. 26).

How can these terrible knowledges turn into an acknowledgment?

6.4.3. The Devil to Pay in the Badlands: A Brazilian Epic of Battle against the Real Other

"War holds back from these things; it is relating them that is implausible. But whoever tells the whole truth is hardly lying." *Grande Sertao: Veredas* (Guimarães Rosa 1956, p. 306),[46] translated into English under the title *The Devil to Pay in the Badlands*, is the masterpiece of the Brazilian novelist Joao Guimarães Rosa. Written in the manner of oral tradition, this epic deals with the battle against the devil, represented by the perverse law of a certain Hermogenes, a man who likes to kill in order to destroy. The narrator, Riobaldo, is the leader of a warrior band of *jagunços* who impose law on the lawless *sertao*. The truth is that each of them may be tempted to collude with Hermogenes, overstepping the fragile bounds where resistance in the name of survival turns into sadism and neutrality into cowardice.

The analyst is confronted with precisely these fragilities and temptations when demons appear in the field. He is not sure he will not flee, surrender, or sell his soul. In the same boat as his patient, it is urgently necessary that he hold steady in his promise no matter what, in situations that tend to rule out this promise or give the lie to it. The path is risky, for the demons demand their share of sacrifices and suicides. The question: "Isn't living very dangerous?" (p. 46) is a leitmotiv of the book.

The time frame throughout the epic involves a preoccupation with a betrayal that must be avenged: "As long as he could not avenge the historical past of his father, he remained haunted" (p. 42). *He* is Diadorim, the *therapôn*, Riobaldo's second in combat.

To perceive these demons, there is no need to be an expert in demonology or animist religions. We are not spiritualists, we do not believe in ghosts, but our patients clutter up our offices with them. The analyst, as we have seen in many of the examples here, encounters the demonic in those moments of arrested time when, willy nilly, he is driven to enter into the world of boredom and hatred beyond desire and memory, where the impersonal murder of bodies and souls runs wild.

The Devil to Pay in the Badlands begins with the proximity of a

---

46. This book tells the epic story of the bands of *jagunços*, private armies in the service of the great landowners of the Brazilian interior, who engaged in actual battles at the beginning of the twentieth century.

doctor, Guimarães Rosa, and the aged Riobaldo, who has become infirm. This is how Riobaldo greets his visitor:

> "You clearly know the right way to think about things in addition to having your medical credentials. So I thank you. Your company brings me great pleasure. Strictly speaking, I'd like you to live here, or nearby; that would be a help to me. There's no one around here who can teach one anything. The *sertao*. The *sertao* is where our thinking is formed, stronger than the power of the place. Living is very dangerous. What? You aren't going to leave yet, are you? Not today. Not tomorrow. I won't allow it. Forgive me, but, in the name of our friendship, you're staying." [p. 38, trans. S. F.]

The power of the place[47]: the speech that is going to well up also springs forth from a bygone era. Like Elias Lönrott, the Finnish doctor who brought together fragments of the oral tradition and magic songs of the Finns to compose the *Kalevala* (Lönrott 1835, 1849), the Brazilian doctor deploys his skill toward a culture on the verge of dying. His epic sings of the death of a time at risk of disappearing and no longer being understood. On the border of two temporalities, the end of the chivalric eras is contemporaneous with all eras. This myth simply tells of the chronic degradation of the fragile dimension of the Symbolic. Like Don Quixote raving about the heroic times that are always in the past, like the Faulkner of the defeat of the South, like the Homer of the Trojan War, Guimarães Rosa is the beneficiary of a narrative that arrives belatedly—that is to say, too late:

> But do you seriously intend to travel all over this sea of territories from one end to the other to compare the assortment of what exists? You have your reasons. Now—I'm saying to myself—you come: you have come too late. The times have gone by; customs have changed. From the practical point of view, there is little, even nothing, that is legitimately authentic anymore. The great bands of valiant, brave men have been scattered; many who were *jagunços* are struggling, begging on street corners. [Guimarães Rosa, p. 38, trans. S. F.]

Oddly enough, the loss of ideals is the basis of the possibility of speaking the *epos*. After catastrophes, speech has been disqualified, and whoever takes it up again places himself in the rift from which it will

---

47. On the difference between a cartographic place (topos) and an existential place (khôra), open to otherness and to ancestors, see Berque 2000.

be able to spring forth like a confession of what is unheard of. Such an inaugural moment comes about very precisely and ritually when the medicine man, as a preamble to a Sioux ceremony, may describe the symptoms of his childhood and the vision that have marked him out with the incompleteness through which words well up and that set him on the difficult path to becoming a medicine man.

"I'm looking for your madness the way a dog looks for its master," a young woman said to the analyst. She had just left prison, where she had been sent after shooting at a policeman. To pass through the disaster zones, the analyst must to some extent confess how he acquired some personal knowledge of the field of trauma; for his patient, concealment registers as a prohibition of thought.

Riobaldo is presented as an invalid, as though, in order to be written, the *epos* needed the infirmity of the body and the wounds in the soul: "If it were not for my weakness due to the ulcer and the rheumatism, I'd gladly come. I'd guide you everywhere" (p. 38). Since he cannot be the traveling companion, he will be the speech companion, a speech closely related to the kind that wends its way in an analysis to describe lost time. Then another ghostly double may enter the narrative, Diadorim, the companion at arms whose presence haunts him: for he will be killed at the end of the book.

Up to the end there remains the enigma, for everyone, of the sexual identity of the *therapôn*. Once he is dead, he will be found to be a woman warrior.[48] The time of this courtly love has stopped, like the time of the warriors. Diadorim is the near and distant Lady. She plays the part of that which guarantees the insistence of life in the face of perverse attacks on linking (Bion 1967) and generalized destruction. We are using the word *perverse* here to describe both the instrumentalization of the human being and all undertakings of desubjectivation. Don Quixote's madness is precisely the antidote for this.

6.4.4. Don Quixote's Lady

In such clashes, imaginary reference points no longer hold good, not even those that distinguish male from female. This is, once again, the

---

48. In the series of woman warriors see Tasso 1581, Kleist 1808, and Tomoé in the Nô theater.

nature of these catastrophic zones: sexual identity is blurred in the same stopping of time. On the other hand, all the details of this story—constantly told, almost without pausing for breath—remain engraved in memory: "I know how I know. The body does not translate it, but it knows!" (p. 41). In this case, though the body's knowledge is inalterable, its form is not.

The Lady's body does not always occupy the poetic heights of the ideal. It rises and falls as catastrophes dictate. Dulcinea, as Sancho describes her, is a heavy, mannish girl who swears like a trooper; she smells of garlic and sweat and is nearly a pushover. But no matter: for Don Quixote, she is, as it were, the star, the empty place where all his thoughts and poems go; she is the one to whom he speaks, the interstice and brief interval of his freedom in the face of those who want to "take care of" him and lock him up.

In the second part of the novel, written in defiance of a forger, the hero yields for a time to the seductions of a duke and duchess. In their castle, Sadean *avant la lettre*, Don Quixote and Sancho are, without knowing it, reified and instrumentalized for the pleasure of their hosts. A perverse social link, named as such by Cervantes, is from then on the target of the hero's battles, until he finally extricates himself and regains his freedom.

In this ordeal he is helped by an avatar of Dulcinea: no lesser personage than an aged and menopausal duenna. To escape this accursed circle in which pleasure is taken at his expense, he avenges the honor of this ridiculous old woman before setting out on his way again. A musical comedy in which bearded duennas sing and dance shows the extent to which the Lady takes the place of the symbolic Other, the guarantor of trust when the name-of-the-father has collapsed. This feminine entity beyond the pleasure principle, beyond all the imaginary clichés of seduction, beyond mommy and daddy, simply represents someone in whom to trust, whatever her appearance. She is the new place that makes speech possible.

6.4.5. The Thing and Words

When they reach the analyst's office, on the brink of hospitalization or already hospitalized, these Don Quixotes and Sancho Panzas who know so much, know too much, certainly do not look like fighters; they look more like vagrants. They seem to be wandering between two worlds on the edge of our world. On the fringes of the city, they are marked out as apotropaic beings who no doubt enable us to sleep soundly at night. They are watchmen of another world: What other world?

"To think that that's what we fought for!" Uncle Emile used to say. An officer in the Alpine light infantry, he had landed at Dunkirk, penniless, on the way back from the victory at Narvik in Norway (April 1940), his bayonet at the ready. He had then joined the resistance in Savoy, been taken prisoner, escaped, been recaptured, and then sent to the concentration camp at Mauthausen. When he returned, he sent all his medals back to the minister in Paris.

A heavy burden weighs on the shoulders of descendants. What unfinished battles have these warriors bequeathed to them, and, at the same time, to all of us? Their war is snatched away by forgers who know how to take advantage of it; their story is cut away from the fabric of history, at the price of the stopping of time for their descendants. This is what our patients, in a final challenge, bring to be analyzed: an initial recognition that follows an itinerary closer to that of Antigone, persisting in burying her dead, dishonored brother, than to the Oedipus complex.

Thus we see what madness and war have in common. The common denominator is not a metaphorical use of the word *war* applied to family situation, streets, cities, suburbs. What is involved is a zone of overlap between the space-time of the warrior, of the mortal sacrifice always on the horizon, and the coordinates of a process of military engagement on the front of the Real, which is the very dynamic of madness.

Far from diagnoses of deficit, the analytic act in cases of madness may be compared to an arrow of language repeatedly shot at the Real Thing in order to force it to enter the realm of speech.[49] The analyst who foresees this combat becomes one of its actors, transferentially, in

---

49. "I need suicide in order to live," a patient told the analyst in such a challenge. After all possible explanations and interpretations, all of which were useless, she finally forced the analyst to invent, in a way that was minimal but not suppressive, the dictionary as the place of the word *suicide*, a place where they could both look it up, if need be, instead of crossing to the other side of the street—at the risk of finding something worse on that side.

an *agôn* (this ancient Greek word, meaning "fight," is at the center of classical tragedies) taking place at the end of time: the end of heroic times, the end of the times of memory, as much as at the end of the times of psychoanalysis. Don't we hear just about everywhere that, given the success of psychotropic drugs, psychoanalysis has had its day?

What if this were true? What if this were the cost of peace at any cost? History teaches us how much that kind of peace costs. But the psychoanalysis of the Real does not hear peace this way. It can be reached only through a battle to find the dimension of the subject of speech, of a symbolic otherness, a battle from which, to be sure, the protagonists return a bit numb. They are far from the triumphalism that rewards the winners up on the dais. And yet, most of all they expect to be expected with what they show us.

7

Expectancy: The Trustworthiness of the Other

7.1. *YES*: AN INITIAL AFFIRMATION

7.1.1. Trauma Speaking to Trauma[1]

In the middle of peacetime, the dissociated lessons of history are waiting for us around the corner of madness. In the universe of chaos it produces, proximity constructs the coordinates of a possible space, and immediacy constitutes the specific dimension of time. With expectancy, the third of the Salmon principles, we come to the symbolic dimension of alterity.

For madness can be defined as the state in which there is no other to respond to it. Indeed, what other could there be to preside over foreclosure, denial, betrayal, erasure, and the wearing down of traces and boundaries, if not a totalitarian other for whom otherness is reduced to subjugation—in other words, an other without true otherness?

The word *expectancy* certainly does not refer to the delays so familiar to analytic practice, in which matters are always put off until tomorrow and speaking is restarted the next time.

Quite the contrary: the term expresses the hope for life when life has been banished from the horizon. It sketches the outlines of an otherness that awaits you against all expectation, all logic, all common sense. In wartime, it emphasizes those others who hope that the wounded buddy will rejoin them and count on the inestimable value of their relation-

---

1. The reference is to the broadcasts of Radio London, received secretly in France after General de Gaulle's appeal of June 18, 1940, which began, "London here; the French speaking to the French."

ship. Now this new loyalty is the only thing of value from now on: the *therapôn* is, first and foremost, among them.

Logic would have it that the wounded soldier or the tranquilized madman be sent home to forget "all that": one must be humane, as the saying goes. But, when the mirrors are broken and the devil is hanging on your coattails, this return home does not always take place in the dimension of the humane. In this case, the dissolution of any place that might guarantee good faith had become a fact, and other people have become no more substantial than masks. When you have returned home, what gaze, empathic or scornful, can compare to the gaze of those who have helped you survive, those whom you have left behind like doubles, alter egos, who believe in your survival even if they are no longer in this world, who are anxious for you to live even beyond your own wish to live? And vice versa.

Expectancy is the expectation that an other will take over for you when you are exhausted, someone you count on the way you count on yourself, and more so, to feed you and soothe you. Food, drink, sleep: the vital needs are the only ones that seem to count, but they would be only mechanical feeding without the face, the voice, the gesture, and the gaze. The water or potato peelings that save your life, the eyes that cry out to go to sleep when danger arises, the warmth of a back when, in normal times, the lack of privacy would be unbearable: all survivors bear witness to the impossibility of surviving alone (Delbo 1970a,b), without an other, present or, if necessary, hallucinated. Our parents will never forget the anonymous person who secretly helps you cross the border, the unknown person who saves your life with a nod of his head and who will never be seen again, or who sends you a warning on a ragged scrap of paper: someone of whom you know nothing, of whom you would have expected nothing in ordinary times.

We have given the name *plural body* to such an otherness, a solidarity that Faulkner (1936) compares to that of maggots in cheese when "the old mindless, sentient undreaming meat that doesn't even know the difference between despair and victory" (p. 250) rummages around for survival. After all, the maggots will metamorphose into insects that are sometimes humble, sometimes splendid, and will take flight. We are speaking of them here on the basis of experience: our patients have led us to become part of this plural body to the point where flight can be envisaged, and freedom: above all, freedom of speech.

7.1.2. Blue Flower[2]: Freedom of Speech

In the common room of the first psychiatric hospital we worked in, a chronically mute woman patient used to stand near a radiator, always the same one. This was a typical asylum in northern France, placed around a former abbey not far from the front and the cemeteries of the last wars. The analyst got into the habit of joining her each week; he, too, would stand with his back to the wall, describing aloud to her what was going on in the room or sometimes simply whatever came into his mind. This small talk, addressed to the woman as though to himself (since she said nothing) had the effect that, after more than a year, on a day like other days in the ordinary life of this hospital, she began to speak and to tell a story as though it had taken place yesterday.

It was wartime. One day, she followed her mother toward the fortifications of the little town where they lived. She caught her mother quickly leaving a German soldier. Back home, her mother had lifted her skirt over her nakedness and screamed at her astonished daughter, "You want to know what I'm doing? OK, take a look!" From then on, the little girl had canceled herself out as a subject until she reached her forties, which seemed to go on forever.

Some time later, she calmly explained to the analyst what had motivated her to speak: "That day, when you passed in front of me, I heard a big YES,[3] and I knew I could talk to you."

The analyst had obviously said no such thing; he had only shown his eccentric persistence in standing alongside her, attracted by the dignified way she held herself and by her wide-eyed, childlike gaze.

The first narrative emerged, bizarrely, from the waves of the canal into which she had then thrown herself. The fish were surprised to see her sink into the water; the algae opened to receive her. Then the sailor from the "Come to Think of It" jumped in to save her from drowning, brought her back to the canal bank, and set her down near a mushroom.

It took some time for the analyst, who was as surprised as the fish, to understand that "Come to Think of It" was the name of a barge

---

2. In French, the term *blue flower* has the connotation of innocence.

3. The analyst had never before been so close to the solidity of the *Bejahung*, the primal affirmation that expects the word of the other.

moored near the lock that her mother was in charge of while her father was away at war, that the "mushroom" was what sailors call a bollard (*bitte*),[4] and that this sailor had no doubt been the last person truly to think about her and her survival. As for the analyst, who was born at the time of these events, he became a father for the first time.

The phrase "Come to Think of It" opens out the space of reverie but also describes the presence of mind of the man who jumped into the water to save the patient's life,[5] when, at the age of 9, she had decided to end it. Without knowing it, the analyst had opened up his thinking to her with the obvious wish that she be reborn to speech. Between the Real of her mother's prostitution and the silence into which she had enfolded herself as a subject, taking refuge in the only dignified bearing that remained to her as she stood in mute vigil near her radiator, a kind of surrealistic collage had been set in place: concrete words, wishes, bodies, and things had reconstructed the explosion of the world—though without denying it—and enabled the subject of speech to be reborn.

Between the Real *bite* of the German and the signifier of paternity, an incongruous mushroom had been there to moor this set of meanings, unexpected and at the same time irreplaceable. Sometimes word-things grow along the canals of France and in all humility manage to engender initial metaphors, without which language dies in the depths

---

4. In French, *bitte* is an exact homophone of *bite*, a slang word for penis. (This kind of homophony, detached from meaning, is one of the characteristics of the signifier for Saussure as well as Lacan.) Moreover, in the imagination, the phallic form of the bollard immediately calls to mind the shape of the erect male genital. We may reflect on the braid that ultimately links the unnamable Real genital of the German; the patient's father, betrayed while he is away at war; the mushroom bollard of her savior's barge; the "thinking" that saved her life; the presence of the analyst at her side; and the phallus that is the signifier of desire or wish: the desire that she live and that she speak, and the analyst's wish to become a father. For Lacan (1958), "The phallus is the privileged signifier of that mark in which the role of the logos is joined with the advent of desire" (p. 287).

5. The setting of this story evokes Jean Vigo's 1933 film *L'Atalante*. The sailor of the "Come to Think of It" might have had the unforgettable head and voice of Michel Simon.

of dictionaries. In a dialect of the north, this woman's name was reminiscent of Blue Flower.

Sometimes inspired by such women, like Breton's Nadja, Lacan's Aimée, or Bataille's Laure,[6] at the time of an earlier war the Surrealists practiced the creation of this kind of space-time. Marcel Duchamp (1934) even invented, for the occasion, the definition of "prime words, divisible by themselves and by one" (p. 48) to bring about, from these "prime elements whose intertwining is the essence of the logos" (Plato, *Theaetetus* 202b),[7] the genesis of an language game when all values have collapsed.

Nadja, who inspired Breton's *amour fou* ("crazy love"), ended up in an asylum. Aimée, Lacan's chief case for his thesis, was discharged from the asylum during World War II to become a cook for her psychiatrist's father; she complained that Lacan never gave her back her own writings, thanks to which his thesis had been praised by the Surrealists. Nadja disappeared among the mad, whereas the book named after her won renown. Laure's fate was marked by the tragedy of loss and child abuse despite the fact that she spent her last four years alongside Bataille's fame. The three writers were thrilled and inspired by these women's madness but, while using their knowledge, won on the front of the Real, to nourish their genius, they hardly served them in the role of *therapôn*. Hadn't Nadja, Laure, and Aimée, just after World War I, Blue Flower, just after World War II, and so many others remained unyielding children in this regard?

---

6. All three come from death zones. Nadja (Breton 1928) was from Lille, in the same northern province—periodically devastated—as Blue Flower. Aimée (Marguerite Anzieu [1889–1992], the mother of the psychoanalyst Didier Anzieu) had the same first name as a sister who had been burned alive (Allouch 1994, Lacan 1932). Laure had lost her father and uncles, the Peignot brothers, in the war of 1914. Jérôme Peignot (1977) cites his aunt, Colette Peignot (Laure), who lived from 1904 to 1938: "I lived not in life but in death. As far as I recall, corpses stood up right in front of me. . . . Feeling somewhat like a monster, I no longer acknowledged the human beings whom I nevertheless loved. Finally I slowly turned to stone, until I became a mere stage prop" (p. 23; cf. Barillé 1997.)

7. Our interpretation of this famous passage is as follows: "For it is the intertwining of nouns that is the essence of the logos. . . . Thus the [nonintertwined] elements are outside of speech and knowledge but are [pure] sensation."

7.1.3. The Children of Terezin[8]

For abused children do not lack resources. They deploy a wealth of invention to counter their ordeals. At an age in which the ego is not yet very coherent or stable, they draw from the porosity of boundaries a strength that far exceeds their capacities, producing an exceptional energy paradoxically derived from contact with the Real.

Among numberless extraordinary stories, here is the well known one of the children of Terezin. We repeat it here because it exemplifies the dimension of expectancy; moreover, the expression *plural body* occurred to us as we read about them. We must add that the analyst who told us about them—and, after all, we ourselves—came within a hair's breadth of knowing the same fate.

Beyond these tragic facts, the story of the children of Terezin must be seen here as a paradigm of all situations, including current ones, private or public, individual or large scale, in which children find themselves reduced in this way to being able to count for survival only on the specific tie that unites them.

Anna Freud gives a surprised account of such child power outside the norm, power that street children on all continents continue to deploy, as do the child warriors of Sierra Leone (Kourouma 2000), Sri Lanka, Colombia, and the like.

Let us review the facts, which date from the end of World War II. In November 1945, six children of about 3 years of age, who had lived in the transit camp of Terezin, were brought to England. They were to stay in a country house, Bulldog's Bank, in a village in Sussex amid fields and forests. They had come as babies to the camp, separately, and placed in the section for motherless children. Their parents had been deported and killed. Their earliest years had been spent in contact with adults who themselves were deported, taking care of the children until, one after the other, they disappeared, transferred to extermination camps.

Pediatric nurses and toys awaited these children in England, where they would stay for one year. In writing about them, Anna Freud can-

---

8. Terezin is the Moravian city best known in its German form, Theresienstadt, on account of the concentration camp of the same name. On the children, see A. Freud 1954 and Landau 1990.

not have failed to think of her aunts, Freud's sisters, of whom her brother Martin writes movingly (M. Freud 1958). They all died, at Auschwitz, even at Terezin, and perhaps at Treblinka after having passed through this camp.

When the children arrived in England, it was a disaster. In no time, they completely demolished the fine arrangements made for them and transformed the pretty house into a field of ruins similar to the concentration camp that was their sole frame of reference. No one could get near them. They insulted the grownups in the coarsest German terms, spat on them, and attacked them in the depths of their good intentions. Impervious and invulnerable, they had paid for their survival in the camp with all feeling for other people. Yet the nurses taking care of them were struck by their extraordinary resilience.[9]

These nurses described the phenomenon unfolding before their eyes: the children behaved in a manner exactly opposite to what would be expected at their age.[10] They could not be separated. Isolating them was out of the question, when one of them contracted measles, nor could their unit be divided up to go for a walk. Intense feelings of affection and solidarity welded them together, a paradox in these children who seemed so hard to their nurses. But they did not have the kind of relationship with one another found in very young children who share games and tears in the playground. When one of them, a little girl, saw the empty bed of one of the members of the little group one day, she said tersely, "*Tot* [dead]" and went on to other things.

It was as though each of these weak children could lean on the others to increase the survival abilities of the body. More than a mere addition of strengths is involved here. According to Clausewitz (1834),

---

9. On the term *resilience*, see Cyrulnik 1999.

10. According to Grim (1998), in France, one year earlier, children like this might have been diagnosed as maladjusted, following the nomenclature officially established by the Technical Advice on Deprived or Morally Endangered Childhood sponsored by the collaborationist Laval government. The "classification of maladjusted youth" presented in January 1944 by Heuyer and Lagache differentiated among "those who can be rehabilitated, those who can be partially rehabilitated, and those who cannot be rehabilitated" (pp. 19–20). It resulted in the setting up of "Public Offices of Social Hygiene" over all this territory, intended to fund Observation and Triage Centers. We know what ideology and practices are barely concealed by these words in those years. Only the liberation of Paris in August 1944 would stop the infernal machine.

the resulting moral tenacity goes beyond quantification. In what does this determination consist, then?

It is based on forgetting oneself, and one's self, for the good of the whole. Moreover, the plural body is not an intangible totality, since one of its limbs can be amputated at any time. Other children, who died earlier at Terezin, had probably been part of this plural vitality. In contrast to the collective movement of an organized grouping, such a set of people has no mirror or official leader. Nor does it function as a sect or stand solidly behind a tyrant.

An event that is ordinary and at the same time exceptional never fails to surprise the analyst. During meals, at the age when children do not like to share and social behavior comes down to "me first, the biggest piece for me," declared all the more firmly as the "me" in question is still insecure, the children of Terezin exhibited a paradoxical attitude. The one who got the biggest piece carefully shared it with all the others and would not eat until everyone had some. During the battle of Waterloo, the young Fabrizio del Dongo has the same experience (Stendhal 1839).[11]

Among these children, the role of the emergent leader, recognized ever since wars began on the basis of an immediate tendency to take care of others in times of danger, might be played by one or another of them depending on circumstances. The material survival of the group, food, sleep while another keeps watch, took precedence over individual gratification. The invulnerability and the odd strength that enabled them to triumph in the adult world, as with a wild animal that keeps its distance and does not let itself be tamed, was only rarely shaken. Terror seized them only when they saw dogs or trucks. The only ob-

---

11. Stendhal describes the incident as follows:

The little troop now consisted of only three soldiers, the corporal, and Fabrizio. When they were less than a league from the higher road, one of the soldiers said, "I can't go on." "Me neither," said another. "Nice news! We're all together," the corporal snapped. "Follow my orders and you'll get through." He had noticed five or six trees along a little ditch in the center of a huge wheat field. "Get to those trees," he told his men. "Lie down here," he ordered, once they had reached the trees, "and not a sound. But before you sleep, who's got bread?" "I do," said one of the soldiers. "Give it here," the corporal commanded. He cut the bread into five chunks and took the smallest for himself." [p. 55]

jects of value in their eyes were spoons, which they called "the little things." These were the only possessions allowed to the deportees.

Between the Thing, from which emanated an omnipresent dread that they brought with them to their land of refuge, and the little tame things to eat with, there gradually slipped another type of food, also passing through the mouths of the adults who took care of them: the English language for naming new things came to replace the filthy German curses. One after the other, the children became increasingly attached to these women, though never giving any one of them the privilege of exclusivity.

We have therefore given the name *plural body* to this artifact of survival set up against the perversions of barbarity and even against the best intentions. The children of Terezin hold no patent on this concept. Many other children find themselves needing to invent it every day, in the face of the infantile and murderous imbecility of supposed adults who are, nevertheless, all-powerful on the domestic or political scale.

7.1.4. The Plural Body: The Authority of the Lady

Such an organism obeys a law, a form: "Till death do us part." The implicit promise linking these children put each one's qualities to good use but did not stop there. No *curriculum vitae* oversees their recruitment, no ideal profile or preset flow chart. And yet it is effective beyond all expectation. Confronted with this all-out energy, like the one that kills the *satori*, Anna Freud was astounded. As are we, in the presence of patients who are maladjusted in the normal world and high-performing in danger situations: all the patients we have mentioned in this book.

They had to deal with the vagaries of a world in perpetual change. Subject to arbitrariness and exhausted from having to keep trying, they came to the certainty, among themselves, that nothing could be expected from anyone. Thus they trained themselves to discern the intentions beneath words and acts with a practical knowledge that could be mobilized at any moment. This intelligence was much higher than is normal for their age. Immediately able to analyze all the parameters of absurd situations, these children were resistant, particularly when it came to complying with pacified ideologies, even those tinged with psychoanalysis, that attempted to cradle them in this welcoming England. They remained on a war footing, like the veterans of all wars. They were a living incarnation of the Salmon principles: immediacy, proximity, expectancy, simplicity. But the solidity of the bond that united them was, in our opinion, based on the dimension of expectancy. What can people expect, after all, when they expect nothing?

The abolition of pretense, unvarnished access to the truth of situations, and tearing the veil from the weakness of adults free up an energy usually held back by repression. We have already noted the way body boundaries are broken through in the extreme situations surrounding the berserk stake and the raging euphoria of daredevils. When death is your companion, your Lady, courted, challenged, you know very well that it is she who awaits you. She is part of your life. We may wonder whether it is not Lady Death who cements the giving of one's word. "Till death do us part,"[12] as we have seen, is not the same as "Long live death." Morbid fascination has no place here.

The death that links them is the mother, the mother of the monuments to the dead or the mother crazy with grief[13] whom they left behind and who is protecting them from back home. She functions as the feminine

---

12. Translator's note: In French, this is "to life, to death."

13. See also the converse situation (Bazin 1926) in which, at the end of World War I, a crazy mother scours the countryside, hanging bread, banknotes, and letters from tree branches. She is looking for her son, missing in the ranks of the enemy, since she lives in the part of the province of Lorraine that became German in the war of 1870. Her encounter with some young French soldiers, recently victorious, is deeply moving:

> With her hand, which was still holding banknotes, she drew a broad line in the air, designating the entire countryside around the woods. And since these young people had surely guessed, by now, that her mind was disturbed, some of them began to laugh; others took pity on her. One man said, looking back, "She's crazy!" and a second, in a lower voice, "Shut up! There's nothing wrong with being crazy at heart!" "Quiet, all of you" shouted Prunier. "Let her talk. You can see she's a mother." Marie Baltus had become young again. Her faded lips regained their pink color. Hope, so often her companion, had returned and was helping her. "I beg you, you're soldiers like him, tell me what *you* know about the missing men who've been seen coming home?" [p. 164]

entity called upon by all the wounded on all the battlefields in the world. She is the one addressed by their speech, traces of which are found in their pockets, afterward: letters never sent. It is not certain that the envelopes piously addressed, in the aftermath, to the families, the godmother, the fiancée, will reach their destinations this way. For the real address is not the motherland but Mother Earth,[14] for and on which they are fighting, who remains the refuge on which they press themselves and who will bury them.

Under these circumstances, the Name-of-the-Father, which Lacan has posited as the inscription of the guarantee of the Symbolic, collapses, and the authority that ensures the transmission of names no longer functions. Besides, the Name-of-the-Father is not reserved for "daddy." It may be, in various cultures, the name of a clan, a totem, a rock, an animal in animist societies, a name handed down by women in matrilineal societies. In all societies, when the foundation of the symbolic order of transmission crumbles, another agency of otherness is required for sheer survival: a response, however minimal, to one's cries, a reflection, however faint, in a gaze, when mirrors no longer give anything back. This was the agency of symbolic recourse that our wounded grandfathers and fathers called "Mommy" all over the battlefields.

7.1.5. The Plural Body with Ancestors

This is the origin of the speech that linked the children of Terezin, in what we may call a madness transference that was the only thing keeping them alive in the face of the madness of circumstances. The proof is that, little by little, the promise "till death do us part" yielded to

---

14. "Earth! Earth! Earth! Earth, with thy folds and hollows and holes into which a man may fling himself and crouch down. In the spasm of terror, under the hailing of annihilations, O Earth, thou grantest us the great resisting surge of new-won life. Our being, almost utterly carried away by the fury of the storm, streams back through our hands from thee, and we, thy redeemed ones, bury ourselves in thee, and, through the long minute in a mute agony of hope, bite into thee with our lips" (Remarque 1928, p. 55). Erich Maria Kramer (1898–1970), who went by the name of Remarque, was born in Osnabrück, Germany. He went into exile in the United States, when Hitler came to power, and was naturalized in 1947.

another, much more nourishing, set of words. Anna Freud noted that their mutual bond was stretching, and that they were becoming more individualized as they learned English, not as one learns a language at school but in a transference to their therapist, who gradually replaced the plural body.

At risk, then, of walking in a new aloneness, these children went through a very critical phase that one might call regression. Here, too, we can imagine how troubling this was to their caregivers. There seemed to have been an unwelcome exchange of the previous invulnerability for a return to babyhood, dependent and dangerously vulnerable to all the infectious diseases. Perhaps they even feared for the little ones' lives—and this time it would be their fault. It is as though the children now had to go through all the stages they had skipped, paying with the loss of their supernatural strength for the simple restoration of the boundaries prematurely broken through by brutality.

Among our patients are children of heroes and children of heroic children. When the heroes do not manage to pay the ransom price for their excessive strength so as to return to normality, their descendants come to see us to exhibit the weakness that their ancestors were not permitted to show. Thus it happens that we congratulate patients when they come down with physiological illnesses in the course of our work together, ratifying the obligatory stages of their route: "Finally, a real illness!" We welcome it as a friend, an ally speaking to us from beyond armor that has become too heavy, sketching the new boundaries of the body and the care that must be accorded it.

They come to the analyst like old children who have formed a plural body with those who fought in the last wars and can, as subjects, bring forth their words, their text, if they meet up with an analyst whose history awaits them on the field of operations. In *Another World*, the novelist Pat Barker (1998) describes a man of today who sees his own children caught up in a fratricidal war close to the nightmares of his grandfather. At the age of 101, the veteran of the war of 1914 relives each night the trip he made in the muddy no-man's-land of the Ardennes to finish off his own brother, screaming in death agony on the barbed wire, his guts ripped out.

Though not honored in literature, our fathers, too, relived their last war each night in bad dreams and fistfights. Why, they would sometimes ask, isn't the memory of very old people limited to pleasant things only? Why these nightmares all the time? No doubt so that they could transmit something of this to their grandchildren, skipping over the intermediate generation, ours.

Thus a plural body is established among the kids of today and the old kids who set out for war without a care in the world, only to return with too many years on their shoulders. Writings lined up in old leatherette notebooks await the death of their authors in order to be deciphered by the descendants. These manuscripts, whose ink is beginning to fade, sometimes try to make a connection, across time, between these young people marked by too much knowledge of the Real and the knowledge of their descendants. One hopes to find secrets there, sensational deeds. But hunger is inscribed on each page of the prisoner's life; even if every day is the same, no one knows what tomorrow will be like. Most important of all is the survival of the buddy, who must be fed and cared for, . . . if only they are not separated.

When one of them comes for analysis, rather unwillingly, it is sometimes in his own name but sometimes in the place of others left in abeyance[15] in the course of generations. The crisis that brings him in encompasses the current field of the ancestors' traumatization.

The therapist's first word amounts to the Yes heard by Gilda and also, really, Ms. Blue Flower, although the analyst did not utter it. It was not to pass the time of day and play a bit part in the hospital that he settled down near the radiator, but in the name of a trust born from the bearing and dignity of this woman. This first Yes from the analyst is a primal affirmation that in fact presides over the judgment of existence we have spoken of and opens out the field of speech: "Yes, something happened, something happened to *you*; it's not all in your head, and what you're showing is the only way you could bear witness to it. No, these events are not the cause of your condition but the object of your investigation."

What authorizes this Yes? Analysts remain quite discreet about the place in them from which the expectancy of such patients proceeds.

---

15. Translator's note: *laissés en souffrance*, "left in abeyance," is literally "left in suffering."

7.2. WE DO NOT CHOOSE THE MOUTH THAT SAYS, "YES, I AM WAITING FOR YOU"

7.2.1. Who Is Waiting for Whom?

Mario Isotti (1978), an analyst in Milan, describes just such a dreadful beginning. The whole story begins with a Yes to wake the dead. Summoned in the morning to diagnose a patient unreachable by any treatment, Isotti does indeed consider her incurable from the way she presents, squeezed into a corner and showing no reaction. That night, he wakes up with the certainty that she is in mortal danger. He immediately phones the head of the hospital; in the middle of the night the two of them rush to the bedside of this woman who had occasioned such extreme fright in him and find that she is actually in a coma: she had swallowed medication that she had been secretly keeping in reserve for some time. Then the work of psychoanalysis began, and it was like a Sisyphean effort that would last for many long years, first in the hospital and then on the outside. At the end of the analysis, she becomes a painter in Paris.

We know nothing more of the mad reason that leads Isotti to repeat this Yes each time this patient's madness brings him back to square one in the analysis. In accordance with the rhythm of the immediacy of psychotic transferences, there is never a permanent accrual of progress. As though to draw from the disaster zone a new "piece of the Real" (Lacan 1976)[16] to be analyzed, everything is periodically put back into play in the transference, with everything at risk up to the boundary of life. In fact, the striking series of relapses always leads to the point where the analyst is waiting for the patient and has to repeat the Yes. Sometimes Isotti tells her his own dreams that arose in the transference.

At the end of her analysis, this patient will sum them up one by one in his honor, along with all the key moments that were so crucial for new articulations. She had registered them perfectly and had used them as levers at a time when she had been completely delusional and

---

16. "The true Real implies the absence of the law. The Real has no order. This is what I mean when I say that the only thing I'll perhaps manage to articulate for you one day is something about what I've called a piece of the Real" (Lacan 1976, p. 11).

the analyst believed that she was unreachable by what he said to her, especially about his own dreams and the impressions made by this madness that was so impressive. But Isotti tells us nothing about the speck of surreality that attracted him to an encounter like this and that made her wait for an occasion to pay him back. We shall try to explain this and explore it.

The bits of the Real that can be intertwined (Plato, *Theaetetus* 202b) as transference do not know the rhythm of scholastic or institutional progress. The patient remains the sole judge of this assessment. As Martin Cooperman says in one of his aphorisms, a psychoanalysis takes two weeks, but it takes over two years to get to those two weeks; in the meantime, we may even wonder which one the analyst is.

The knotting, the intertwining, that in fact constitutes the analysis in these cases comes about only when the analyst is ready. It is an event that may occur in the urgency of an initial confrontation, but it may also take years. It may even happen that, years later, the patient comes back to see whether the analyst has made progress— in other words, whether in the meantime other patients have taught the analyst what aspects of his own history he is involved with and especially the ways in which he can make use of them in the transference.

7.2.2. The *Tunnel* Awaiting Louise and Her Analyst

Louise, one of the analyst's first patients, came back to see her twenty years later. She had certainly not found, in the first stage, what "was waiting for her." And yet it had been possible for her, at that time, to put into words a history of war and trauma sufficient to make her life alive. In her benevolent neutrality, however, the analyst had not completely joined her on the front of the Real.

When she returned, her hair had begun to go gray, as had the analyst's. She liked her life; she was living and painting in a town near Paris with her second husband, a well-known craftsman, in a large house where they had their studios. They had no children but often played host to their nephews and nieces, and they were planning to return to her native province, where her family had been established for a long time.

She had in fact come back to the analyst with a very precise question concerning her brother. A perpetual source of concern to his siblings, he lived like an outlaw. His addictive behaviors had landed him in a series of institutions, each of which he left, using the psychoactive drugs for dealing. The analyst did indeed recall that, of all her brothers and sisters, Louise had felt particularly responsible for him. When their parents died, Louise related, she had arranged for his hospitalization in an institution near where she lived, so that she could visit him easily and have him over when he was on leave.

Now she had to come to a decision and was seeking the analyst's advice. There was going to be a trial of electroconvulsive therapy; she had been told that, in a comfortable form, this had become a common and effective treatment. She could not bear the idea of electroshock, which, for her, was equivalent to brainwashing: "You understand, after what our parents went through! I want to get him discharged and have him come to live with me. I need your advice and your help for that."

Their mother had had brain surgery when they were children, following multiple epileptic seizures. It was said that these crises began when her father returned from deportation unrecognizable, as were all these revenants. The father, a notable of old provincial stock, had been a hero in the Resistance and was sent to a concentration camp. He came back at the end of the war with a memento: drawings of life in the camp, done by another prisoner who had died there. In the first part of her analysis, Louise has spoken a lot about this set of drawings hung on the walls; wordless images of the cruelty of deportation, they had haunted her childhood. Without saying a word, her father had made them share everyday life in the camps. He often said to his son, who was already having problems, that he would end up behind bars. Now, at the age of 50, Louise wanted to avert this fate.

At this moment, the analyst once again had a very vivid sense impression, one that had come over her from the time of their first meeting but had quickly been written off as subjective and hardly in keeping with the conception of her work that she then had. It was the smell of old stones, along with the image of a medieval dungeon in the castle of Chinon, that, though saying nothing about it and contrary to

all historical fact, she had associated with the captivity of Joan of Arc.[17]
Once this olfactory sensation had been swept aside to make way for
benevolent neutrality, the analysis could begin.

This time, when the repressed sensation that she had made no use
of before returned for no apparent reason, the analyst confided to Louise
that she, too, had made some headway in the meantime. She had since
become more closely interested in the war, which had even become a
hobbyhorse.

Louise asked why. Simple, the analyst replied: her patients had
made her realize that she, too, had been born during the war, that she
had very nearly come into the world in prison, where her mother had
been locked up by the Germans.[18] All these prisons led her, today, to
tell the story of the children of Terezin so as to convey that, as children of war coming together in this office, analyst and patient could
both stand on this common ground to imagine Louise getting her
brother discharged and bringing him into her home. The analyst
promised to help her in this. Continuing in this vein, she told Louise
about the principles of war psychiatry. Then, when the patient had
left, she reproached herself, as she often did, for not having been able
to hold her tongue in accordance with the rules.

Louise spoke to her brother about these sessions with the analyst
and about her plans. She arranged for him to live in a separate apartment in an outbuilding of her house, on condition that he undertake
not to drink or use drugs anymore and to look after the place. Diagnosis and treatment receded into the background. She even dared to tell
her brother about an intuition she had: she had always thought that
their father had handed down to him, his son, something of the camp.

In the course of the sessions, the analyst learned that, after several
trial runs, the brother was true to his word. He had found work to do

---

17. Joan of Arc did in fact meet King Charles VII for the first time in the castle of
Chinon, in the middle of the tiny kingdom that he won in the war with the English:
she recognized him in the middle of the court when he had voluntarily put on garments like those of the others in order to test the Maid. The prison in this castle, carved
on a level with the rock, had made an impression on the analyst in her childhood,
though Joan of Arc had obviously never been held there.

18. Hence perhaps the oddly vivid odor of the stones of a cell during Louise's
first visit. Once again, stones speak when mouths are silent.

in her husband's studio and was keeping his apartment clean. Together, they spoke of their father, who had never given up certain ways of acting like a prisoner, for example, an uneasy and taciturn proximity, as though the boundaries between people had to be blunted in order to be more resistant to the arbitrariness that could befall one at any moment.

"Could it be that, in a certain sense, my father betrayed his own son by leaving him all alone in the midst of this silence?" Louise asked one day.

The analyst found the word *betrayal* a bit strong. But it reminded her of the way Jonathan Shay (1995) defines traumatization, and she cited this in reply:

"The author of a book called *Achilles in Vietnam* links the trauma of the Greek warrior or the American GI to the horrors of war, of course, but especially to the betrayal by his own people."

Louise then mentioned a detail never spoken of before. Her father had been handed over by a friend, who had personally opened the door of the car in which the military police were waiting. Believing that he was going to a secret meeting of the Resistance, he had been taken, unbeknownst to him, to his arrest and later deportation. The friend redeemed himself with a fine political career in the postwar period. Her father had told her about this shortly before his death, asking her to say nothing about it: "Why stir all that up again?"

The analyst had often heard this expression from her own father's mouth in connection with the period of the war. And that was that. But it was not certain that the daughters' silence was enough to seal off the betrayal. Things speak when mouths are silent. As we have seen, this is one of the leitmotivs of this book.

One day, Louise noticed a book beside the analyst, called *The Tunnel* (Lacaze 1978), which the latter had decided to read. Louise had had it at home, right under her eyes, for at least ten years.

"How did you find it?" she asked suddenly.

Surprised by her question, the analyst replied without thinking that this book had been given to her own father by his brother, Uncle Emile, who had been deported during the war. When asked what he had gone through, Emile, like Louise's father, would say nothing. One day, however, he gave his brother this book, which had just been published: "If you want to know what I went through, read this. A pal of mine from over there wrote it." As if talking to herself, the analyst added that she didn't know why she had waited so long to open it. It must be said that, asked what it was about, her father had made it sound unremarkable:

"It's a story about folks who were deported, like Emile, and dug a tunnel between Austria and Yugoslavia. The hero is a hoodlum, as 'resistant' as those who made a career of it after the war. History is being rewritten every day. When the war was over, everyone was a resister, and people like Emile didn't want to talk about it anymore: 'You had to have been there; you can't understand.'"

The usual refrain. All at once, the analyst summarized the book for Louise:

"The tunnel is the one at Loibl Pass, dug across the Alps by the people who had been deported to the camp at Mauthausen to allow German tanks to reach the Adriatic in all seasons. The story is told by one of the deportees, a Parisian street urchin, a bit of a pimp, who had gotten caught by chance. The author, André Lacaze, makes his life in this camp into a narrative that's horrifying and invigorating at the same time. His antihero refers to no conventional ideal but the survival of his buddies, few of whom made it through in the end."

Louise interrupted the summary: "It was my father's favorite book. After he died, my mother kept it on her bedside table. I recognized the dark red cover. I never read it either. Can you lend it to me?"

She kept going without a transition: since the time of her analysis, she said, one symptom persisted, but she considered it minor. She found it impossible to drive a car, though she had had her license for a long time. Her husband often kidded her about this, saying that she couldn't get up the courage. Her excuse was a back ailment that hardly ever left her.

"Since when?" asked the analyst.

"Oh, probably since my rape," replied Louise simply.

This remark, made in passing, hit the analyst full force. How could she have heard this whole story already and rested content in the belief that it had only to be spoken to be inscribed?

The pain was there, waiting faithfully. But, this time, analyst and patient were together in the place to which *The Tunnel* had brought them. The analyst asked Louise to tell everything all over again, since she realized that, between ignorance and negligence, including her own history, she had allowed horrors to be spoken of in everyday terms. Hadn't she been complicit in this intellectual detachment that enables one to say everything without saying anything, perpetuating the lesion in otherness that we have identified? For the first time, an obvious link was being made between the murder of soul and body of which Louise had been the object and scientifically organized mass murder. Horrified at her collusion with this banalization of evil, the analyst listened more carefully.

Thirty years earlier, Louise had been on the campus of her university. Instead of taking the bus to get back to town, she got into a car at the invitation of two young men who looked like students. She clearly remembered saying to herself at the time, "I shouldn't," perhaps the words her father had said to himself in similar circumstances.

They had stopped in front of a building on the outskirts of the city, and one of the men got out to look for something. Today Louise told herself that she could still have fled. What he had been looking for was a gun that he now held to her back to keep her from crying out. The car quickly headed toward the countryside, where he raped her while the other man held the barrel of the gun to her neck. Then they threw her out of the car. She walked to a café, where she felt too dirty to speak, undressed by people's eyes. She could not get up the courage to phone anyone.

The first time around, the analyst had not been fully enough present when Louise had looked death in the face. The police did no more than tell her that men who murdered young women were at large in the vicinity at that time. The incident was filed away without follow-up. Several years later, well before her analysis, Louise's first husband hadn't reacted when she pointed out one of the two criminals, whom she recognized in the street: "That's him." She became pregnant by this first husband shortly thereafter, miscarried, divorced, and had not tried to have children thereafter.

This time, the analyst was not bound by the ideal of neutrality. She, too, as Louise now knew, had since made contact with this terrible knowledge imprinted on the body: *The Tunnel* was waiting, at the crossroads of their two histories, with all the obviousness of the dissociated unconscious. For the first time, Louise brought in the drawings of the camp. Remarkably sharp in their outlines, highly colored, they depicted the horrors with a humorous detachment that, to this day, defied the *Nacht und Nebel*[19] planned by the Nazis. They arose from the same source of inspiration as *The Tunnel*, in contrast to the sinister grayness under which the analyst had at first imagined them. Louise later decided to donate them to a local museum of the Resistance.

She then decided to relate this whole story—her own, the analyst's, the story in the book—to her brother and her husband so as to validate facts that had long been kept apart from memory. Dormant facts had brought them together like children of war instead of mere passive victims of dramatic circumstances. Today, all three have returned to their native province, where her brother is now living independently.

Let us sum up. The tragic kidnapping of their father obviously had no causal relation to Louise's rape and her circumstances. What enables us to say this? Causalities are always constructed in retrospect. In the face of the Real, therefore, it cannot serve as a therapeutic tool. According to what Wittgenstein (1930–1933) calls "the stupid superstition of our time" (p. 6e),[20] explaining and understanding something is all that is needed to effect change. The fact remains that we do not stop producing understanding and causality: we rattle like machine guns with whys and hows, as Sullivan (1945) jokes,[21] to the point where we take guilt on ourselves when we find no other explanation, or project it onto a scapegoat, individual or collective. The tragic flaw[22] takes over here,

---

19. *Night and Fog*. The Alain Resnais (1957) film of that name publicly revealed pictures from the archives of the Final Solution.

20. The passage is as follows: "How could fire or fire's resemblance to the sun have failed to make an impression on the awakening mind of man? But not 'because he can't explain it' (the stupid superstition of our time)—for does an 'explanation' make it less impressive? . . . After the description of any such magical cure we'd like to add: If the illness doesn't understand *that*, then I don't know *how* one ought to say it" (pp. 6e–7e).

21. "In the world of people, explanations are very easily obtained for almost any act of any person. All you have to do is say: 'And why did you do that?' and he rattles like a machine gun with great streams of words, verbal statements; and if you go away, he is apt to use streams of words in a letter to complete the demonstration of how unutterably easily he deceives himself into feeling that he knows what he is doing, which is apparently all that most people need in order to feel comfortable" (p. 206).

22. Cf. Saïd 1978. In Greek tragedy, the flaw in the family line, clan, or hero is called *hamartia* (from *hamartano*, which literally means "miss the target"). This flaw

embodying the inevitability of a blind fate that had descended upon an entire family line.

But Louise could certainly say much more about "her rape" the second time around: it was no longer a brief news item, possibly called upon to explain what came afterward, nor was it a destiny tragically brought about by her father's ordeals. What was said changed on account of the analyst's book. The way the analyst listened was necessarily modified. The resonance had been picked up and further amplified, and a certain knowledge had been transferred.

For, as a result of the torture she had experienced, Louise found herself plunged into a state of complete abandonment familiar to her father and brother and also to her mother. They had survived; they were connected to one another by all that, endowed with that certain knowledge that remained unspoken. We have called it the knowledge of the Real, a knowledge without a subject. Only a plural body can support such knowledge. Analysts often neglect this unique configuration until they agree to return to it temporarily in order to confront that stubborn Thing incarnated in minds or bodies that are too small to contain it before a therapist is found who enables its placement in history to be mobilized and felt.

On the level of the petty details of history, Louise's back pain disappeared. She began to drive, even the van for their move. She decided to pay for her sessions in the manner of the children of Terezin. Since she did not have much money, she brought the analyst some of the good wine and foie gras from her native region. The analyst agreed to be fed in return.

The analyst's analysis makes it possible to ratify the impact of impressions such as the one received in the first meeting with Louise, and to question these impressions. In this regard, Lacan always stated that the training analysis is nothing other than the analyst's personal analysis, the one that enabled him to analyze the origin of his wish to become the person to whom symptoms are addressed. Perhaps one of his enigmatic formulas can be clarified here: the analyst is the one who identifies with his symptom. Isn't this an acknowledgment that such

---

is tragic in that it affects all the members of a lineage without distinction, victim and executioner alike.

training[23] proceeds in a way not very different from that of the Sioux medicine man? Here the flaw binding him to the locus of speech, to "the words of the tribe" (Mallarmé 1876) is affirmed right from the outset. In his analysis, but also when he is sitting with a difficult patient like this, it is from just such a shaky point that he must constitute the pieces of broken representations and fit them together.

7.3. DREAMS THAT SAY NO

7.3.1. Dreaming in a Totalitarian Situation[24]

The effects of totalitarian regimes have sometimes lasted beyond the fall of the empires. Analysts have had to practice their trade under the worst conditions of dictatorship, for example in Argentina, where it was necessary to devise in advance a pretext for the sessions in case the police descended. Why inject this sinister note in the case of a practice that, one might think, at the very least calls for freedom of speech simply in order to exist?

The reason is that analytic discourse, whatever its form, is an anti-totalitarian tool par excellence, since it posits the locus of the free other no matter how constrained; in these extreme cases, madness appears to be its best ally. Thus, in circumstances of imprisonment and solitary confinement in Uruguay, the psychoanalysts Maren and Marcelo Viñar (1989) describe how one of the prisoners who had been tortured owed his health to his ability to hallucinate frequent visits from his friends. The latter were astonished at the certainty with which he thanked them for their visits once he got out, for, on the rational level, it had been absolutely impossible for them to meet with the prisoner or even imagine doing so.

Thus madness is sometimes the only possible opening in the compactness of the Real. More an instrument than a destiny, it breaches the total, or totalitarian, order: it is at the same time a symptom and a means of getting out. This is especially so when the foreclosure of all

---

23. In the sense, Lacan specifies, of formations of the unconscious. Translator's note: in French, "training" is *formation*.

24. See Gaudillière 1997.

possible living speech is deliberately undertaken by murdering people, body and soul.

For one does not choose the mouth, or the dream, or the hallucination that says No. In saying this, we are not suggesting that dreams "know" negation, but, quite the contrary, that, by the very act of dreaming, they may say No to those who try to prevent one from dreaming. These are, first and foremost, dreams that say No to attacks on the unconscious. Conversely, it is possible to make a traumatized person crazy by clinically preventing him from dreaming (Barrois 1998).[25] Sometimes, then, it is up to dreams to record history, while they wait to come upon an other to whom to speak.

In 1933, Dr. C. came home after a long day of work. Tired, he sat down on a couch and dozed off. He dreamed that he had to treat Hitler and agreed to do so; he awoke weeping.

Charlotte Beradt (1966), a young German woman from the period between the two world wars, collected some three hundred dreams like this, brought to her between 1932 and 1938, either directly or through friends, doctors, or priests who were waiting for them without knowing how or why. They were indispensable intermediaries, weaving a connection between dreamers who did not know one another and the astonished readers of these texts, which were published in the 1960s. The dreams record facts that were not yet documented in history and that most people did not want, or were unable, to see. Like traumatic

---

25. Barrois writes as follows:

We all know how likely neuroleptics, benzodiazepines, and many other psychotropic substances are to bring about alterations in the different stages of sleep. . . . Sleep disturbances in psychotraumatic syndromes are well known, and it is clear that any medicinal interference with the structure of sleep is likely to change dream activity significantly. . . . I have come to formulate the hypothesis that this nocturnal activity of a hallucinatory-oneiric type (the nightmares of traumatic neuroses) was literally blocked by psychotropic medication acting on the various cerebral structures responsible for sleep; it is as though there were a sort of pressure, of internal constraint on the figuration or irruption of traumatic scenes and uncontrollable functions of recall. . . . As a result, treatment must therefore begin right from the first seconds of the interview by an attitude of unconditional acceptance of the subject's word. . . . [A]ntipsychotic treatment runs the risk of pushing the subject into a long-term progression of the illness. [p. 33]

dreams that try to inscribe the impact of the Real, these lack a subject but stubbornly try to constitute one. After the First World War, Freud (1920) made a clear distinction between such dreams and dreams of wish fulfillment.[26] They are dreams that Wittgenstein (1945–1949) asked to be analyzed, proclaiming himself a critical disciple of Freud: when he returned from the front, like all the others he must have been burdened by this kind of dream.

Beradt carefully collated the texts of these dreams. As the totalitarian machine gradually revealed itself, she encoded the obvious signs: Hitler became Uncle Henry, the Nazi Party the family. She hid her notes in the pages of the books in her library and finally left Germany in 1938 when the situation became impossible. She managed to have all these books sent to her in the United States.

Some years later, she published her notes, with a gripping introduction, first in Munich and then in America. Beradt was part of the first circle of German friends of Hannah Arendt and her husband in their New York exile. We know enough about their strong reservations when it came to psychoanalysis to appreciate the full value of the encouragement they gave this publication.[27]

Beradt, who was not a psychoanalyst and had not personally experienced the hell of the camps, emphasizes the clear differences be-

---

26. Freud writes:

But it is not in the service of [the pleasure] principle that the dreams of patients suffering from traumatic neuroses lead them back with such regularity to the situation in which trauma occurred. We may assume, rather, that dreams are here helping to carry out another task, which must be accomplished before the dominance of the pleasure principle can even begin. These dreams are endeavouring to master the stimulus retrospectively, by developing the anxiety whose omission was the cause of the traumatic neurosis. They thus afford us a view of a function of the mental apparatus which, though it does not contradict the pleasure principle, is nevertheless independent of it and seems to be more primitive than the purpose of gaining pleasure and avoiding unpleasure. *This would seem to be the place, then, at which to admit for the first time an exception to the proposition that dreams are fulfillments of wishes.* [p. 32, emphasis added]

27. This is the recollection of the mother of a Parisian analyst who shared part of an Italian vacation with Arendt and Beradt, during which there was talk of the need to publish these dreams collected during the Nazi period.

tween the dreams she calls political and those customarily reported in classical psychoanalysis, which finds in them the royal road to the unconscious and repressed wishes. In the former case, the outlines are extremely precise; no associations are evoked; and, when they return to the dreamer several years later, they do so with exactly the same text, almost down to the comma. They mark out the territory of the Real and do not involve the workings of metaphor and metonymy that govern the half-saying of the truth in repressing dreams of desire.

Despite their lucidity and their prescience bordering on a social prescience, the dreams collected by Charlotte Beradt must be included among these traumatic dreams that have always defied interpretation in terms of wish fulfillment. Their very sharp outlines give the impression that analytic discourse was working toward the secret constitution of a shadow language in the very country in which totalitarianism wanted to be in charge of everything right down to dreams (Gaudillière 1997).[28] Her book was entitled *The Third Reich of Dreams*. The risks she ran were not small. The proximity of danger was no doubt responsible for the extraordinary effectiveness of her commentary and gave her the courage of her undertaking.

In the dreams she reports, we hear the crying of the stones from the houses that collapsed everywhere, the weeping of windows closed by barbed wire, the shouting of loudspeakers ordering people to keep in step as they marched, the trembling of bodies being spied on and scorned. It is not only the event that is traumatizing but also the jamming of information, forcing the body to become the refuge of resistant messages on the threshold of speech, on the border of the abstract and the concrete.

Things speak on a stage different from that of the repressed unconscious, for the other does not respond, or it screams absurd and murderous demands. It is that otherness that we have called the Real Other. In the same period, Freud was dealing with it as he once again took up his *Moses and Monotheism* (1939) on the eve of the burning of his books and of the first accounts of the concentration camps, which he had read (Schur 1972). He uses the example of a crime that cannot

---

28. According to Reinhart Koseleck (1979), the Nazi leader Robert Ley observed, in a 1938 speech in Munich, that the only person who can still lead a private life in Germany is the person who is sleeping.

be spoken of and poses the question of the subject of a historical truth who emerges from the absence of traces. What remains are the almost concrete impressions, like those from the hammering of graven images, whose madness or innocence[29] would constitute anti-memory in a latency of time.

7.3.2. A Dream of Wittgenstein's

In these same troubled times, we once again find Ludwig Wittgenstein, whose three older brothers killed themselves. The fourth, Paul, the pianist, lost his right arm in the war of 1914. Ravel wrote his piano concerto for the left hand for him. In 1929, after a decade-long interruption in his philosophical work, Ludwig left Austria, returned to Cambridge, and had a dream that Beradt could have added to her series of political dreams. We know of it from a letter he wrote to his friend, Moritz Schlick, to whom he felt the need to relate it (Monk 1990).[30]

It depicts a figure who is at one and the same time Jewish, a labor leader, and educated like a rich Scottish lord. At one point, this figure, riding a motorbike, opens fire on a cyclist and then on a girl, whom people see writhing on the ground and dying. At the end of his account to Schlick, Wittgenstein admits that he is embarrassed at being himself of Jewish origin and that the case of this figure is his own case as well.

What especially interests him in this dream is the figure's name, the successive deformations of which, in the text, pass through the lines

---

29. Freud's fourth sister, Dolfi, an adorable old maid, will die of hunger in Terezin. Martin Freud (1958) describes her as "subject to impressions, or forebodings, of coming disasters which we thought ridiculous and even a little silly" (p. 16). In her simplicity, she thus saw what many did not want to see, things that the dreams collected by Charlotte Beradt recorded night after night: "I remember walking with her one day in Vienna, when we passed an ordinary kind of man probably a Gentile, who, so far as I know, had taken no notice of us. I put it down to a pathological phobia, or Dolfi's stupidity, when she gripped my arm in terror and whispered, 'Did you hear what that man said? He called me a dirty stinking Jewess and said it was time we were all killed' (p. 16).

30. Educated in the aristocratic manner, Wittgenstein will be tempted, in 1935, to emigrate to Soviet Russia, from which he will hastily return, disenchanted.

of fracture marked by the ideologies and social movements of the century. First he is called Vertsag; several lines later, Verzagt (in German, *verzagt* means discouraged). *Versagung* is the very word Freud uses for denial. At this time, Wittgenstein had moved to England, but he was not unaware of the anti-Semitic threats making themselves evident in his country of origin. The message of this dream was more widely disseminated in 1937, after his return from Russia, in a kind of urgent confession he made to some of his friends. He doubtless admitted to them that his family had renounced their Jewish origin in the preceding century, and that he himself had never denied the aristocratic origins lent to his family by a princely name (McGuinness 1988). We are in the period leading up to the Anschluss (Rhees 1984).

We, for our part, are writing from Europe at the dawn of the twenty-first century. The patients who come to speak to us, unreconciled despite the amnesties, constantly bring us back toward the fault lines opened by all the totalitarianisms of the century. Hannah Arendt approached these events and their origins as a historian and a philosopher. She describes the Real Other that we have kept on running into in this book and that, at times, has even been able to recruit psychoanalysis institutionally, along with the rest. Against the background of genocide, the question asked by Yolande Mukagasana (1997), whose Tutsi husband and their three children were massacred in Rwanda, is this: When all the traces have been erased, what still motivates someone to make an inscription beyond all reason? This is Freud's very question.

Freud, who was in the bad graces of both totalitarianisms, was perfectly aware of how inadequate the theoretical instruments of classical psychoanalysis were for living up to this expectation, since the process and the lifting of repression presuppose a continuity of the signifying chain. Now this chain is broken with the implementation of murder and destruction, organized in the name of a pseudo-science, with the adherence of millions of people including, sometimes, well-known scientists. In the name of the primacy of the collective, numberless massacres pile up. Seeking a reply to this question, Freud thus has every reason to reject the notion of a collective unconscious, whose confusion promotes the fictitious arguments of totalitarianisms.

And yet he must describe the unconscious that is awaiting the hour when it will inscribe history on the ruins of speech: "It is not easy for us to carry over the concept of individual psychology into group psychology, and I do not think we gain anything by introducing the concept of a 'collective' unconscious. The content of the unconscious, indeed, is in any case a collective, universal property of mankind" (Freud 1939, p. 132). What does he mean by this?

On the basis of traumatic dreams and the myth of a traumatic history, *The Third Reich of Dreams* (Beradt 1966) and *Moses and Monotheism* (Freud 1939) confirm in practice and in theory that, in approaching the Real, these two fields are one, that the subject produced by analytic discourse in the grip of the Real is, as in an analysis of madness, the subject of a historical truth cut off from history. The otherness of expectancy is equal to those stakes.

The same delay that makes war traumas wait on the threshold of a possible inscription freezes the voices coming from the totalitarianisms of the twentieth century. During all this time, these questions have been considered collective and hence alien to the discourse of psychoanalysis, which had been hastily put in order in individual cases. All the clinical work we have been showing here, all the "facts" emerging from the repressed unconscious, do not tolerate this summary dichotomy. In view of our experience, such contrasts are irrelevant. To conform to them, psychoanalysis is content to march to the politically correct tune of the moment.

7.3.3. The Psychiatry of the Nazi War[31]

The psychiatrists of the Third Reich, too, took a keen interest in the psychic health of fighters and collectivities. Their results even made some English psychiatrists envious, to the point where they interrogated German prisoners on their methods of selecting officers and on the secrets of such a dazzling psychic "form." In this regard, Nazi war psychiatry is a grotesque counterexample of the Salmon principles.

"Graciously" (Colonomos 1987, p. 106) offered by the German Psychoanalytic Society to Nazi ideology in 1936, after the exile of Jewish psychoanalysts, the Psychoanalytic Institute of Berlin, under the name German Institute of Psychological and Psychotherapeutic Research, was

---

31. See Brecht and colleagues (1985).

directed by Matthias Heinrich Göring, cousin of Marshall Göring.[32] Considerable financial resources were put at its disposal by Matthias Göring. He took personal charge of the mental health of the Luftwaffe officers, while Werner Kemper[33] drew up the directives on what to do in the face of war neuroses in the infantry. It was also necessary to devise techniques for brief therapies, to detect and take charge of homosexual soldiers, and to study the consequences of air raids on the population. In short, the Institute was declared to be of strategic importance on account of its crucial mission: to determine the foundations and laws of human personality development and collective personality development.

In 1944, Göring gave a lecture on the contribution of psychotherapy to the conduct of the war as a whole, in which he mentioned research on ethnopsychology. On these foundations, heavily worked over by propaganda, what did the substitutes for the Salmon principles become on the German front?

Proximity, seen there as overcrowding, implied the dangers of psychic contamination. Hence it was strongly advised that the defective individual, a virus compromising the effectiveness of the group, be removed as far away as possible and his return prevented. The role of the psychiatrist was thus to diagnose weak, anxious, and hysterical personalities, and to send them immediately to the rear. Immediacy had to do with the speed with which these orders were carried out, and also with the summary executions of recalcitrant soldiers, whose number increased drastically with time. Expectancy—what awaited them— was thus at best a brief and efficient therapy via reeducation. In cases of backsliding or strong characterological deformation, the medics were invited to take special measures (Shephard 2000).

When madness in turn sees psychoanalysis graciously offered to the ideology of the moment, it knows what is been sought in order to

---

32. The names of the founder of psychoanalysis and of the Berlin Institute's sponsor, Max Eitingon, were suppressed, and analytic terminology was changed, so that the former theory, suitably disguised, would become unrecognizable and the theft perfect, especially since there was no longer any trace of a plaintiff. For an account of this episode, see Colonomos 1987.

33. He continues to exert an influence in Brazil (Besserman Vianna 1997).

eradicate Freud's discovery: to be precise, the transferential dimension, from which the history of the analyst's lineage cannot be eliminated.

7.4. THE SUBJECT OF "HISTORICAL TRUTH"[34]

7.4.1. Edwige, *Sunken Red*: A Cruel Truth

Edwige came into the office one day, having been sent by a former patient of the analyst's. Overwhelmed, the analyst spent the time of the interview wondering to whom she would be able to refer her. She did not come up with someone for her, as though it were impossible to imagine who could see her. Toward the end of the appointment, Edwige mentioned timidly what her main concern was: her baby, a little girl she felt like hurting. The analyst immediately decided to take her into treatment.

After Edwige left, the analyst asked herself about her sudden wish to erase this patient from her sight almost as soon as she saw her. She at first blamed the fact that Edwige looked so retiring, so distant and restrained, so as not to have to admit to herself that what she felt was

---

34. With regard to the "incubation period" of traumatic symptoms following a railway accident, Freud (1939) asks: "How are we to explain a delayed effect of this kind, and where do we meet with a similar phenomenon?" (p. 66). "There is no difficulty," he says, in finding an analogy between group and individual psychology: "a discrepancy was able to grow up between the written record and the oral transmission of the same material—*tradition*" (p. 68). Later in this work, Freud writes:

> It is worth specially stressing the fact that each portion which returns from oblivion asserts itself with peculiar force, exercises an incomparably powerful influence on people in the mass, and raises an irresistible claim to truth against which logical objections remain powerless . . . . This remarkable feature can only be understood on the pattern of the delusions of psychotics. *We have long understood that a portion of forgotten truth lies hidden in delusional ideas,* that when this returns it has to put up with distortions and misunderstandings . . . . We must grant an ingredient such as this of what may be called *historical truth* to the dogmas of religion as well, which, it is true, bear the character of psychotic symptoms but which, as group phenomena, escape the curse of isolation. [p. 85, emphasis added]

very close to cruelty, hidden in her own indifference. When Edwige returned, she described her days, which passed by dully while her husband was at work. Nothing interested her, nothing moved her anymore. She spent long hours looking at people from her window, wondering what life was and how they managed to live.

She did not have much to say about her family. They had been rich in the past, when they lived in the Netherlands. Her mother's father had been a businessman in Indonesia, where the mother was born; at the time, this country was part of the Dutch Indies. She knew nothing about a ruin that went back to before her birth. Besides, she wasn't interested in all that. The only remaining advantage in this family background was a good education and a certain refinement.

The sessions dragged on forever, with no change in the murderous impulses toward the baby. It was in vain that the analyst asked what was going on in her at those moments; all she could reply was that she looked at her daughter with eyes of stone and had no feelings toward her. This was the same gaze with which, unbeknownst to her, she looked at the analyst.

And so one day—why that day?—the analyst calculated the dates quickly and guessed that Edwige's mother had been in Indonesia during the last war. She asked her whether she knew what her family's fate had been during this troubled period. Edwige looked at her in shock. The analyst felt uneducated.

Time went by. On another day, the analyst broke the rules even more, going beyond everything established as appropriate to her function: "I recently saw in a history book the photo of a little Dutch girl, taken in by the Red Cross after leaving a Japanese camp."

She was careful not to tell Edwige that she had been struck by a family resemblance between this little girl and the patient. The same shocked look greeted this information, as though the analyst had yielded to an indiscreet curiosity. Going all the way to a serious breach of good manners, including professional manners, she dug herself further into the hole: "If I'm saying this to you, it's because I've seen this same stony look in the eyes of my own mother, who had been imprisoned by the Germans during the war."

These words were greeted by a polite silence, and the analyst was immediately sorry she had said too much.

More time passed. The void was still there. Once, the analyst saw the young woman's gaze wander toward the cover of a paperback book beside her. Another book! The cover unambiguously depicted a Japanese soldier armed with a machine gun and a prisoner on the other side of barbed wire. Although Edwige hadn't asked about it, the analyst replied to the question in her furtive glance and told her at length how this book, *Give Us This Day* (Stewart 1956), had arrived there: "The author just sent it to me. His name is Sidney Stewart; he's a psychoanalyst, Joyce MacDougall's husband. I met both of them at Umea, in northern Sweden,[35] at a conference entitled 'Identity Survival.'"

Even as she tried to put a stop to this flood of words, the analyst continued:

"Sidney is one of the very rare survivors of the 1942 march of Bataan, in the Philippines, in which American prisoners marched for ten days without eating or sleeping. The Japanese finished them off for the least failing. He was able to stay on his feet thanks to five buddies who all held each other up so that none of them would fall. They were confined in one camp after another, and his story takes us down from circle to circle, as in Dante's *Inferno*: it seems as though they've been through the worst, but the worst always lies ahead.

"Among these five men, there was one, not very trustworthy, always on the point of collaborating with the enemy, whom the others caught each time and firmly brought back to them, since, like a plural body, they needed him if they were to keep going. Sidney Stewart, the last survivor of the little group, was left for dead in Japan, in a freezing garage, where the Red Cross saved him at the last minute. He's a tall, vigorous man, who chose this title for his book in memory of an army chaplain who died while reciting the prayer 'Give us this day' for the others, in a boat where the prisoners were piled up in the hold.

"He mentioned this saga in his talk in Sweden. On that occasion, he began discussing an episode in which one of the prisoners, as he was dying, saw his buddy looking intently at the ration of rice he was

---

35. The countries of northern Europe have had a long tradition of offering therapeutic treatment to refugees from various war and torture zones on earth. See Lavik (1994), which was sent to us by the psychoanalyst Sverre Varvin, director of the Psychosocial Center for Refugees at Oslo University.

still holding in his hand. Without having read the book, I had the impression that the dying man's buddy was Sidney. At that moment, he stopped short; the lights were too bright, he said, and he could not read his paper anymore. He abruptly left the dais. We met up with him on the line in the university cafeteria, where his wife was speaking softly to him. Sidney's eyes were full of tears.

"The ground was shaking under our feet as well. They had jumped from the boat, taking advantage of an American air raid. Until I read his book, I didn't understand what he meant when he said that they had jumped into the sea, and their air force pulled them out."

The analyst was practically the only one to speak during this session. Was she trying to bring this young woman out of her galactic void in order to include her in the plural body of survivors formed by Sidney, his buddies, Joyce, Edwige, and the analyst?

Little by little, the session became livelier. Edwige announced that she had felt a wish to learn how to make picture frames. She excelled in this, despite the ironic comments of her family. She also took courses in art history, in which she discovered the monstrous creatures of Hieronymus Bosch, who was born in her ancestral province.

Several months later, she learned from one of her parents' friends, entirely by chance and without her mother's knowledge, that her mother had indeed spent four of her teenage years in a Japanese concentration camp in Jakarta. She made inquiries at the Dutch Cultural Center but found few documents. She quickly decided to begin studying psychology and also to take part in dramatics, at which she proved brilliant. She had other children, took correspondence courses, and passed all her examinations with impressive energy and persistence. She had given her children the words with which to confront the cruel history transmitted by her mother: her stony gaze, elusive and incomprehensible in this gentle, calm woman, had been its sole vector.

Afterward, her husband's work took the family abroad. From there, she had a letter sent to the analyst, asking her urgently to buy a Dutch book, *Sunken Red* (Brouwers 1981),[36] that had just been translated into French. In this way, the great silence that had buried the Japanese

---

36. Born in 1940 in Batavia (now Jakarta), the capital of the former Dutch Indies, Jeroen Brouwers is one of the most widely read and famous authors in the Netherlands. Marked by his stay in a Japanese internment camp during his childhood in

internment camps in Indonesia was being publicly lifted for her. The author explained how, long after their return, he had never been able to speak with his mother about their common past in Jakarta, nor could he even go to her funeral. Before his little boy's eyes, she had been horribly humiliated there by a cruelty different from that of the gulags or extermination camps.

Brouwers then wrote this book after his mother's death, without sparing his own childhood cruelty toward her: the book was a grave monument, the kind of text with which poets of the past used to honor the dead, piously wrapping them, finally, in a shroud woven of words that could not be said when they were alive.

Does this mean that the return of the subject exiled by totalitarian discourses does not occur without cruelty?

7.4.2. The Theater of Cruelty

A book, an object, a dream, or a song may thus await a patient—a certain dream of the analyst's as well, provided it is put into a narrative and delivered to its co-owner. Like all precision instruments, this must obviously be used with care. The field is specific: this is the same analytic discourse, but this time with a grip on the silences of history.

The analytic discourse that Freud glimpsed on the eve of the Second World War came from mass destruction in the making. It thus concurs with the experience of therapists at the front, which we have been citing throughout this book.

A theater of cruelty opens out where things without a name have an impact and make it necessary to find an other who is able to hear the inaudible, to put words to the unnamable. Now the other called upon to respond does not have a response readily available. The analyst's silence, summoned in the depths of its entrenched dissociation, is, in this case, irresponsible.

As naive as Percival, initially the most innocent of the knights of the Round Table, the analyst may be fascinated by the extraordinary stories he is being told. He may sit there without saying a word, en-

---

Indonesia, he is the author, among other works, of an autobiographical trilogy, of which *Sunken Red* is the second volume.

chanted by the bleeding lance, the urn filled with sacrificial blood, and the young people in the procession. The silence to which Percival was trained refuses to give the words for its impressions and questions, however naive these may be. And yet they would have treated the pain and healed the wound in the belly of the Fisher King, that is, of the man injured on the battlefield and traumatized physically as well as morally.

The king, too, waited for several centuries to find his poet. This is the time of latency, of expectancy, in which Freud observes that group psychology is similar to that of the single subject. As Freud (1939) notes, it corresponds to the time lapse between the development of oral literature and its being fixed in writing. Associating madness and trauma, he states that a portion of forgotten truth lies hidden in delusional ideas, and he extends this to the social field. According to Schiller, Freud writes, "What is to live immortal in song must perish in life" (p. 101, n. 1).

On the basis of an analogous experience of the shipwreck of time, the analyst may finally come to question what is being shown to him. For what is at issue is emergence from a stupor so that both analyst and patient will not go under. Here one comes close to the shores of the *terrae incognitae* indicated by monsters on old maps. Thus the analytic transference with madness is like a history of social cataclysms in which the figure of the analyst is forced by Madness to get into the same boat (cf. Brant 1494) and deal with the same risks of navigation.

Madness cannot speak to us if it is not summoned to the analyst's place by another character: a double, not at all similar, not an alter ego, since in this context there is no longer an ego or an *alter*, no other in the mirror. Demobilized from the ego and from the desires that make up our whole life, people who, as Plato (*Phaedrus* 244a) says, have reason to be mad focus on an invisible target in their search for the antagonist who will give them a reply. Such is the therapist who awaits the patient in the analyst.

Now, Folly is difficult, an unwilling partner. In its case, the transference consists in rejecting in turn all good intentions, all skills, all theories, pouncing on the one who lies in wait for it: an other appearing in the place of the analyst, always unexpected and enigmatic. It has nothing to do with resemblance or empathy, for the good reason that, in this context, nothing looks like anything anymore. For what comes onstage at the border of the human and the inhuman has nothing to do with the psychology of the characters but instead with what Antonin Artaud (1931–1936) calls an event[37] that has never gained acceptance. In analytic work, this theater is the royal road to the dissociated unconscious, just as the interpretation of dreams gives access to the repressed unconscious.

At this point, whether cataclysm or a mere accident of transmission, the tool of names gets broken, as Wittgenstein (1945–1949) puts it, producing what Artaud (1936) calls "a break between things and words, ideas and the signs that represent them." In his madness, the poet seeks the concrete place, the platform on which to deploy "the need for speech more than speech already formed, poetically repeating the journey that ends in the birth of language" (p. 12).

In May 1933, a year that we have encountered more than once in this book, before returning to enter a psychiatric hospital he wrote prophetically: "It is a question of knowing whether, in Paris, before the imminent cataclysms, it will be possible to find enough ways, financial or otherwise, to allow such a theater to live, and this theater will persist, in any case, because it is the future. Or whether a bit of real blood will be necessary, at once, to manifest this cruelty" (Artaud 1931–1936, p. 105).

Confronted with visionaries like this, how do analysts manage to prepare for a transmission and also to recognize themselves a bit?

7.4.3. Telling Secrets

During a trip to Alaska,[38] at the worst moments with Joseph, the analyst phoned him regularly from that end of the world. It was there, so far away, that a colleague gave him an article called "Telling Secrets"

---

37. "The first Theater of Cruelty show," Artaud writes, "will be entitled THE CONQUEST OF MEXICO. *This will stage events rather than men.* Men will appear in their proper place with their emotions and psychology interpreted as the emergence of certain powers *in the light of the events and historical destiny in which they played their role*" (p. 97, emphasis added).

38. In 1984, we were invited to the Summer Institute for Cross-Cultural Studies at the College of Human and Rural Development, University of Alaska Fairbanks, for a conference entitled "Empowering Processes for Native People." Some of the proceedings are reported in Mohatt and Eagle Elk 2000.

(Ridington 1982) by an anthropologist who was an Athapascan Indian from the Canadian Northwest Territories.[39]

The secret terrors of childhood appear here as the crucible of the myths of the community, on condition that they are linked to visions brought back from what medieval literature calls the wild space, the place of Folly (Fritz 1992), in which the child spends some time alone, learning the field of madness. When he returns, his words are received into the theater of the dream that an elder dreamed about him during his absence. The elder tells him the dream.

With this to sustain him, the young man on the way to adulthood will elaborate his childhood secrets and transmit them to a larger and larger circle of people. He will gradually become an elder himself. One day, on the basis of this moment of recounted terror, which has become a link among the generations and the community, he will be summoned to the place of the dreamer able, in turn, to receive the secret visions of a child. In this social link of transmission, called the road of telling secrets, the history of lineages is interwoven with the history of society.

This custom of his society of origin, described by the anthropologist, is not unconnected with the brief moments of signifying coincidences in which the analyst comes to meet the patient from his own familiarity with uncertain zones on the approach to the Real. He thus makes it possible to discern the link connecting analysts of madness to each other in an exacting transmission across generations.

In clinical practice, such dreams of transmission, too, emerge from the space of miracle: the wild space of the Athapascans, the forest in which medieval literature placed the work of madness. The knight enters the forest, where he encounters fairies, loses his sense of time, and fights monsters. He puts himself at risk, like Joseph, Tristan, Gilda, Jacques, Louise, Henry, Edwige, Auguste, Blue Flower, Ernest, . . . and their analysts, to serve as a plaque on which the disasters of the time are inscribed so as to organize the return of words into the social link, where they in turn constitute the myths and stories to be transmitted

---

39. This reference was given to us by Art Blue, Ph.D., himself of Athapascan origin, who is a member of the Department of Native Studies at Brandon University, Manitoba.

to coming generations, vital resources against the return of the Real. Quite simply.

7.4.4. And What about Simplicity?

The reader duly informed by the account of the four Salmon principles is now expecting the chapter of simplicity to follow here. There will be no such chapter. Since 1917, the fourth of these principles has kept all the distance it needed with regard to the jargons that have always revolved around physical or psychic symptoms, babbling authoritatively. We shall therefore not get embroiled in long speeches about the clarity required in situations of expectancy, immediacy, and proximity; instead, in bringing this book to a close, we shall follow our most famous doctor, Master Alcofribas Nasier.[40]

---

40. We shall learn the identity of the famous author of whose name this is the anagram.

8

A Simple Conclusion: Frozen Time, Frozen Words

8.1. "WHAT IS WELL THOUGHT OUT CAN BE CLEARLY EXPRESSED"

Molière, who read this Renaissance doctor carefully in the next century, had already promoted the lung as the universal cause of the illnesses of his imaginary invalid (1673). He had lampooned the idiocy that definitively explains the properties of opium in terms of a "dormitive virtue." Today, as well, pseudo-sciences and psychodiafoiresque[1] theories, and especially their newspeak for internal use, impede access to madness and traumas. With a bit of kitchen Latin, seasoned with a few obscurities borrowed from more firmly grounded discourses, it will always be easy to make an appointment with the chorus of the learned so as to conclude, after some gibberish that has no bearing on the case, that "this is exactly why your daughter is mute" (Molière 1666, II. iv). "It isn't so simple," said Gilda, "simply to meet someone."

In fact, the patients whose stories encountered our story are the first to remind us that this simplicity cannot be taken for granted. It must be won each time we approach the nodal points of the transference, so that we can report it clearly and distinctly. When a patient sharply points out the irrelevancy of our formulations, we face the problems of tuning (in the musical sense) speech where two foreign languages have come up against one another.

To return to methodological rules, Nicolas Boileau (1669–1674), following Descartes, teaches us that "What is well thought out can be

---

1. From the name of Dr. Diafoirus, the ridiculous physician of *The Imaginary Invalid*. His name has "diarrhea" in it.

clearly expressed,/And the words to say it come easily to us" (pp. 153–154). The use we make every day of the principle of simplicity consists in the need to say nothing to a patient that we could not maintain, in the same terms, when speaking to colleagues, and vice versa. On the other hand, the theoretical formulations produced in the transference by patients are always simple, correct, precise.

But simplicity does not mean simplification. For the situation of having someone to talk to serves as an echo chamber for multiple voices that go beyond the classic schema of sender/receiver in a polyphony whose rhythm and color the stories we have been telling here have tried to convey.

These microhistories have not sought to reproduce exactly what went on in the sessions. They have nothing to do with a microphone fitted into the wall or hidden under the analyst's armchair. A protocol of objectivation is absurd when it comes to grasping the efficacy of speech in a setup that, from the first, guarantees its freedom. Those, as we have kept on saying, are the true criteria of the oral tradition of which psychoanalysis is a stubborn survival.

The freedom of the tale, of the *dict*, as it was called in the French Middle Ages, is fully claimed here, with the variants that belong to this mode of transmission (Nagy 1996), even when it is fixed in writing. On these grounds, raw process notes are always unsatisfactory, as though the essence of what is being made and calibrated, in the course of the sessions, had escaped. What is it that is being "made" there, as the poet says who wrote *Making of the Pré* (Ponge 1960; *pré* is "meadow")?

We have spoken of approaches to the Real and of forms found on its borders. What is involved is the birth of a subject of saying, the subject of a story cut out of history. The cases reported here are the re-creation in which such rare moments can be seized: that is the task of the "harsh reality of fiction" of which the brilliant French clown Raymond Devos (1989) speaks. They are never literal transcripts. All the constructions developed in analysis wear out and deteriorate like works of art and medicine drawn in sand: ephemeral, provisional. Surprisingly, elaborations that called for a great deal of effort evaporate. Interpretations that seemed decisive appear futile in retrospect, when taken out of the moment and the narrow context of the transference. *Verba volant.*

It is as though the leftover bits of the Real, unearthed from the rubble of history, were sending cries toward the analyst, sounds and words arrested in mid-flight. They are the prelude to the soaring of a subject. Once all these deafening silences have been able to be articulated and inscribed, the analyst is relegated to the status of a bit player. Quickly discarded, he hardly expects recognition or even the dividends of a success or an investment. All he can do is tell a story.

What remains of such analyses is like the trace in the sky of a bird's migration, which makes it possible to keep account of time and the seasons and to hear songs that one thought had fallen silent long ago. It is not unusual for some people, patients or analysts, who have been on the alert for a long time to be sensitive to fossil messages, apparently without origin or form, coming from worlds that have disappeared, uprooted from the conventional and contrived universes of reason.[2]

But a new social link is formed around these revivals; they, in turn, have become attentive to the silences of the *doxa* and are not afraid of catching frozen words on the wing, cut-out words without a mouth or a subject, that languish where the seas mingle at their edges.

8.2. HEARING FROZEN WORDS

At the borders of the old and the new worlds, in hyperborean latitudes, one had better know one's boat and one's crew. The protection of some debonair[3] giant is not to be neglected. We shall finish our journey in the company of one of our most famous ones.

On his coat of arms, inscribed in his name and that of his family, we are happy to find the gules. In French, the *gueule* is the gullet swallowing all kinds of wines and foods, but also the mouth that, loud and clear, sends words among men. Former divinities of the land, the

---

2. Formerly, in France, the *livre de raison* (reason book) was the notebook given to every new bride for recording household expenses; reason, from the Latin *ratio*, means calculation here. But, in certain extreme circumstances, this notebook could also become the manuscript in which, day after day, were described increasing dangers or the widening of the horrors of war. Anne La Fontaine, a psychoanalyst in Paris, showed us her grandfather's reason book, a notebook that became his confidant in the 1914 war, in the hope that his granddaughter would open it and become a psychoanalyst.

3. Etymologically, of good extraction, good family.

giants Pantagruel, son of Gargantua, himself the son of Gargamelle and Grandgousier,[4] were immortalized by François Rabelais (1534–1551), alias Master Alcofribas Nasier, in the time of the great discoveries in the new world. He was also a doctor, and he is performing a therapeutic action here.[5] In the names of these characters is inscribed their appetite for life, food, and drink, and at the same time their appetite for talking, weeping, laughing, and saying what should not be said.

In Chapters 55 and 56 of Book Four, Rabelais brings the fine crew together for a strange adventure. On its boat, the plural body essentially consists of the famous trio—Pantagruel; his "merry man" (that is, his fool) Panurge; and his warrior, Friar John of the Hashes—to whom their pilot should be added.

On the open sea, while they are "banqueting, . . . feasting and speechifying and telling nice little stories, Pantagruel suddenly jumps to his feet and takes a look all around him. 'Can you hear something, comrades?' he asks. 'I seem to hear people talking in the air. But I can't see anyone. Listen!'" (p. 566).[6]

---

4. Henri Dottenville (1973) notes in connection with Gargantua that he is a giant "whose name is alive only in France and some francophone provinces" (p. 225). The names of these eponymous heroes of the Rabelaisian tribe all contain an etymology in which we immediately read *grand gullet*, sometimes even in their phonetic articulation. These ancient pagan divinities with their big mouths came to meet Rabelais from the depths of time and the oral traditions of tales and fabliaux. Certain eponymous places from the toponymy of the ancient provinces still bear witness to this. Thus there are a number of Mount Gargans, a number of hills called Gargantua's Turd, and a number of valleys that are his footprints from olden times.

5. The very famous Advice to the Reader is written in this sense:

> Dear reader, you who read this book,
> Strip yourself of all affectation,
> And, reading it, do not be scandalized:
> It contains neither evil nor infection . . . .
> When I see the grief that undermines and consumes you,
> It is better to write of laughter than of tears,
> For laughter is peculiar to human beings.
> [Rabelais 1534–1551, p. 36, translation modified]

6. Translations from the text of Rabelais have been modified by the authors.

His companions think he is hearing voices; he seems to be hallucinating. But, despite ears open "like oysters in the shell" (p. 566), no
matter how hard they listen they hear nothing. Pantagruel "continues
to affirm that he can hear several voices on the air, both male and female," until the others are able to discern "whole words, . . . voices and
different sorts of sounds of men, women, children, and horses" (p. 567),
which of course greatly frightens them.

At first this experience arouses great panic, especially in Panurge,
who is known as a coward. Hiding, as usual, behind the monk's
sword, he makes a scene, stirring up the whole troupe to an in-
glorious flight: "Let's run away. Let's save ourselves. I don't say
this because I'm afraid, for I fear nothing except danger" (p. 567).
Here we can easily recognize the analyst's first impulse in such
cases.

The giant, however, agrees to be heckled by these voices; from the
start, he says Yes to their existence: "Let's see first what people they
are. They may happen to be our friends. But I still can't catch sight of
anyone, though I can see a hundred miles all round" (p. 567).

Pantagruel then calls upon his culture as a man of the Renaissance,
trying several successive scientific causalities. He first undertakes a
cosmological interpretation, in which different dimensions of time in-
tersect. Then he goes back to the Homeric definition of words as
"bounding, flying, and moving, and consequently alive." Finally he
refers to the myth of Orpheus and the Orphic tradition. No longer
able to endure Orpheus's sadness, the Thracian women tore him to
pieces and threw his head and his lyre into a river, which carried them
out to sea: "And all the time there issued from the head a melancholy
song, as if in mourning for Orpheus's death, while the lyre, as the
moving winds strummed it, played a harmonious accompaniment to
this lament" (p. 568).

In this list, we recognize our inveterate attempts to find causalist
interpretations in the face of the incomprehensible. But, when confronted with voices and sounds that should not be there, it is better
for the analyst, too, to go on to the next chapter: forget about the cause;
what are these voices saying?

The pilot, who knows this region, takes his bearings and tells them
what is going on. On this immense ocean without any orientation
points, he names and marks off the invisible place where they now

are[7]: the site of a naval battle in which the protagonists disappeared with all their possessions. Their voices wander until someone comes across them, lends an ear, and pays attention:

> "My lord, don't be afraid. This is the edge of the frozen sea, and at the beginning of last winter there was a great and treacherous battle here . . . . The words and shouts of the men and women, the sound of the weapons, the clashing of the armor, the neighing of the horses, and all the other frightful noises of battle then froze in the air. But now that the hardship of winter has passed with the coming of calmness and better weather, they are melting and are heard." [p. 568]

Panurge asks to see one of them, if possible. He has to be shown what cannot be said. Would we, then, have to add visual hallucination to auditory hallucination? But isn't this the very demand of the analyst, who first seeks to see forms, reconstituted catastrophes, on the basis of the aberrations the patient show him?

More time is needed to understand that, knocking at the door from the beyond, are words, to be sure, but Real words, laden with flesh and affect: these are not signifiers or ectoplasms. The pilot is not trying to put ideas into the passengers' heads or to seduce them. There is nothing of the totalitarian helmsman about him. He does not use virtual images to ensure the voluntary servitude of his passengers. He relates history.

Pantagruel, for his part, takes another step on the road of the transference, throwing on the deck "whole handfuls of frozen words, which look like crystallized sweets of different colours" (p. 569). Here we are getting closer to the linkage in which the Real is tied to the Imaginary that permits affects, along with the pure Symbolic of heraldic language. For the colors are those of coats of arms, which will later illustrate the names of lineages on the basis of a trauma of history:

> We see there some gules words, . . . some vert sinople, some azure, some sable, and some or.[8] After we warm them a little in our hands,

---

7. Cf. the story of Mimi-Nashi-Hoîchi in Hearn (1904): night after night, a blind young monk is summoned to a place where he hears and tells about the shipwreck and disappearance of the Heike clan in the course of a naval battle that had taken place in the area many years before.

8. These are heraldic terms for the colors red, green, blue, black, and gold, respectively.

they melt like snow, and we actually hear them, though we do not understand them, for they are in a barbarous language. There is one exception, however, a fairly big one. This, when Friar John picks it up, makes a noise like chestnuts thrown on the embers without being pricked. It is an explosion and makes us all start with fear. "That," says Friar John, "was a cannon shot in its day." [p. 569]

After being heard in their register of truth, words can then be entwined in language games that will give them shelter and tombs, forms of poetry or music intended to bury the unbearable disappearance by converting it into precious creations.

This weaving into a text (Lacan 1959–1960, Nagy 1996) begins here with wordplay. Panurge asks Pantagruel to give him still more frozen words. "But Pantagruel answers that only lovers give their words." "Sell me some, then," says Panurge. "That's a lawyer's business," replies Pantagruel, "selling words. I'd rather sell you silence, though I should ask a higher price for it"[9] (p. 569).

The language games end in songs here, as the refrain says,[10] in music appropriate for echoing each of the words in the register it was uttered in: "Nevertheless he throws three or four handfuls on the deck, and I see some very sharp words among them; bloody words, which as the pilot tells us, sometimes return to the place from which they come— but with their throats cut; some terrifying words; and others quite unpleasant to look at. When they have all melted together, we hear . . ." (p. 569). Here Rabelais makes us hear the onomatopoeias of a famous polyphonic piece of the Renaissance, so as to have human throats, led there by the art of music, sound out the din of Clément Janequin's "La Bataille de Marignan."[11] This commemorative piece begins, like Rabelais' "frozen words" episode and as the analysis of those whom we have brought together here in chorus, "Listen!"

"These are the battle-cries and the neighings of the chargers as they clash together. Then we hear other great noises going off as they melt, some like drums and fifes, others like clarions and trumpets" (p. 569).

---

9. As psychoanalysts do? But Rabelais could not have foreseen this.

10. In France, the refrain of a popular song is "Everything ends in songs."

11. Celebrating the 1515 victory, in Italy, of King Francis I of France over the Emperor Charles V, Janequin makes dazzling use of onomatopoeia. Although he died in great poverty, his work was renowned. This song was known in the sixteenth century as far away as Mexico, under the title "La Batalla de Juaniquin."

Now, we are not dealing here with some sort of tape recording preceding the invention of techniques that would later allow it. The narrator of the episode, here in the guise of someone who loves such immobilizations in formalin, is called sharply to order by Pantagruel himself: "I want to preserve some of the gules words in oil, the way you keep snow and ice, and then to wrap them up in clean straw. But Pantagruel refuses, saying that it is folly to store up things which one is never short of, and which are always plentiful, as gullet words are among good and jovial Pantagruelists" (p. 569).

This is the only membership we want to boast of, here at the end of this book. At the moment of conclusion, Rabelais invites us not to let ourselves be fascinated by the horrible beauty of recorded catastrophes. "Whereof one cannot speak . . .": the putting into story/history of this impossibility bears witness to the path we have had to travel in order to pass it from mouth to mouth and inscribe it. In reality, this "bloody rough way," as Wittgenstein called it, goes through traumas and madness to secure the production of freedom among men.

October 11, 2001

References

Aaron, S. (2002). *Le Non de Klara*. Paris: Maurice Nadeau.

Agee, J. (1938). *A Death in the Family*. New York: Bantam, 1969.

Allouch, J. (1994). *Marguerite ou l'Aimée de Lacan*. Paris: EPEL.

Amadas et Ydoine (13th century), trans. R. G. Arthur. New York: Garland, 1993.

Aranda, E. d'. (1656). *Les captifs d'Alger*, ed. L. Z'rari. Paris: Jean Paul Rocher, 1997.

Arbousse Bastide, P. (1972). *Auguste Comte et la folie*. In *Les sciences de la folie*, ed. R. Bastide, pp. 47–72. Paris: Mouton.

Arendt, H. (1951). *The Origins of Totalitarianism*. New York: Harvest, 1976.

—— (1959). Reflections on Little Rock. *Dissent* 6(1):45–56.

—— (1963). *Eichmann in Jerusalem: A Report on the Banality of Evil*. New York: Penguin, 1994.

—— (1971). *The Life of the Mind*. New York: Harcourt Brace.

Artaud, A. (1936). *Le théâtre et son double*. Paris: Gallimard, 1964.

—— (1931–1936). *Selected Writings*, vol. 4, trans. V. Corti. London: Calder, 1974.

Aubailly, J.-C. (1984). *Le monologue, le dialogue et la sottie. Essai sur quelques genres dramatiques de la fin du moyen-âge et du début du XVI° siècle*. Paris: Champion.

Bailly, L. (1996). *Les catastrophes et leurs conséquences psychotraumatiques chez l'enfant. Descriptions cliniques et traitement*. Paris: ESF.

Balzac, H. de. (1832). *Colonel Chabert*, trans. C. Cosman. New York: New Directions, 1997.

Barillé, E. (1997). *Laure, la sainte de l'abîme*. Paris: Flammarion.

Barker, P. (1992). *Regeneration*. New York: Dutton.

—— (1994). *The Eye in the Door*. New York: Dutton.

—— (1995). *The Ghost Road*. New York: Dutton.

———— (1998). *Another World*. New York: Penguin.

Barrett, D. (1996). *Trauma and Dreams*. Cambridge, MA: Harvard University Press.

Barrois, C. (1988). *Les névroses traumatiques*. Paris: Dunod.

———— (1993). *Psychanalyse du guerrier*. Paris: Hachette.

———— (1998). Psychoses aigües, subaigües et au long court. Complications et expressions des syndrômes psychotraumatiques (ou PTSD des auteurs Nord Américains). *Annales Médicopsychologiques* 156:30–36.

Barrois, C., and Andro, J. P. (1991). *L'Effroi des hommes* [*Human Dread*]. Paris: Télévision FR3.

Baudelaire, C. (1861). *The Flowers of Evil*. London and New York: Oxford University Press, 1998.

Bazin, R. (1926). *Baltus le lorrain*. Paris: Calmann-Lévy.

Becker, A. (1998). *Oubliés de la grande guerre. Populations occupées, déportés civils, prisonniers de guerre*. Paris: Editions Noèsis.

Beckett, S. (1953). *L'Innommable*. Paris: Editions de Minuit.

———— (1961). *Comment c'est*. Paris: Editions de Minuit.

Beers, C. (1908). *A Mind that Found Itself*. Pittsburgh: University of Pittsburgh Press, 1981.

Belau, L., and Ramadanovic, P. (2002). *Topologies of Trauma. Essays on the Limit of Knowledge and Memory*. New York: Other Press.

Benedetti, G. (1971). *Paziente e Terapeuta nell' Esperienza Psicotica*. Turin: Bollati Boringhieri.

———— (1980). *Alienazione e Personazione nella Psicoterapia della Malattia Mentale*. Turin: Giulio Einaudi.

———— (1996). The splitting between separate and symbiotic states of the self in the psychoanalytic dynamic of schizophrenia. *International Forum of Psychoanalysis* 5:23–38.

Beradt, C. (1966). *The Third Reich of Dreams*. Chicago: Quadrangle, 1968.

Bergman, I., dir. (1977). *The Serpent's Egg* (film).

Berque, A. (2000). *Ecoumène. Introduction à l'étude des milieux humains*. Paris: Belin.

Besserman Vianna, H. (1997). *Politique de la psychanalyse face à la dictature et à la torture. N'en parlez à personne*. Paris: L'Harmattan.

Bion, W. R. (1946a). *Experiences in Groups*. London: Tavistock.

———— (1946b). Leaderless groups. *Bulletin of the Menninger Clinic* 10: 77–81.

———— (1959). *Cogitations*. London: Karnac, 1994.

———— (1962). *Learning from Experience*. London: Heinemann.

———— (1963). *Elements of Psycho-Analysis*. London: Heinemann.

———— (1967). *Second Thoughts*. London: Karnac.

———— (1975). *A Memoir of the Future. Book I. The Dream.* London: Karnac, 1991.

———— (1977). *Taming Wild Thoughts.* London: Karnac.

———— (1982). *The Long Week-End, 1897–1919.* London: Karnac.

———— (1997). *War Memoirs, 1917–1919.* London: Karnac.

Bitbol, M. (1990). *L'Elision.* Paris: Seuil.

Bloch, M. (1940). *L'Etrange défaite.* Paris: Gallimard, 1990.

Boileau, N. (1669–1674). *L'Art poétique.* Paris: Garnier Flammarion, 1989.

Bollas, C. (1987). *The Shadow of the Object. Psychoanalysis of the Unthought Known.* New York: Columbia University Press.

Braceland, F. (1946). Psychiatric lessons from World War II. *American Journal of Psychiatry* 103:587–593.

Brant, S. (1494). *The Ship of Fools.* New York and London: Dover, 1991.

Brecht, K., Friedrich, V., Hermanns, L., et al. (1985). *Hier geht das Leben auf eine sehr merkwürdige Weise weiter. Zur Geschichte der Psychoanalyse in Deutschland.* Hamburg: Kellner.

Brécourt-Villars, C. (1988). *Yvette Guilbert l'Irrespectueuse (1865–1944).* Paris: Plon.

Breton, A. (1928). *Nadja.* New York: Grove, 1962.

Briole, G., Lebigot, F., Lafont, B., et al. (1994). *Le traumatisme psychique: rencontre et devenir.* Congrès de Psychiatrie et de Neurologie de Langue Française. Paris: Masson.

Brouwers, J. (1981). *Sunken Red,* trans. A. Dixon. New York: New Amsterdam Books, 1990

Cantor G. (1960). *La théorie Bacon-Shakespeare. Le drame subjectif d'un savant,* ed. E. Porge. Clichy: GREC, 1996.

Capurro, R. (1999). *Auguste Comte, Actualidad de una Herencia.* Montevideo: Edelp.

Carroll, L. (1865). *Alice's Adventures in Wonderland and Through the Looking-Glass.* New York: Signet, 1960.

Cervantes, M. (1605, 1614). *Don Quixote,* trans. J. Rutherford. New York: Penguin, 2003.

Chrétien de Troyes. (1181). *Le conte du graal ou le roman de Perceval,* ed. C. Mela. Paris: Librairie Générale Française, 1990.

Clausewitz, K. von. (1834). *On War,* trans. A. Rapoport. New York: Viking, 1982.

Cocteau, J. (1934). *The Infernal Machine,* trans. A. Berme. New York: New Directions, 1964.

Coignet, C. (1850). *Les cahiers du Capitaine Coignet. Mémoires d'un officier de l'empire, achevés le 1 Juillet 1850.* Paris: Documents Historiques Editions Deux-Trois.

Colonomos, F. (1987). L'Institut de Psychanalyse de Berlin avant 1936. In *Contribution à l'histoire de la psychanalyse en Allemagne, 1907–1960*, pp. 80–108. Paris: Association Internationale d'Histoire de la Psychanalyse.

Conrad. J. (1902). *Heart of Darkness.* New York: Penguin, 1995.

Cooperman, M. (1983). Some obervations regarding psychoanalytic psychotherapy in the hospital setting. *The Psychiatric Hospital* 14:21–28.

Crocq, L. (1999). *Les traumatismes psychiques de guerre.* Paris: Odile Jacob.

Cyrulnik, B. (1999). *Un merveilleux malheur.* Paris: Odile Jacob.

Damasio, A. (1995). *Descartes' Error. Emotion, Reason, and the Human Brain.* New York: Avon.

———— (1999). *The Feeling of What Happens: Body and Emotion in the Making of Consciousness.* New York: Harvest.

Dante Alighieri. (1309). *The Divine Comedy of Dante Alighieri. Inferno,* trans. A. Mandelbaum. New York: Bantam, 1982.

Davenson, H. (1946). *Le livre des chansons, ou introduction à la chanson populaire française.* Neuchâtel, Switzerland: Editions de la Baconnière, 1977.

Davoine, F. (1989). Potential space and the space in between two deaths. In *The Facilitating Environment. Clinical Applications of Winnicott's Theory,* ed. G. M. Fromm and B. L. Smith, pp. 581–603. Madison, CT: International Universities Press.

———— (1990). Delusion as a way of knowledge. In *Illness in the Analyst. Implications for the Treatment Relationship,* ed. H. J. Schwartz and A. L. Silver, pp. 47–71. Madison, CT: International Universities Press.

———— (1992). *La folie Wittgenstein.* Paris: EPEL.

———— (1998). *Mère folle.* Strasbourg: Arcanes.

Déguignet, J. M. (1999). *Mémoires d'un paysan bas-breton, 1834–1905.* Paris: Editions An Here.

Delbo, C. (1970a). *Auschwitz et après. I. Aucun de nous ne reviendra.* Paris: Editions de Minuit.

———— (1970b). *Auschwitz et après. II. Une connaissance inutile.* Paris: Editions de Minuit.

———— (1971). *Auschwitz et après. III. Mesure de nos jours.* Paris: Editions de Minuit.

Delmas, L. (1988). *Visages d'une terre lorraine occupée. Le Jarnisy 1914–1918.* Charleville-Mézières: Ardenn'Offset.

Demiéville, P. (1972). *Entretiens de Lin Tsi. Traduction et commentaire.* Paris: Fayard.

Descartes, R. (1618–1637). *Oeuvres philosophiques 1618–1637.* Paris: Garnier, 1963.

———— (1637). *Discourse on the Method*, trans. G. Hefferman. St. Paul, IN: Notre Dame University Press.

———— (1641). *Méditations philosophiques*. Paris: Gallimard, 1958.

Devos, R. (1989). *A plus d'un titre*. Paris: Olivier Orban.

Dodds, E. R. (1959). *The Greeks and the Irrational*. Berkeley, CA: University of California Press.

Dor, J. (1985). *Introduction to the Reading of Lacan*, trans. S. Fairfield. New York: Other Press, 1998.

———— (1994). *The Clinical Lacan*, trans. S. Fairfield. New York: Other Press, 1999.

Dottenville, H. (1973). *Histoire et géographie mythique de la France. Géographie de Gargantua*. Paris: Maisonneuve.

Dubois, W. E. B. (1921). *The Seventh Son: The Black Man in the Revolution of 1914–1918*, ed. J. Lester. New York: Random House, 1986.

Duchamp, M. (1934). *Duchamp du signe. Ecrits*. Paris: Flammarion, 1975.

———— (1967). *Ingénieur du temps perdu. Entretiens avec Pierre Cabanne*. Paris: Belfond.

Ducharme, R. (1976). *Les enfantômés*. Saint-Laurent-Paris: Lacombe-Gallimard.

Dufournet, J. (1974). *Adam de la Halle à la recherche de lui-même. Le jeu dramatique du Jeu de la Feuillée*. Paris: SEDES.

Eccles, J. C. (1994). *How the Self Controls Its Brain*. Berlin and New York: Springer.

Eliot, T. S. (1922). The waste land. In *Collected Poems, 1909–1962*, pp. 50–74. New York: Harcourt Brace, 1991.

———— (1929). Dante. In *Selected Essays, 1917–1932*, pp. 199–240. New York: Harcourt, 1950.

Erasmus, D. (1508). *The Praise of Folly*, trans. L. F. Dean. New York: Packard, 1946.

Ey, H., Bernard, P., and Brisset, C. (1967). *Manuel de psychiatrie*. Paris: Masson.

Fabre, D. (1992). *Le carnaval ou la fête à l'envers*. Paris: Gallimard Découvertes.

Fabre, J.-H. (1979). *Insects*, ed. D. Black. New York: Scribner's.

Faulkner, W. (1936). *Absalom, Absalom!* New York: Vintage International, 1990.

Ferenczi, S. (1919). *Psychoanalysis of War Neuroses*. London: International Psychoanalytic Press, 1921.

Fleischmann, P., dir. (1968). *Hunting Scenes from Bavaria [Jagdszenen aus Niederbayern]* (film).

Ford, J., dir. (1962). *The Man Who Shot Liberty Valance* (film).

Foucault, M. (1961). *Madness and Civilization. A History of Insanity in the Age of Reason.* New York: Vintage, 1988.

Freud, A. (1954). An experiment in group upbringing. In *The Writings of Anna Freud*, vol. 4, pp. 163–229. Madison, CT: International Universities Press, 1968.

Freud, M. (1958). *Sigmund Freud, Man and Father.* New York: Vanguard.

Freud S. (1895). Project for a scientific psychology. *Standard Edition* 1:281–397.

——— (1907). *Delusions and Dreams in Jensen's "Gradiva."* Standard Edition 9:1–95.

——— (1911). Psycho-analytic notes on an autobiographical account of a case of paranoia (dementia paranoides). *Standard Edition* 11:1–79.

——— (1918). From the history of an infantile neurosis. *Standard Edition* 17:1–122.

——— (1919). The "uncanny." *Standard Edition* 17:217–256.

——— (1920). *Beyond the Pleasure Principle. Standard Edition* 18:1–64.

——— (1925). Negation. *Standard Edition* 19:233–239.

——— (1933). *New Introductory Lectures on Psycho-Analysis. Standard Edition* 22:1–182.

——— (1939). *Moses and Monotheism. Standard Edition* 19:1–137.

Freud, S., and Breuer, J. (1893–1895). *Studies on Hysteria. Standard Edition* 2.

Freud, S., and Jung, C. G. (1974). *The Freud/Jung Letters. The Correspondence Between Sigmund Freud and C. G. Jung*, ed. W. McGuire, trans. R. Mannheim and R. F. C. Hull. Cambridge, MA: Harvard University Press.

Friedkin, W., dir. (1971). *The French Connection* (film).

Fritz, J. M. (1992). *Le discours du fou au moyen-âge, XII°-XIII° siecles. Etude comparée des discours littéraire, médical, juridique et théologique de la folie.* Paris: PUF.

Fromm, M. G., and Smith, B. L. (1989). *The Facilitating Environment. Clinical Applications of Winnicott's Theory.* Madison, CT: International Universities Press.

Fromm-Reichmann, F. (1946). *Psychoanalysis and Psychotherapy.* Chicago: University of Chicago Press, 1959.

Fuentes, C. (1990). *Valiente Mundo Nuevo.* Mexico City: Fondo de Cultura Economica.

Gaide G., Mérendet, O., and Penna, J.-L. (1996). *Un col, des hommes. Le Petit Saint Bernard.* Montmélian: La Fontaine de Siloé.

Gaudillière, J.-M. (1995). Mesures pour mesures. *Epochè* 5:15–21.

——— (1997). Rêver en situation totalitaire. *Critique* 603–604:641–650.

Ginzburg, C. (1980). *Le fromage et les vers. L'Univers d'un meunier du XVI⁰ siècle.* Paris: Aubier.

——— (1989). *Le Sabbat des sorcières.* Paris: Gallimard, 1992.

Glass, A. J. (1956). *Management of mass psychiatric casualties.* Paper presented at the 62nd Annual Conference of Military Surgeons, Washington, DC, November.

Glucksman, A. (1987). *Descartes, c'est la France.* Paris: Flammarion.

Goffman, E. (1961). *Asylum.* New York: Doubleday.

Gorney, J. E. (1994). On limits and limit setting. *Psychoanalytic Review* 81:259–278.

——— (2000). Bulimia as metaphor: twinship and play in the treatment of a difficult patient. In *Progress in Self Psychology*, ed. A. Goldberg, vol. 16, pp. 141–154. Hillsdale, NJ: Academic Press.

Gouhier, H. (1931). *La vie d'Auguste Comte.* Paris: Librairie Philosophique J. Vrin, 1997.

Graves, R. (1929). *Goodbye to All That.* New York: Doubleday, 1989.

Greenberg, J. (1964). *I Never Promised You a Rose Garden.* New York: New American Library, 1989.

Grim, O. R. (1998). Inadaptation et handicap. De la clinique à l'histoire. *Le Carnet Psy* 39:19–20.

Grinker, R. R. (1945). Psychiatric disorders in combat crews overseas and in returnees. *Medical Clinics of North America* 29:729–739.

Groddeck, G. (1917–1934). *Ça et moi. Correspondance entre Groddeck et Freud.* Paris: Gallimard, 1977.

——— (1923). *The Book of the It.* London: Vision Press, 1949.

Grossman, D. (1995). *On Killing.* New York: Back Bay Books.

Gudmundsson, E. M. (1993). *Angels of the Universe*, trans. B. Scudder. New York: St. Martin's Press, 1997.

Guimarães Rosa, J. (1956). *The Devil to Pay in the Badlands.* New York: Knopf, 1963.

Harrison, T. (2000). *Bion, Rickman, Foulkes, and the Northfield Experiment: Advancing on a Different Front.* London: Jessica Kingsley.

Hearn, L. (1904). *Kwaidan: Stories and Studies of Strange Things.* London: Tuttle Shokai, 2002.

Hearne, V. (1986). *Adam's Task: Calling Animals by Name.* New York: Knopf.

Heers, J. (1983). *Fêtes des fous et carnavals.* Paris: Fayard.

Heisenberg, W. (1971). *Physics and Beyond.* New York: Harper & Row.

Herodotus. *The History of Herodotus*, trans. G. Rawlinson. New York: Tudor, 1932.

Highsmith, P. (1957). *Deep Water.* New York: Penguin, 1974.

Holloway, H. C., and Ursano, R. J. (1984). The Vietnam veteran: memory, social context, and metaphor. *Psychiatry* 47:103–108.

Homer. *The Iliad*, trans. W. H. D. Rouse. New York: Signet, 1999.

—— *The Odyssey of Homer*, trans. R. Lattimore. New York: Harper, 1965.

Howard, R., dir. (2001). *A Beautiful Mind* (film).

Hsiung, P. M. (1984). *Zhang Xu et la calligraphie cursive folle*. Paris: Collège de France, Institut des Hautes Etudes Chinoises.

Hugo, V. (1862). *Les Misérables*. Paris: Gallimard.

Hunt, L. (1992). *The Family Romance of the French Revolution*. Berkeley, CA: University of California Press.

—— (2002). *History and psychoanalysis*. Paper delivered at the colloquium "Why Psychoanalysis?" Radcliffe Center for Advanced Studies, Cambridge, MA, February.

Huxley, A. (1932). *Brave New World*. London: Grafton, 1977.

Isotti, M. (1978). *Amore Mio Nemico*. Milan: Rizzoli.

Isozaki, A. (1978). La notion d'espace-temps au Japon. In *Ma: espace-temps au Japon*, pp. 8–9. Exhibition Catalog, Musée des Arts Décoratifs, Paris, October–December.

Izutsu, T. (1978). *Le kôan Zen*. Paris: Fayard.

Janequin, C. (1485–1558). *Chansons françaises. La guerre: la bataille de Marignan*. Arles: Harmonia Mundi, 1982.

Jay, J. (1991). Terrible knowledge. *Family Therapy Networker* 15:18–29.

Kant, I. (1766). *Dreams of a Spirit-Seer*, trans. E. F. Goerwitz. London: Thoemmes, 1998.

Kentsmith, D. K. (1986). Principles of battlefield psychiatry. *Military Medicine* 151:89–96.

Kerouac, J. (1957). *On the Road*. New York: Viking.

Keynes, J. M. (1947). *Newton the Man*. Cambridge, UK, and New York: Cambridge University Press.

Kimura, B. (1972). *Hito To Hito No Aïda*. Tokyo: Kobundo.

Kleist, H. von. (1808). *Penthesilea. A Tragic Drama*, trans. J. Agee. New York: HarperCollins, 1998.

Koseleck, R. (1979). *Vergangene Zukunft: Zur Semantik geschichtlicher Zeiten*. Frankfurt am Main: Suhrkamp, 1990.

Kosminsky, P., dir. (1999). *Peacekeepers* (film).

Kourouma, A. (2000). *Allah n'est pas obligé*. Paris: Seuil.

Kuhn, T. (1970). *The Structure of Scientific Revolutions*. Chicago: University of Chicago Press.

La Boétie, E. de. (1548). *Anti-Dictator: The Discours sur la Servitude Volontaire of Etienne de la Boétie*, trans. H. Kurz. New York: Columbia University Press, 1942.

Lacan, J. (1932). Le cas Aimée ou la paranoïa d'autopunition. In *La psychose paranoïaque dans ses rapports avec la personnalité*, vol. 2, pp. 151–303. Paris: Seuil, 1975.

——— (1947). La psychiatrie anglaise et la guerre. In *Autres Ecrits*, pp. 101–120. Paris: Seuil, 2001.

——— (1949). The mirror stage as formative of the function of the I. In *Ecrits: A Selection*, trans. A. Sheridan, pp. 1–7. New York: Norton, 1977.

——— (1953). The function and field of speech and language in psychoanalysis. In *Ecrits: A Selection*, trans. A. Sheridan, pp. 30–113. New York: Norton, 1977.

——— (1954). Réponse au commentaire de Jean Hyppolite sur la Verneinung de Freud. Seminar, February 10. In *Ecrits*, pp. 369–399, Paris: Seuil, 1966.

——— (1955–1956). On a question preliminary to any possible treatment of psychosis. In *Ecrits. A Selection*, trans. A. Sheridan, pp. 179–221. New York: Norton, 1977.

——— (1957). The agency of the letter in the unconscious or reason since Freud. In *Ecrits. A Selection*, trans. A. Sheridan, pp. 146–175. New York: Norton, 1977.

——— (1958). The signification of the phallus. *In Ecrits: A Selection*, trans. A. Sheridan, pp. 281–291. New York: Norton, 1977.

——— (1959–1960). *The Seminar of Jacques Lacan. Book VII. The Ethics of Psychoanalysis*, trans. D. Porter. New York: Norton, 1992.

——— (1960). The subversion of the subject and the dialectic of desire in the Freudian unconscious. In *Ecrits: A Selection*, trans. A. Sheridan, pp. 292–325. New York: Norton, 1977.

——— (1964). *The Four Fundamental Concepts of Psychoanalysis*, ed. J.-A. Miller, trans. A. Sheridan. New York: Norton, 1978.

——— (1966). *Ecrits*. Paris: Seuil.

——— (1969–1970). *Le Séminaire, livre XVII. L'Envers de la psychanalyse*. Paris: Seuil, 1991.

——— (1971–1972). *Le Séminaire, livre XIX. . . . Ou pire*. Unpublished.

——— (1972–1973). *The Seminar of Jacques Lacan, Book XX*, ed. J.-A. Miller, trans. B. Fink. New York: Norton, 1998.

——— (1974). *La troisième. Petits ecrits et conférences*. Unpublished.

——— (1976). *Le sinthome (consacré à J. Joyce)*. *Ornicar?* 6–11, 1977.

——— (2001). *Autres écrits*. Paris: Seuil.

Lacaze, A. (1978). *Le Tunnel*. Paris: Julliard.

Lafont, B., and Raingeard, D. (1992). Les principes de Salmon à l'épreuve de la guerre du Golfe. *Médecine et armées* 20:95–100.

La Halle, A. de. (1276). *Le jeu de la feuillée*, ed. J. Dufournet. Paris: Garnier Flammarion, 1989.

La Mettrie, O. de. (1746). *L'Homme machine*. Paris: Pauvert, 1966.

Landau, M. (1990). Les enfants de Terezin. *Le temps du non: Psychanalyse et Idéologie* 5:45–51.

Laroque, F. (1988). *Shakespeare et la fête*. Paris: PUF.

Lavik, N. J., ed. (1994). *Pain and Survival: Human Rights Violations and Mental Health*. Oslo: Scandinavian University Press.

Le Clézio, J. M. G. (1971). *Haï*. Geneva: Skira.

Legendre, P. (1989). *Le crime du caporal Lortie*. Paris: Fayard.

Le Goff, J., and Schmit, J. C. (1981). *Le charivari*. Paris: Mouton.

Levi, P. (1958). *If This Is a Man*. New York: Abacus, 1987.

Lönrott, E. (1835, 1849). *The Kalevala, or Poems of the Kalevala District*, trans. F. P. Magoun, Jr. Cambridge, MA: Harvard University Press, 1963.

Loo, H., Carvalho, W. de, Hartmann, F., and Amado, B. I. (1994). Les électronarcoses d'entretien. Actualités sur l'électroconvulsivothérapie. *Psychologie Médicale* 26:565–575.

Loraux, N. (1990). La métaphore sans métaphore. À propos de l'Orestie. *Revue Philosophique* 2:115:139.

Loriga, S. (1991). *Soldats. Un laboratoire disciplinaire. L'armée piémontaise au XVIIIe siècle*. Paris: Mentha.

Lumière, L., dir. (1894). *L'Arroseur arrosé* (film).

Machiavelli, N. (1513). *The Prince*, trans. H. C. Mansfield. Chicago: University of Chicago Press, 1985.

Malamoud, C. (1989). *Cuire le monde. Rite et pensée dans l'Inde ancienne*. Paris: Editions la Découverte.

———— (2002). *Le jumeau solaire*. Paris: Seuil.

Mallarmé, S. (1876). *Le tombeau d'Edgar Poe*. Paris: Gallimard Pléiade, 1961.

Marshall, S. L. A. (1944). *Island Victory*. Washington, DC: Zenger, 1982.

Maupassant, G. de. (1887). *Le horla et autres contes d'angoisse*. Paris: Presses Pocket, 1989.

Mauss, M. (1924). *The Gift. The Form and Reason for Exchange in Archaic Societies*, trans. W. D. Halls. New York: Norton, 1989.

McCaughey, B. G. (1986). The psychological symptomatology of a U.S. naval disaster. *Military Medicine* 151:162–165.

———— (1987). U.S. Navy Special Psychiatric Rapid Intervention Team (SPRINT). *Military Medicine* 152:133–135.

MacDougall, J. (1989). *Theaters of the Body*. New York: Norton.

McGuinness, B. (1988). *Wittgenstein: A Life*, vol. 1. *Young Ludwig (1889–1921)*. London: Duckworth.

Melville, H. (1853). Bartleby the scrivener. In *Billy Budd, Sailor and Other Stories*, pp. 59–99. New York: Penguin, 1985.

Milgram, S. (1974). *Obedience to Authority*. New York: Harper & Row.

Missios, C. (1985). *Toi au moins, tu es mort avant*. La Tour d'Aignes: Editions de l'Aube, 1991.

Mohatt, G., and Eagle Elk, J. (2000). *The Price of a Gift. A Lakota Healer's Story*. Lincoln, NB: University of Nebraska Press.

Molière. (1662). *The School for Wives*. In *Comedies of Molière*, vol. 1, trans. F. Green, pp. 241–290. New York: Dutton, 1937.

——— (1666). *The Mock Doctor*. In *Comedies of Molière*, vol. 1, trans. F. Green, pp. 395–427. New York: Dutton, 1937.

——— (1673). *The Hypochondriac*. In *Comedies of Molière*, vol. 2, trans. F. Green, pp. 411–472. New York: Dutton, 1937.

Monk, R. (1990). *Ludwig Wittgenstein: The Duty of Genius*. New York: Penguin.

Montaigne, M. de. (1580). *The Complete Essays of Montaigne*, trans. D. M. Frame. Stanford, CA: Stanford University Press, 1958.

Moore, W. (1989). *Schrödinger. Life and Thought*. Cambridge, UK, and New York: Cambridge University Press.

Mozart, W. A. (1786). *The Marriage of Figaro (Le Nozze di Figaro)*. New York and London: Dover, 1979.

Mukagasana, Y. (1997). *La mort ne veut pas de moi*. Paris: Fixot.

Muller, J. P. (1995). *Beyond the Psychoanalytic Dyad: Developmental Semiotics in Freud, Peirce, and Lacan*. New York and London: Routledge.

Muller, J. P., and Richardson, W. J. (1982). *Lacan and Language: A Reader's Guide to Ecrits*. New York: International Universities Press.

——— (1988). *The Purloined Poe. Lacan, Derrida and Psychoanalytic Reading*. Baltimore, MD: Johns Hopkins University Press.

Musil, R. (1930–1942). *The Man Without Qualities*, trans. S. Wilkins. New York: Vintage, 1996.

Nadeau, M. (1944). *Histoire du surréalisme*. Paris: Seuil, 1964.

Nagy, G. (1979). *The Best of the Achaeans: Concepts of the Hero in Archaic Greek Society*. Baltimore, MD: Johns Hopkins University Press.

——— (1996). *Poetry as Performance. Homer and Beyond*. Cambridge, UK, and New York: Cambridge University Press.

Nasar, S. (1998). *A Beautiful Mind*. New York: Simon & Schuster.

Nelli, R. (1974). *L'Erotique des troubadours*, vols. I and II. Paris: Union Générale d'Editions.

Nerval, G. de. (1854). *Les chimères*. Paris: Gallimard La Pléiade, 1960.

O'Connell, M. R. (1985). *The Falklands experience, 1982*. Paper presented at the Fourth Annual Workshop on Combat Stress, Fort Sam Houston, TX, March.

O'Drury, M. (1973). *The Danger of Words*. London: Routledge & Keagan Paul.

———— (1981). Some notes on conversations with Wittgenstein. In *Recollections of Wittgenstein*, pp. 76–171. London and New York: Oxford University Press.

Pankow, G. (1969). *L'homme et sa psychose*. Paris: Aubier Montaigne.

Parker, B. (1972). *The Mingled Yarn*. New Haven, CT: Yale University Press.

Pasolini, P. P., dir. (1975). *Salo: The 120 Days of Sodom* (film).

Pécaut, D. (1987). *L'Ordre et la violence. Evolution sociopolitique en Colombie entre 1930–53*. Paris: Editions de l'EHESS.

Peignot, J. (1977). *Ecrits de Laure*. Paris: Pauvert.

Plato. *Gorgias*, trans. W. C. Helmbold. New York: Prentice Hall, 1952.

———— *Phaedrus*, trans. A. Nehamas. New York: Hackett, 1995.

———— *The Republic*. In *Great Dialogues of Plato*, trans. W. H. D. Rouse, pp. 118–422. New York: New American Library, 1956.

———— *Theaetetus*, trans. R. A. Waterfield. New York: Viking, 1989.

Poe, E. A. (1845). The facts in the case of M. Waldemar. In *The Complete Poems and Stories of Edgar Allen Poe*, vol. 4, pp. 656–663. New York: Knopf, 1946.

Ponge, F. (1960). *Making of the Pré*, trans. L. Fahnestock. Minneapolis: University of Minnesota Press, 1982.

Rabelais, F. (1534–1551). *Gartantua & Pantagruel*, trans. J. M. Cohen. New York: Penguin, 1955.

Red Bird, S. (1984). Personal communication. Summer Institute in Cross-Cultural Studies, University of Alaska, Fairbanks.

Remarque, E. M. (1928). *All Quiet on the Western Front*, trans. A. W. Wheen. New York: Fawcett, 1995.

Renou, L. (1978). *L'Inde fondamentale. Etudes indianistes réunies et présentées par Charles Malamoud*. Paris: Hermann.

Resnais, A., dir. (1957). *Night and Fog* (film).

Revel, J. (1996). Microanalysis and the construction of the social. In *Histories. French Constructions of the Past*, ed. J. Revel, R. Nadaff, and L. Hunt, pp. 492–502. New York: New Press, 1998.

———— (2001). *Qu'est-ce qu'un cas?* Paper presented at the colloquium "Casus Belli," Ecole des Hautes Etudes en Sciences Sociales, Paris, June.

Rey-Flaud, H. (1980). *Pour une dramaturgie du moyen-âge*. Paris: PUF.

——— (1985). *Le charivari. Les rituels fondamentaux de la sexualité*. Paris: Payot.

Rhees, R. (1984). *Recollections of Wittgenstein*. London and New York: Oxford University Press.

Ridington, R. (1982). Telling secrets. Stories of the vision quest. *Canadian Journal of Native Studies* 2:213–219.

Rivers, K. (1976). *Memories of Lewis Carroll. Library Research News* 3.4. Hamilton, Ontario: McMaster University.

Rivers, W. H. R. (1918). *Dreams and Primitive Culture*. Manchester, UK: Manchester University Press.

——— (1922). *Instinct and the Unconscious*. Cambridge, UK and New York: Cambridge University Press.

Rouget, G. (1980). *La musique et la transe*. Paris: Gallimard.

Rousseau, J. J. (1768). *Complete Dictionary of Music*. New York: AMS Press, 1979.

Sacks, O. (1973). *Awakenings*. New York: Vintage.

——— (1985). *The Man Who Mistook His Wife for a Hat*. New York: Touchstone.

——— (1995). *An Anthropologist on Mars*. New York: Knopf.

Sacy, S. de. (1985). *Descartes*. Paris: Le Seuil.

Saïd, S. (1978). *La faute tragique*. Paris: Maspero.

Salmon, T. W. (1917). *The Care and Treatment of Mental Diseases and War Neuroses (Shell Shock) in the British Army*. New York: War Work Committee of the National Committee for Mental Hygiene.

Sapir, E. (1949). *Selected Writings of Edward Sapir on Language, Culture and Personality*. Berkeley, CA: University of California Press.

Sargant, W., and Slater, E. (1944). *An Introduction to Physical Methods of Treatment in Psychiatry*. New York: Jason Aronson, 1973.

Sass, L. A. (1992). *Madness and Modernism. Insanity in the Light of Modern Art, Literature, and Thought*. Cambridge, MA: Harvard University Press.

Sassoon, S. (1937). *The Complete Memoirs of George Sherston*. London and Boston: Faber and Faber, 1972.

Saussure, F. de (1915). *Course in General Linguistics*, trans. W. Baskin. New York: McGraw-Hill, 1965.

Schem, S. (1997). *Mount Misery*. New York: Ivy.

Schmitt, J.-C. (1990). *La raison des gestes*. Paris: Gallimard.

——— (1994). *Les revenants. Les vivants et les morts dans la société médiévale*. Paris: Gallimard.

Schönberg, C.-M., and Boublil, A. (1987). *Les Miserables* (musical).

Schrödinger, E. (1954). *Nature and the Greeks and Science and Humanism*. Cambridge, UK and New York: Cambridge University Press, 1996.

———— (1956). *Mind and Matter*. Cambridge, UK and New York: Cambridge University Press, 1990.

Schur, M. (1972). *Freud, Living and Dying*. Madison, CT: International Universities Press.

Searles, H. (1960). *The Nonhuman Environment*. Madison, CT: International Universities Press.

———— (1965). *Collected Papers on Schizophrenia and Related Subjects*. Madison, CT: International Universities Press.

Sebald, W. G. (2001). *Austerlitz*, trans. A. Bell. New York: Modern Library, 2002.

Sévigné, Madame de. (1660–1696). *Lettres choisies*. Paris: Gallimard, 1988.

Shapiro, E., and Carr, A. W. (1991). *Lost in Familiar Places. Creating New Connections between Individual and Society*. New Haven, CT: Yale University Press.

Shay, J. (1995). *Achilles in Vietnam. Combat Trauma and the Undoing of Character*. New York: Touchstone.

Shephard, B. (2000). *A War of Nerves: Soldiers and Psychiatrists in the Twentieth Century*. Cambridge, MA: Harvard University Press.

Sieffert, R. (1979). *Nô et kyôgen, printemps eté. Théâtre du moyen âge*. Paris: Publications Orientalistes de France.

Silver, A. (1989). *Psychoanalysis and Psychosis*. Madison, CT: International Universities Press.

———— (1996). Frieda Fromm-Reichmann: Loneliness and deafness. *Forum of Psychoanalysis* 5:39–46.

Sophocles. *Oedipus at Colonus*, trans. R. Fitzgerald. In *Sophocles I. Four Tragedies*, pp. 77–155. Chicago: University of Chicago Press, 1954.

———— *Antigone*, trans. E. Wyckoff. In *Sophocles I. Four Tragedies*, pp. 157–204. Chicago: University of Chicago Press, 1954.

Soury, P. (1986). *Chaînes et noeuds*, ed. M. Thomé and C. Léger. Private publication.

Starobinski, J. (1971). *Les mots sous les mots. Les anagrammes de Ferdinand de Saussure*. Paris: Gallimard.

Steinberg, M. P. (1995). Aby Warburg's Kreuzlingen lecture: a reading. In *Images from the Region of the Pueblo Indians of North America*, pp. 59–114. Ithaca, NY: Cornell University Press.

Stendhal. (1839). *The Charterhouse of Parma*, trans. M. Mauldon. London and New York: Oxford University Press, 2000.

Sterne, L. (1759–1767). *The Life and Opinions of Tristram Shandy, Gentleman*. New York: Penguin, 1997.

Stewart, S. (1956). *Give Us This Day*. New York: Avon, 1990.

Stravinsky, I. (1918). *The Soldier's Tale* (musical composition).

Strindberg, A. (1897). *Inferno*, trans. M. Sandbach. New York: Penguin, 2001.

Strouse, J. (1981). *Alice James: A Biography*. Cambridge, MA: Harvard University Press.

Sullivan, H. S. (1945). *The Fusion of Psychiatry and Social Science*. New York: Norton, 1971.

——— (1946). *Conceptions of Modern Psychiatry*. New York: Norton.

——— (1974). *Schizophrenia as a Human Process*. New York: Norton.

Sutherland, J. D. (1989). *Fairbairn's Journey into the Interior*. London: Free Association.

Swedenborg, E. (1749–1756). *Dictionary of Correspondences, Representatives, and Significatives*. New York: Kessinger, 2003.

Swick Perry, H. (1982). *Psychiatrist of America: The Life of Harry Stack Sullivan*. Cambridge, MA: Harvard University Press.

The Tale of Tristan's Madness (1978), trans. A. S. Fredrick. Hammondsworth, UK: Penguin.

Tasso, T. (1581). *Jerusalem Delivered*, trans. J. M. Esolen. Baltimore, MD: Johns Hopkins University Press, 1979.

Tavernier, B., dir. (1992). *La guerre sans nom* (film).

Textbook of Military Medicine (1994). Vol. I.2: *Military Psychiatry: Preparing in Peace for War*. Falls Church, VA: Office of the Surgeon General.

Textbook of Military Medicine (1995). Vol. I.3: *War Psychiatry*. Falls Church, VA: Office of the Surgeon General.

Thom, R. (1977). *Stabilité structurelle et morphogénèse*. Paris: Interéditions.

——— (1983). *Paraboles et catastrophes. Entretiens sur les mathématiques, la science et la philosophie*. Paris: Flammarion.

——— (1990). *Apologie du logos*. Paris: Hachette.

——— (1991). *Prédire n'est pas expliquer. Entretiens avec Emile Noël*. Paris: Eshel.

Thompson, G., and Thompson, S. (1998). Interview with Dr. Otto Allen Will, Jr. *Contemporary Psychoanalysis* 34:289–304.

Tierney, P. (2000). *Darkness in El Dorado: How Scientists and Journalists Devastated the Amazon*. New York: Norton.

Valéry, P. (1921–1922). *Charms*, trans. J. L. Brown. New York: Forsan, 1983.

Van Damme, D. (n.d.). *Erasme, sa vie, ses oeuvres*. Anderlecht, Belgium: L'Administration Communale d'"Anderlecht.

Verlaine, P. (1866). *Poèmes saturniens*. Paris: Gallimard Pléiade, 1948.

Verlet, L. (1993). *La malle de Newton*. Paris: Gallimard.

Vigo, J., dir. (1933). *L'Atalante* (film).

Viñar, M., and Viñar, M. (1989). *Exil et torture*. Paris: Denoël.

Virgil. *The Aeneid*, trans. R. Fitzgerald. New York: Vintage, 1990.

Visconti, L., dir. (1969). *The Damned* (film).

Voltaire. (1759). *Candide*, trans. J. Butt. New York: Penguin, 1990.

Wang, H. (1987). *Reflections on Kurt Gödel.* Cambridge, MA: MIT Press.

Westfall, R. (1993). *The Life of Isaac Newton.* Cambridge, UK: Cambridge University Press.

Winnicott, D. W. (1971). *Playing and Reality.* New York: Penguin.

——— (1974). Fear of breakdown. *International Review of Psycho-Analysis* 1:103–107.

Wittgenstein, L. (1914–1916). *Notebooks 1914–1916*, ed. G. E. Anscombe and G. H. von Wright. Chicago: University of Chicago Press, 1984.

——— (1918). *Tractatus Logico-Philosophicus.* London and New York: Dover, 1999.

——— (1929–1930). A lecture on ethics. *Philosophical Review* 74:3–12, 1965.

——— (1930–1933). *Remarks on Frazer's Golden Bough*, ed. R. Rhees, trans. A. C. Miles. Atlantic Heights, NJ: Humanities Press, 1979.

——— (1933–1934). *The Blue and Brown Books.* New York: Harper Torchbooks, 1965.

——— (1934–1936). Notes for lectures on "private experience" and "sense data." *Philosophical Review* 77:275–320, 1968.

——— (1938). *Lectures and Conversations on Aesthetics, Psychology, and Religious Belief*, ed. C. Barrett. Berkeley, CA: University of California Press, 1997.

——— (1945–1949). *Philosophical Investigations.* Oxford: Blackwell, 1958.

Xingjian, G. (2000). The case for literature. *www.literature-awards.com/nobelprize_winners/sitemap.htm/.*

Zeami. (1420). *La tradition secrète du Nô. Traduction et commentaires de René Sieffert.* Paris: Gallimard, 1960.

Zola, E. (1898). "J'Accuse!" In *The Dreyfus Affair. "J'Accuse" and Other Writings*, trans. E. Levieux, pp. 10–13. New Haven, CT: Yale University Press, 1998.

Zumthor, P. (1978). *Le masque et la lumière. La poétique des grands rhétoricqueurs.* Paris: Seuil.

Index